MODERN NOVELISTS

General Editor: Norman Page

MODERN NOVELISTS

Published titles

Forthcoming titles

MODERN NOVELISTS

PATRICK WHITE

Mark Williams

St. Martin's Press   New York

© Mark Williams 1993

All rights reserved. For information, write:
Scholarly and Reference Division,
St. Martin's Press, Inc., 175 Fifth Avenue,
New York, N.Y. 10010

First published in the United States of America in 1993

Printed in Hong Kong

ISBN 0–312–08990–2

Library of Congress Cataloging-in-Publication Data
Williams, Mark, 1951–
Patrick White / Mark Williams.
p. cm. — (Modern novelists)
Includes bibliographical references and index.
ISBN 0–312–08990–2
1. White, Patrick, 1912– —Criticism and interpretation.
2. Australia in literature. I. Title. II. Series.
PR916.3.W5Z947 1993
823—dc20 92–29033
CIP

To Jan

Contents

Acknowledgements

This book began as an M.A. thesis at the University of Auckland in the mid-1970s. My thanks to Bill Pearson and Ken Larsen who guided me through my early writing on Patrick White. Bill New and Diana Bydon at The University of British Columbia were my guides as I broadened my interests in White, writing a doctoral dissertation. Thanks are due to all the above and to Adrian Mitchell at The University of Sydney. I also wish to thank Gregory O'Brien for, once again, providing a great cover.

I also wish to thank the University of Waikato Research Committee and the University of Canterbury English Department for generously supporting the work with grants and Christina Stachurski who helped with proofreading and indexing.

Some of the ideas in the book were developed in articles published in *Westerly*, *Kunapipi* and *World Literature Written in English*.

General Editor's Preface

The death of the novel has often been announced, and part of the secret of its obstinate vitality must be its capacity for growth, adaptation, self-renewal and self-transformation: like some vigorous organism in a speeded-up Darwinian ecosystem, it adapts itself quickly to a changing world. War and revolution, economic crisis and social change, radically new ideologies such as Marxism and Freudianism, have made this century unprecedented in human history in the speed and extent of change, but the novel has shown an extraordinary capacity to find new forms and techniques and to accommodate new ideas and conceptions of human nature and human experience, and even to take up new positions on the nature of fiction itself.

In the generations immediately preceding and following 1914, the novel underwent a radical redefinition of its nature and possibilities. The present series of monographs is devoted to the novelists who created the modern novel and to those who, in their turn, either continued and extended, or reacted against and rejected, the traditions established during that period of intense exploration and experiment. It includes a number of those who lived and wrote in the nineteenth century but whose innovative contribution to the art of fiction makes it impossible to ignore them in any account of the origins of the modern novel; it also includes the so-called 'modernists' and those who in the mid- and late twentieth century have emerged as outstanding practitioners of this genre. The scope is, inevitably, international; not only, in the migratory and exile-haunted world of our century, do writers refuse to heed national frontiers – 'English' literature lays claim to Conrad the Pole, Henry James the American, and Joyce the Irishman – but geniuses such as Flaubert, Dostoevsky and Kafka have had an influence on the fiction of many nations.

Each volume in the series is intended to provide an introduction to the fiction of the writer concerned, both for those approaching him or her for the first time and for those who are already familiar with some parts of the achievement in question and now wish to place it in the context of the total *oeuvre*. Although essential information relating to the writer's life and times is given, usually in an opening chapter, the approach is primarily critical and the emphasis is not upon 'background' or generalisations but upon close examination of important texts. Where an author is notably prolific, major texts have been made to convey, more summarily, a sense of the nature and quality of the author's work as a whole. Those who want to read further will find suggestions in the select bibliography included in each volume. Many novelists are, of course, not only novelists but also poets, essayists, biographers, dramatists, travel writers and so forth; many have practised shorter forms of fiction; and many have written letters or kept diaries that constitute a significant part of their literary output. A brief study cannot hope to deal with all these in detail, but where the shorter fiction and the non-fictional writings, public and private, have an important relationship to the novels, some space has been devoted to them.

NORMAN PAGE

Preface

When Patrick White died in 1990 he left a legacy of twelve novels, two volumes of short stories, half a dozen published plays and an autobiography. Since his death David Marr's major biography has appeared. It is possible, then, to see his work whole and to trace the intricate connections between the life and the work. It is also possible to arrive more securely at an estimation of his place in twentieth-century writing than it was while the work remained incomplete. This book offers an overview of White's development as a novelist from the late 1930s to the late 1980s and sets his work in the context of the modern novel.

Because the stress here is on the *overall* development of his art, particular attention is directed at the period before the Second World War when White, as a marginal figure in the 1930s English literary scene, set about learning his trade as a writer. Here we see White struggling to come to terms with various personal, ideological and formal problems. The formal and stylistic indecisions that mark White's early work are crucial to an understanding of his subsequent development. White did not emerge *ex nihilo* as a major novelist some time around 1957 on a small farm outside Sydney. His post-war writing cannot be divorced from his experience as a young man living as a kind of reverse remittance man on £400 per annum in the London of the thirties and soaking up the cultural milieu.

In White's first two published novels, *Happy Valley* (1939) and *The Living and the Dead* (1941) we see a young 'English' writer struggling to assimilate the various fashionable styles, literary and political, of the time. His very dissatisfactions with the culture in which he found himself are characteristic of young English writers in that period.

In the novels of the late 1940s and 1950s we see White, after returning permanently to Australia from Europe, setting out to relearn the business of novel-writing. As he puts it in his 1958 essay,

'The Prodigal Son', '[w]riting, which had meant the practice of an art by a polished mind in civilised surroundings, became a struggle to create completely fresh forms out of the rocks and sticks of words'. In *The Aunt's Story* (1948) White farewells the European 'civilisation' towards which he feels powerful ambivalences and traces its breakup in the Second World War. The next two novels, *The Tree of Man* (1955) and *Voss* (1957), use the epic form as a means of encompassing the historical and imaginative experience of Australia.

In the novels of the 1960s White dramatises his divided response to Australia itself. *Riders in the Chariot* (1961), *The Solid Mandala* (1966) and *The Vivisector* (1970) include more and more of the Australian scene, even suburbia towards which White consistently expressed a profound antipathy. In this period we also find that varieties of religious thought and imagery assume a prominent place in White's fiction.

White's late fiction shows an increasing tendency towards a self-conscious manner and an unprecedented openness about the homosexual interest that had long informed his fiction, however unobtrusively. For White, homosexuality, which he associates with disguise and ambivalence, becomes a kind of metaphor for artistry itself. Yet, for all the playfulness with language and representation in his late fiction, White never retreats into postmodernist game-playing, if by 'postmodern' we mean that the writer snips the ties between art and life. In stressing the artificiality of fiction, he asserts its closeness to, not its distance from, life.

None of the familiar categories of current critical discourse – modernist, postmodernist, post-colonial – are adequate to a novelist like White. His work is rich and various enough to be interpretable in the terms of all of these, depending on the critic's interpretive scheme. White borrows where he chooses and takes elements from an immense variety of literary styles and fashions, linguistic registers and religious systems. But he keeps his distance from all, obliging his would-be exegetes to attend to that elusive, capacious, always ironic voice that moves through his fiction.

Neither an 'English' nor an 'Australian' novelist in any narrow sense, White has become a truly international writer, whose major fiction begs comparison with the work of contemporaries like Malcolm Lowry, Janet Frame and Salman Rushdie. Like these, White deals on equal terms with history and myth, fact and imagination, language as the vehicle of moral critique and language as play.

Introduction: Places, Tribes, Dialects

Dylan Thomas once described himself to an American audience as a 'remittance bard'.[1] The epithet, though witty, is not quite just. The point about remittance men is that the income which allows them to indulge their vices in distant places must come not from abroad but from home. Thomas was simply following that line of English poets and novelists who have toured America in search of cash. However outrageous his behaviour, no respectable relative was sufficiently scandalised to pack him off to the colonies. However appealing to him was the notion of remittances, no-one was prepared to pay to keep him out of England. The life of Malcolm Lowry, on the other hand, is a late classic in the remittance man tradition. Lowry was a true remittance bard. The youngest son in a wealthy, Methodist, Liverpool family, Lowry decided early in life to rebel against the virtues of his background. He would have no truck with respectability, church going, money making, sobriety and filial piety. So he fled abroad to exotic places and ended up in one of those English-speaking back-waters which remained for Lowry's tribe, the English Imperial middle class, right up to the Second World War 'the colonies'.

Patrick White's life story, considered in the remittance-man tradition, has an unfamiliar twist: unwilling to fit into the colonial grazier world of his parents, he was supported in London throughout the late 1930s by remittances from Australia. Born in London in 1912, three years after Lowry and two years before Thomas were born, White spent his childhood in Australia and was sent back to England at age 13 to be educated, or '[i]roned out' as he himself has put it, at a militaristic public school, Cheltenham.[2] White came from a section of the colonial landed gentry which wished to eradicate the taint of being 'colonial'. He was educated

1

in the manner appropriate to a prospective member of the English ruling class. Thus he was left with the problem that in Australia he was suspected as an Englishman with a posh accent and in England he was always 'colonial'.

After coming down from Cambridge in 1935, White was no more able to return to his class, the Australian version of the English country gentry, and act out the expected role as grazier than Lowry, when he came down in 1932, was able to return to the bosom of the provincial Imperial middle class to cultivate an interest in the fate of oil and cotton stocks. White, like Katherine Mansfield before him, began to write as a reverse 'remittance man'. Far from being sent to the colonies for alcoholic or other scandalous reasons, he was maintained comfortably in London by a puzzled but tolerant father unsure what to make of the cuckoo hatched in an otherwise tidy nest: a writer. White's homosexuality does not seem to have been a problem for his family as was Lowry's drinking, if only because it was more easily ignored. As far as White himself was concerned on his return to Australia after the war, his fatal brand of separateness was the fact of being an artist.[3]

In the pre-war period it was the desire to escape a provincial background tainted by philistinism that led White, like many other Australian writers and artists between the two wars, to settle in London where he wrote pale poems, derivative novels and unstaged plays. The distance he managed to establish from his family in this period would survive his repatriation and be unmistakeable three decades later. There is a photograph of Patrick White in a *Time-Life* study of Australia and New Zealand published in 1964 in which we see a stylishly dressed urbane figure against a background of modernist paintings and bric-à-brac.[4] This same book also contains a series of photographs of the White family sheep station, Belltrees.[5] As White's autobiography, *Flaws in the Glass*, reveals, Belltrees is one of the several farms of the White brothers, Patrick's father and uncles, whom we see in all their Edwardian confidence in a photograph in *Flaws in the Glass*.[6] What is striking is the similarity of the Whites of Belltrees in 1964 to the solid Edwardian group in *Flaws in the Glass*. In both groups we sense an unassailable stability, a fixed conviction of belonging to a superior class, and a supreme confidence that one's family and its privileges will endure in spite of time and change. Depicted at dinner on resplendent mahogany, the modern grazier Whites might have leapt from the pages of one of their cousin's novels set in the 1910s. It is significant that the *Time-Life* book does not allude to the connection between the novelist and the graziers. To outward appearances White has escaped their world; he is no longer identifiable with his origins. Yet in his fiction of the 1950s and 60s White returns again and again to the vanished world of Edwardian colonial graziers. In his novels the world of 'the White brothers' continues to figure as a point of stability, although contemporary history is everywhere recorded as a series of savage declines.

Like Lowry, then, White never completely freed himself from his origins, and as with Lowry, the period in which he first asserted his independence of his background was one in which he relied upon remittances from home to finance his creative self-expression. White made his less dramatic break with family, class, and nation during the late 1930s when he set himself up as a writer on the faintly raffish borderland between gentility and bohemia on four hundred pounds per annum remitted.

Ebury Street, where White lived on coming down from Cambridge, was still stylish in the 1930s, though declined from its former splendours. Situated where Belgravia slips into Pimlico, it had been elegant enough in the pre-war period for George Moore to have rooms there. Osbert Sitwell recalls visiting Moore there around that time.[7] Ebury Street, circa 1914, is mentioned in Virginia Woolf's *The Years* (1937) as a suitable place in which to install an upper-middle-class bachelor of taste.[8] Certainly, Ebury Street was not in the late 1930s quite as raffish and bohemian as White paints it in *Flaws in the Glass*.[9] Ebury Street allowed him to make his first telling gesture of independence, even if his flamboyant denial of origins was made possible by a generous allowance from home. Having made this gesture White was able to return to Australia in 1947 without being swallowed by family and class. He had transcended the rebel's need to announce his rebellion by means of a flamboyant personal style. Henceforth he would express his flamboyance in his writing. He bought a small farm outside Sydney at Castle Hill, a semi-rural suburb in those days, where he set himself to cultivate humility. The White of this period stares at us mournfully from beside the flank of his 'illicit cow'.[10] At Castle Hill, White was able to observe his former tribe – both Hunter Valley Whites and his mother ensconced in moneyed Sydney inner suburbia – from a safe distance.

Patrick White at a crucial point in his career left the London milieu in which, however marginally, he was on the way to becoming established as a minor novelist who might yet produce major work. He moved as far as possible from the city which until the Second World War was the intellectual centre of the English-speaking world. He did not content himself with a cottage in the Sussex countryside and the option of commuting to London. He did not choose to settle in any of the favourite watering holes of expatriate English literati around the Mediterranean littoral. The Mediterranean was very popular in the 1920s and 30s among writers who, like Norman Douglas and the Australian Martin Boyd, found the English-speaking world 'chaste and castrated' (the phrase is Ezra Pound's).[11] White, evidently, found such a lifestyle attractive after the war, more attractive anyway than that offered by an exhausted England. He narrowly rejected the life of a Hellenic beach-comber in favour of Australia in 1946–47.[12]

White was by no means unusual in his dissatisfaction with England in the late 1930s. The title of Osbert Sitwell's book written at the end of the decade, *Escape with Me*, bespeaks the mood of a generation of English intellectuals eager to discover some part of the globe not 'made and governed in the image of Manchester or Detroit'.[13] Whether from horror of the ghosts of grandfathers, of reigning dullness, or of impending bombs, England by 1939 was widely held to be a place to leave. White is unusual in the unlikely place for which he traded a depressed and depressing England. He chose a place where he could expect to find little in the way of literary communities or significant new reading publics. Of course, there was the attraction of a remembered landscape to pull him back to Australia, but he found the inhabitants of the desired landscape intolerably dull. Moreover, he missed in Australia the 'civilised surroundings' he had known in London.

It was a landscape without figures to which he chose to return. It is worth considering just how unlikely was Australia, far less Castle Hill, as a residence for White in the 1940s. Australia, according to White, was a backwater inhabited almost exclusively by philistines. It was provincial and John Bullish. Moreover, Australia was that part of the English-speaking world least tolerant of White's particular 'vice'. White, the homosexual, chose to set up house with his Greek lover in Australia at a time when Greeks were considered black and 'poofteroos', if they were suspected, were altogether beyond the pale.[14]

Much of what White has written about life in Australia is so scathing that one is forced to wonder how or why he managed to endure his long stay. There is a quality of hysteria in the reaction. White's survey of contemporary Australia in 'The Prodigal Son', an essay written in the 1950s that is part *apologia*, part manifesto, recalls T. S. Eliot's view of the modern world in *'Ulysses*, Order, and Myth' as an 'immense panorama of futility and anarchy'.[15] Everywhere there is ugliness, futility, the sprawling emptiness of a fallen democratic world. White piles image upon image of the ugly, the banal, the fatuous. For White, Australia with its levelling and rancorous democratic spirit is a fallen world. White's modernism expresses itself chiefly as a disdain for modernity and Australia is the modern world in its most characteristic, hence unacceptable, form. The cult of the average that satisfies the desires of the 'common man' produces inevitably for White a spiritual wasteland. Such an authorial attitude is to be found, sometimes concealed, sometimes overt, throughout White's Australian fiction. It is a view that finds its most concentrated and deeply negative expression in *Riders in the Chariot*.

From around the late 1960s, however, White's stance towards suburbia, the representative experience of modern Australian life, undergoes a change. *The Vivisector* (1970) is a crucial transitional text in this respect. Here a complicity is acknowledged between the figure of the artist and the fallen common world with its consumerism and materialism. In his fiction of the fifties White had selfconsciously chosen to focus on the 'ordinary' world in order to uncover the 'extraordinary' possibilities that lay concealed within it.[16] But, however much his novels had affirmed the existence of a 'mystery' and a 'poetry' locked within the quotidian, it was clear that the novelist regarded the world he had chosen to explore as lacking in fullness, less rich and satisfying than the European world left behind. With *The Solid Mandala* (1966), however, this stance begins to be modified and in *The Vivisector* a partial transformation occurs. Suburbia, which staged the crucifixion of the visionary Jew, Himmelfarb, in *Riders in the Chariot*, solicits the artist's attention as did the desert in *Voss*.

White's own attitude towards his country, however, remained carping and negative. From the late sixties White chose to become much more active and prominent in public life, commenting on Australian political and cultural life, but his stance as a public figure was generally oppositional. He supported the Australian Labour Party, during the Whitlam years, chiefly because he hoped the government might share his own antipathies. He spoke out against Australian involvement in the Vietnam war. After Whitlam's fall from power he vehemently condemned the Govenor General who sacked him. He enthusiastically supported the environmental movement and opposed the nuclear industry.

Nevertheless, throughout the post-war period White's fiction shows an increasing acceptance of the positive role of his country *as a whole* in his art. In his epic novels of the early post-war years, *The Tree of Man* and *Voss*, it is the landscape that receives the author's reverence while Australian social life is depicted as antagonistic to art. White's method here, stylistically and formally, is not so much to depict as to aestheticise 'ordinary' experience. In 'The Prodigal Son' White makes clear that his intention from his arrival in Australia was to render from a symbolist perspective and with high romantic colourings the traditional material of Australian realist fiction. In this aestheticism which finds expression above all in White's style we find most clearly evidence of his distaste for the common experience of Australia. It is as though the style is designed to hold at arm's length the vulgar matter of the narrative. Stan Parker in *The Tree of Man* may be the common man dignified, but it is the spiritually significant and unique inner self that White values, not the unremarkable social self.

Nevertheless, White's Australian fiction records a slow movement towards acceptance. In a development very similar to that of the New Zealand novelist, Janet Frame, who began writing as a vatic social critic, railing against the materialism of the citizens and has moved towards a more playful and accepting sense of the artist's relation to society, White moves in his post-war fiction progressively (albeit reluctantly) towards an acknowledgement of the dependence of the artist on the forms of mass society. In *The Vivisector* Hurtle Duffield discovers that his creativity has been 'fertilised' by the vulgar grocer, Cutbush, on his Sydney park bench.

Nevertheless, White has an instinctively dualistic habit of mind which infects not only his handling of character but also his ability to see whole his chosen country. White's Australia, especially in the fifties and sixties, is either a landscape which encourages mystical possibilities or the endless banality of suburbia. It is true that White's later fiction experiments with various means of including these dualities within larger wholes, but he never entirely abandons his initial divided response to the country in which he chose to live and write. Given his contempt for the society he found in his backwater and given the novelist's usual preference for a rich social life on which to draw, why did White remain in Australia through the barren and dissatisfied years of the fifties?

The simple answer to this question is that White was averse to society in nearly all its contemporary forms and preferred nature uncluttered by human figures. Such an explanation at least serves to account for the degree of isolation he accepted. White settled down on a small farm outside Sydney, cultivating a stormy but intermittently blissful domesticity while raising dogs, goats, flowers and vegetables. Here White found a microcosm of the White world of the Hunter Valley without the explicit class structure. A major source of what satisfaction he did find at Castle Hill is suggested by the bucolic activities to which he turned: milking an illicit cow, growing cabbages, observing the seasons. In a world of technology, utility, motion, and masses we detect the ring of a Ruskinite litany. White is fighting his way back against the dirty stream of contemporary history and has, it would seem, stumbled on a still unspoiled world of organic virtue, in spite of his various dissatisfactions with the Castle Hill experience.

There were, of course, plenty of rural backwaters in the England of the 1940s loaded with charm, history, and thatched cottages. Moreover, the modern world had unequivocally reached semi-rural New South Wales by the end of the Second World War. White's retreat was engulfed during the 1950s and 60s by the red-brick march of Sydney suburbia. There was, however, a signal advantage that Castle Hill enjoyed over an English cathedral town or a pleasant backwater like Zennor, a town where D. H. Lawrence and Mansfield had stayed, which Auden favoured as a holiday spot and in which White wrote Housman-inspired poems in the mid-1930s.[17] The advantage was simply that modernisation was felt to have gone further in England, its presence was felt more ubiquitously. According to contemporary cultural critics like F. R. Leavis, it was difficult in England by the 1930s to find any place where the traditional ways didn't merely linger on as quaint relics of the past but actually possessed more than a remnant of their former life. The connection between the past and present had been too sharply broken. It was possible to mourn the old ways but not to offer them as a still viable way of life.

In England during the 1920s and 30s, according to Leavis, the process of the eradication of traditional ways of life was more or less consolidated. The 'old organic' world was expunged from the countryside by the new towns, ribbon developments, modern factories in the south, mock-Tudor suburbia, and arterial highways. This process was opposed most vehemently by Leavis, but it was opposed also by a large number of 1930s writers not all of whom shared Leavis's social perspectives. It was opposed, for instance, by C. Day Lewis, George Orwell and John Betjeman. Surprisingly diverse English writers in the 1930s felt that a point of no return had been reached. Modernity was triumphant and only a few pockets of tradition, a few last outposts of the old order, remained to be mopped up.

At Castle Hill White deliberately positioned himself on a frontier between the traditional rural world in which people supposedly felt themselves to be part of natural process and the modern world in which humans are alienated from natural process. Fifty years previously, as Raymond Williams observes in *Culture and Society* (1958), D. H. Lawrence had found himself on just such a frontier at Haggs Farm where he loved Jessie Chambers, the 'Miriam' of *Sons and Lovers*.[18] At Haggs Farm, Lawrence was able to observe and evaluate the new reality from the standpoint of a vanishing one. The advantage of Castle Hill for White was that it offered what Haggs Farm had offered Lawrence: a perspective from within what he felt to be an intact 'organic' world that was threatened but not yet on the point of being squeezed out of reality. In England by the 1930s Williams's 'frontier', a word which suggests a demarcation between separate and roughly equivalent forces, had collapsed. According to Leavis by the early 1930s the organic community of the old England 'had so nearly disappeared from memory that to make anyone, however educated, realize what it was is commonly a difficult undertaking'.[19]

Yet Leavis claimed not only that its traces were detectable in England but also that such communities continued to exist outside England. *Scrutiny* writers used two books in particular as evidence that such a thing as 'the organic community' had once existed and that its passing ought to be considered a loss. One of these was Stuart Chase's *Mexico*, a work which Malcolm Lowry knew and admired. In Mexico during the late 1930s and then in British Columbia after 1940, Lowry was seeking evidence of that 'organic' way of life which White was to seek at Castle Hill a few years later.

The second book Leavis and his followers used as evidence that the organic community was not a myth but an authentic party of the

English past was George Sturt's *The Wheelwright Shop* (1923). Leavis quotes a passage from this work in his *Culture and Environment* (1933) which reveals the shape of the nostalgia that afflicted Leavis, Lowry, and White:

> The men, unlettered, often taciturn, sure of themselves, muscular, not easily tired, were in a sort of way an epitome of the indomitable adaption of our breed to land and to climate. As a wild animal species to its habitat, so these workmen had fitted themselves to the local conditions of life and death. Individually they had no special claim to notice; but as members of old-world communities they exemplified well how the South English tribes, traversing their fertile valleys, their shaggy hills, had matched themselves against problems without number, and had handed on, from father to son, the accumulated store of experience. If one could know enough, one might see, in ancient village crafts like that of the sawyers, the reflections as it were of the peculiarities of the countryside – the difficulties and dangers, the daily conditions – to which these crafts were the answer.
> . . . they themselves, you found, were specialists of no mean order when it came to the problem of getting a heavy tree – half a ton or so of lumber – on a saw pit and splitting it longitudinally into specified thicknesses, no more and no less. What though the individual looked stupid? That lore of the English tribes as it were embodied in them was not stupid any more than an animal's shape is stupid. It was an organic thing, very different from the organized effects of commerce.[20]

This is precisely the world of Stan Parker at Durilgai in White's *The Tree of Man*. Stan Parker, White's pioneer small farmer, is 'muscular', 'taciturn', and on the face of it 'stupid'. In Durilgai we see a community composed of peasants of English stock (except for the Irish) in the process of fitting itself to a habitat. When Sturt claims that 'the peculiarities of the countryside' are reflected in the lives of the people we may think of White's praise of a novel by the New Zealander Maurice Shadbolt in which White speaks of Shadbolt's ability to convey the ways in which 'the tremors and often disastrous eruptions' of the land are reflected in the lives of 'its only superficially bland inhabitants'.[21] These words are more appropriate to *The Tree of Man* than to Shadbolt's novel, *A Touch of Clay* (1974). When Stan Parker teaches young Joe Peabody to

fence we see the handing on from one generation to the next of
'the accumulated store of experience'. Stan's inability to hand on
what he knows to his son, Ray, is one of the chief signs in the novel
of the breakdown of the organic community under the impact of
a rootless modernity. Cut off from his origins, Ray becomes utterly
fragmented, yet visited in spite of himself by moments of nostalgia
for the golden-grained world of childhood.

In *The Tree of Man* we find a quite unexpected sense of affirmation. To turn from *The Living and the Dead* to *The Tree of
Man* is to turn from a novel caught up by the movement of
disintegration it traces to one in which the possibility of human
wholeness is not merely suggested but is actively affirmed. In
the earlier novel we find intimations of possible wholeness, of
ways of life more rounded and satisfying than those that are the
norm in a European civilisation slipping into the Second World
War. Invariably, these alternatives are located *outside* the worlds
which the novel describes and invariably they are unable to resist
the furious bias of contemporary history towards disaster which
the novel records. In the latter work there is an elegiac tone, a
recognition of the precariousness of what has been recovered and
that it exists not so much by virtue of place as by authorial act of will
or desire. Yet this elegiac tone does not negate the affirmation. The
desired alternatives to contemporary civilisation offered in *The Tree
of Man* – natural cycle, religious vision, sexual love – are not merely
unlikely and unconvincing gestures. They are the fixed points from
which the novelist now writes.

To gauge the effect of this mood of affirmation on the writing
of Patrick White we need only to compare *The Tree of Man* with
the fiction of the 1930s and of the early war years. Nothing is so
striking in *The Living and the Dead* as the sense of the inadequacy
of the available language to the novelist's task. There is an obsessive
recording in the novel of the effects of advertising, jazz and the
cinema on the ability of people to think, feel, or act clearly. The
novel recognises reluctantly that it must employ the currency of
a language that has been debased by contemporary usage and
feels itself infected by what it records. White's farm at Castle Hill
signifies a desire on the part of the novelist to bypass modern social
organisation and to return to a simpler mode of connection that
supposedly prevailed when humans saw themselves not as masters
of but as part of natural process. In his literary version of the earthy
paradise, 'Durilgai', we glimpse part of the reason that White left

England and settled in what he saw as a provincial, philistine backwater. His reasons for staying through four decades were to prove more complex and various, but the preference for a simpler and more complete way of life than that of modernity remained constant.

1

The 'English' Patrick White

The 1930s Context

Patrick White, although it seems odd to think of him in such a context, falls belatedly into 'the Auden generation'. He too was born between 1904 and 1915, was educated at public schools and Oxbridge. He began publishing in the middle thirties, by which time the Auden group was well established. His first three novels, all now lost, were written in the late thirties before *Happy Valley* which appeared in 1939.[1]

Like the writers of the Auden group, he found himself as a young writer overshadowed by, and deeply ambivalent about, the writers of the twenties – Eliot, Joyce, Lawrence. Like them also, he expressed a sympathy for and attraction to working-class people, although his sympathies were prompted less by socialist conviction than by nostalgia for the family servants who had befriended him as a boy. David Marr points out that White's affair with a Spanish fascist aristocrat showed how easily he was swayed towards the right; nevertheless, White's political sympathies in the late thirties were becoming engaged by the plight of the victims of fascism.[2] It was partly the feeling that the working class offered the only viable alternative to fascism and partly a typically thirties confusion of the proletariat with the peasantry which led White in *The Living and the Dead* to turn to the working class as a possible way out of a dying bourgeois culture.[3] Like other middle-class writers in the decade White approached the working class and its putative future with misgivings and evasions.

The 1930s was a decisive decade in White's development as a

writer. In the early thirties White spent some time as a jackeroo on an Australian sheep station then went up to Cambridge where he read languages. The jackerooing experience saw him making serious beginnings as a novelist. Although White abandoned the work produced here, themes central to this period would appear later in more sophisticated guise once he had achieved distance from what he saw as the rawness of Australian life. The trick was to assimilate the ruling styles of contemporary writing to his own perspectives and needs, and this would take a further two decades to achieve. What was crucial after the period spent on the Monaro watching sheep by day and writing by night were the years at Cambridge. Although White would be curiously silent about his Cambridge years in his autobiography, *Flaws in the Glass*, it was here that he encountered the literary influences that were to shape his development as a novelist.

White went up to Cambridge in 1932 and was faced with the problem of choosing among the ideologies, styles, tones, cliques and movements that made up the undergraduate scene. The three main options were dandyism, heartiness and socialism. White, somewhat timidly, was a dandy. Homosexual, theatrical, stylish in dress, modernist in his tastes – the photographs in David Marr's biography show White's transition from the Cambridge freshman with moustache to the London dandy affectedly holding a cane in Roy de Maistre's portrait.[4] But White was not quite up to date; the dandies had been influential in the twenties, they were passé a decade later. Cambridge undergraduates with literary ambitions in the thirties affected working-men's dress; they did not, like White, linger below A. E. Housman's rooms, hoping for a visitation. White's early poetry was similarly outmoded. White was very much a Georgian when he published his second thin, private volume of poems, *The Ploughman and Other Poems*, in 1935, although the Georgians had been laid to rest in *Granta* as early as 1929.[5] A more important, though still not quite fashionable, influence on his early writing was that of modernism. Modernism was idolised, criticised, condemned and emulated throughout the 1930s. For many among the politically motivated writers of the decade it was a distraction at best, a kind of ghost lingering after its time. It was, however, a ghost that would not go away and White was merely one of the thirties novelists who were profoundly influenced by Eliot in particular. The very early novels of Greene, Isherwood and Orwell show the same kind of debt, although modernism was to prove less important in their later, better known works. White's debt to modernism, especially to Eliot and Lawrence, was to prove a vital and fruitful one.

In the late twenties and early thirties, Eliot's influence dominated the advanced undergraduates at Cambridge. In the course of the thirties, it became increasingly fashionable on the literary left to attack Eliot's conservative modernism. As late as 1949 John Davenport, Jack Lindsay, and Randall Swingler, all prominent thirties literary leftists, were attempting to lay to rest Eliot's irritating ghost in an editorial note in an issue of *Arena*.

> Tradition and culture: the words ring like a cracked bell; and indeed the dreary ritual reminds one of a middle-class funeral, even down to the sherry. The loved one died of sleeping sickness – *encephalitis lethargia*, caused by the T.S.E.-T.S.E. fly.[6]

Such a strong desire to have a living author buried suggests a nervousness on the part of the would-be grave-diggers. The stubborn prestige of Eliot, in spite of his political heresies, is confirmed by such adolescent rebellions. Eliot was to be an important stylistic influence on White in the late thirties. More important still was Lawrence who remained a forceful, albeit ambivalently regarded, presence throughout the thirties. Lawrence's organicist mission was explicitly taken up by Lawrence Durrell in his *The Black Book* (1935). He turns up in heroic guise in Auden's *The Orators* (1932) where he figures as a possible healer of the neurotic psyches of young Englishmen.

Lawrence's ghost stalked and troubled the thirties, and is to be found throughout White's first novel, *Happy Valley*. (Lawrence will still be a decisive influence nearly two decades later on *The Tree of Man*.) His ghost would not be exorcised because, however antipathetic his politics were to thirties leftists, Lawrence's uncompromising view of the sickness of English culture after the 1914–18 war concurred with the prevailing view of thirties literary culture, a view shared by the political left, right and the several shades of opinion between.

Despite all the pylons, wirelesses, aeroplanes and locomotives that announce the new age in the poetry of the thirties, Lawrence's organicist mission was by no means forgotten. We may hear it insistently behind the leftist rhetoric of C. Day Lewis who advises prospective communists in 1933 to 'break up the superficial vision of the motorist and restore the slow, instinctive, absorbent vision of the countryman'.[7] We may hear it in John Betjeman's 1937 poem 'Slough' ('Come friendly bombs and fall on Slough/It isn't fit for humans now'), in Durrell's *The Black Book,* and even in Orwell's hankering after Edwardian village life in *Coming Up for Air* (1939). We may also hear it raised very stridently indeed in the early writings of F. R. Leavis whose attacks on the organs of mass opinion-making – radio, cinema, newspapers – in *Mass Civilization and Minority Culture* (1933) have a rancorousness that anticipates White's treatment of the same in *The Living and the Dead.*[8]

By 1933 there was already a politically charged climate at Cambridge. In the course of the thirties the claim of politics on the attention of young English writers became more and more pressing. Poets like Cecil Day Lewis and Stephen Spender felt obliged to 'retreat from liberalism' and join the Communist Party.[9] Young undergraduates like the poet John Cornford and the Marxist critic Christopher Cauldwell went to Spain on the Loyalist side and were killed. Significantly, their deaths took place 'abroad'; at home, despite the fierceness of the rhetoric, the stakes were not so high. In Cecil Day Lewis's *Starting Point* (1937) and in White's *The Living and The Dead,* published four years later, characters leave for Spain and probable death as the novels close. On the continent 'the hard, ferocious theologies of nationalistic and revolutionary idolatry' took root;[10] in England at the universities young middle-class intellectuals affected varying degrees of commitment to ideology, usually on the left.

There is inescapably an air of unreality about the leftist politics of English upper-middle-class writers and intellectuals in the thirties. Grahame Greene describes the problem thus:

We were a generation brought up on adventure stories who had missed the enormous disillusionment of the First War; so we went looking for adventure.[11]

Greene is speaking about the impulse behind the thirties fad of travel books, but he touches on a deeper dilemma. How were these young bourgeois from public schools and Oxbridge to touch not 'adventure', the stuff of boys' fantasies, but 'reality', the world of men? As Christopher Isherwood has pointed out, many among his generation felt themselves to be not quite men, to have missed or failed the decisive 'test' of manhood posed by the First World

War.[12] In their politics, in their enthusiasm for the proletariat, in their romantic obsession with Spain, the writers of the Auden generation revealed their view of themselves as inadequate, ineffectual, removed from the hard, clear detail of the real. To these young bourgeois the lives of working people seemed more 'real' than their own, less clouded by neurosis, sexual ambivalence and self-doubt. History was something which happened to other classes.

The young Patrick White shares the sense of being isolated by class, education and speech from the hard world of historical experience that we commonly find among the young middle-class writers of the late thirties. He adopts in his fiction of this period a formal orientation that in a characteristically thirties fashion attempts to address this problem: his second novel, *The Living and the Dead*, follows the journey of a young bourgeois intellectual away from his self-enclosed world of sensibility towards the 'real' world of things and actions. This is the form adopted by W. H. Auden in *The Orators*, by Lowry in *Ultramarine* (1933) and by Edward Upward in his fabular novel, *Journey to the Border* (1938). These middle-class writers are linked by a common desire to find a way out of their bourgeois preoccupation with subjectivity and to make contact with the historical world for which the thirties literary-left felt a conscience-stricken attraction.

The orthodox view is that the important shift that occurred in thirties writing was that away from the aestheticism of the twenties towards a revived realism, towards the use of the vernacular, and towards historical kinds of discourse. There is much truth in this view, but it needs to allow for important counter-trends and complications. There was a movement away from the emphasis on sensibility and the mandarin style we find in the novels of Virginia Woolf. However, this movement was not seen by Auden, Spender or Isherwood as a retreat from modernism. They felt that they were building on modernism, putting its techniques to their own purposes. Woolf herself followed her own instincts in the thirties, extending the modernist-symbolist line, and her work is as much a part of the thirties as is that of Auden, Day Lewis, Waugh or Greene. Woolf actually sponsored many of the young leftist poets in the production of their first collective magazine/manifesto, *New Signatures* (1932). The *New Signatures* poets had none of the Bloomsbury reverence for 'states of consciousness', but Woolf, whose views on poetry were as conservative as her views on fiction were advanced, does them an injustice when she chides Auden for his allegiance to 'raw fact'.[13] Auden and his followers were no more indifferent to subjectivity than was Woolf. 'All genuine poetry', wrote Auden, 'is in a sense the formation of private spheres out of a public chaos'.[14] The Auden writers were merely more guilty about their subjectivism than Woolf, more reluctant to give it unchecked expression.

In the early thirties, while Woolf's fiction was moving further into the self, Christopher Isherwood, whose prose is definitive of the ruling English style of the day, was developing a narrative method that displays little overt interest in subjectivity. Isherwood's narrators have a naivety that hollows them out and makes them wholly receptive to external events. Isherwood's style strives after transparency; his characteristic language use is without literariness, artificiality, or lyricism. Yet William Bradshaw, the narrator of *Mr. Norris Changes Trains* (1935), is no more an inhabitant of the world of 'raw fact' than are the characters in Woolf's *The Waves* (1931). Bradshaw is a neurotic and isolated young English bourgeois in late Weimar Germany, trapped by his self-imposed role as observer. His dangerous objectivity conceals an underlying complicity with the demented and surreal world he inhabits, and here the characteristically thirties concern of Isherwood to reflect the connections between the private world of the individual and the public world of action is in substantial agreement with that of the young Patrick White.

David Lodge has observed that in the thirties journalistic writing was used by English prose writers to record the increasingly extreme political events. Thirties writing, he asserts, 'tended to model itself on historical kinds of discourse – the autobiography, the eye-witness account, the travel log'.[15] There were, however, significant departures from this trend – Wyndham Lewis, Joyce and Woolf, for example. White remained steadfastly committed to imaginative prose-fiction, not to historical discourse. Nevertheless, he wanted to register in his fiction the impact of history on the consciousness of the individual and to trace the movement of consciousness, however tentatively, out towards political events. Isherwood's prose was not to his purpose. He needed a style more layered, more mandarin, more difficult. Like Lowry, he needed to find a compromise between the aestheticist tendencies of high modernism and the historical sensibility which was in vogue in the thirties.

What White needed were specific formal strategies, what Lowry calls 'design-governing postures', adequate to his understandings of the relations between the inner world of consciousness and the outer world of action.[16] He sought some formal means of reconciling an antagonism in the modern English novel between these two worlds. In the late thirties when he began to publish, the world of action was more alluring than were the worlds of sensibility. Poets were ejecting timid, Prufrockian intellectuals out of their self-enclosed universes of bourgeois sensibility into the 'real' world.[17] Elyot Standish in White's *The Living and The Dead* is a somewhat belated representative figure of this type: he is Prufrock seen through the eyes of an historically-minded, politically conscience-stricken, late-thirties writer. Like Dana Hilliot, the hero of Lowry's *Ultramarine*, he is another of those thirties bourgeois intellectuals self-consciously seeking a way out of his neurotic preoccupations into the rough, real world of men and action.

Another of the formal strategies that White discovered in the thirties was expressionism. White, like Isherwood, was in Germany in the early thirties, and was one of the few English writers of the period to be deeply influenced by expressionism. Auden and Isherwood, it is true, employed expressionist techniques in their play *The Ascent of F6* and there was a minor vogue for expressionism in thirties drama. But the most significant legacy of expressionism among the generation that emerged in England in the 1930s is to be found in Lowry's *Under the Volcano* and White's *The Aunt's Story*, both of which grew out of the thirties although neither was published till after the war. In these two novels the expressionistic tendencies of the prose mirror the political violences and dislocations of the late 1930s. They stand in stark contrast to the cool, objective prose style which, in the orthodox view, dominated thirties English novelists.

In the late thirties and early forties White attempted to work out in his early fiction the various conflicting impulses which are familiar features of the post-war 'Australian' White. In both *Happy Valley* and *The Living and the Dead* we find experiments with modernist techniques, a high modernist disdain for the modern world, a species of social prophesy and a strain of between-the-wars organicist nostalgia which carries over into *The Tree of Man* and is still to be felt in the horror at the impact of modernity on traditional Greek life White expresses in *Flaws in the Glass*.[18] In *The Living and the Dead* these impulses and their stylistic correlatives are most blatantly and thereby most tellingly working against one another. The very strains of these conflicts within the novel indicate

White's dissatisfaction with his place within the literary milieu of thirties England and thereby they suggest both why he was to abandon England immediately after the war and what he was fated to carry with him into his subsequent writing.

Happy Valley

> 1939 was not a year in which to start a literary career.
>
> E. M. Forster

The debts of White's early writing to Joyce, Woolf and Lawrence have often been noted. Less attention has been paid to White's debt to the Victorian novel. In *Happy Valley* the novelist selects representative figures from all strata of a given society. He stands outside that society and views it as a whole. The characters are made to fit neatly and inevitably into a class society whose structure is seen as permanent and unquestionable. The novelist expects his readers to make moral discriminations about the lives of his characters. The narrator does not hesitate to point the reader towards the appropriate judgement. Moreover, like the narrator of the Victorian novel, the narrator of *Happy Valley* presents himself to us as an observer upon whose judgements we can safely rely.

This habit of the narrator of making judgements and of drawing attention to his role as an unfolder of events whose outcome he knows in advance is distracting in a novel with evident pretensions to being 'modern'. Barry Argyle is overcomplimentary in likening the effect of authorial presence to Brecht's 'alienation effect': the effect of White's intrusive narrator on the reader is irritating rather than critically distancing.[19] As Carolyn Bliss notes, the narrative perspective is 'uncertain' with its habit of 'shift[ing] unpredictably from genially Fielding-like first person, through Jamesian central intelligence, garden variety omniscient, and Joycean interior monologue'.[20]

White's grasp of the social range he attempts to encompass is seriously flawed. His working-class characters in particular are very unsure in their execution. Chuffy Chambers, the melancholic simpleton, is a caricature with the illusion of psychological depth thrown in. The townspeople are stereotypes: red-faced, mindless publicans and a malicious chorus of housewives. The bourgeois

Belpers are Dickensian humours without the master's touch of gratuitous life. Even they have more vitality than the timid seekers after more than provincial bourgeois existence has to offer, Oliver Halliday and Alys Browne, who are the novel's central characters.

With rural figures White's touch is surer. The Furlows are confident sketches of a kind that White will later develop with considerable comic effect: the ineffectual squatter and his socially ambitious wife. Sidney, their dissatisfied daughter, and Hagan, her lover, have real energy, a life of their own. These types also will reappear in White's fiction. The wilful, sexually attractive and aggressive woman given, like Emma Bovary, to the confusion of life with romantic fantasy will reappear as Maman Courtney (*The Vivisector*), Elizabeth Hunter (*The Eye of the Storm*) and, comically, as Amy Parker in *The Tree of Man*. The later versions of the type, however, will possess rich and complex inner lives in a way that Sydney, for all her Mallarméan reveries, does not. This line of romantic heroines, which ends as self-parody in Eddie/Eadith Twyborn, joins in a complicated dalliance with a line of Australian proletarian heroes: the red rogue males from Hagan to Don Prowse. Hagan's life is all on the surface. In White's work this type of pure maleness, of Ned Kelly swagger, lacks inner life while the female counterparts to the type, from Sydney to Elizabeth Hunter, possess rich inner lives. A significant shift in this relationship occurs in *The Tree of Man* where Stan Parker, the simple farmer, is granted sensibility. In the love affair between Sidney Furlow and Clem Hagan we find the first, faltering steps in a flirtation White's fiction will trace between the Aussie 'bloke' and the European 'lady' which will end in *The Twyborn Affair* (1979) not with a marriage but with a rape.

A familiar 1930s theme is evident in White's depiction of these lovers. Sidney Furlow, like the middle-class heroes of other 1930s novels, is locked inside her sensibility and sees the external world as brutal and crude. Yet she feels that she ought somehow to make contact with the real world, which she associates with the figure of the foreman, Hagan. Like Dana Hilliot in Lowry's *Ultramarine*, she is drawn to the working class not out of Marxist enthusiasm but from a conviction that working-class life has a more sure grasp of reality than bourgeois life. She is guilty about, or dissatisfied with, her self-absorption, her addiction to inwardness, and sets out to embrace the world of fact. Hagan represents lived reality and the vernacular energies of the language, as do the sailors in *Ultramarine*. His language is earthly, direct, colloquial. His world is active, sensuous, heterosexual. He lacks the thirties bourgeois hero's self-division, his sense of sexual guilt, his neurosis.

Significantly, at this early stage of his writing White is most at home with station life. His feel for the Australian squattocracy has given rise to his most successful pictures of Australian life. White has lovingly recreated the Sydney mansions of the rich squatters. At the heart of these mansions lie the glittering chandeliers that signify transcendence of vulgarity and greed in White's symbolic language which habitually assigns sensibility to the rich and leisured – provided they are uncontaminated by commerce – and 'reality' to the poor and labouring – provided they are uncontaminated by lower-middle-class 'virtue'. The outback homesteads which the squatters visit rather than inhabit have an innocent charm. Even the coarse and greedy squatters with their sheep-obsessed sons are thoroughly convincing. White knows their world from the inside and he shows both the renegade's malice towards his own class and the scion's affection. With suburbia, the typical mode of modern Australian life, White will always be ill-at-ease, often insensitive, sometimes hysterical, unable to decide whether the form appropriate to its depiction is the pastoral or the satire.

Happy Valley is not unsatisfactory, however, merely because of White's obvious predilection for station life. The novel is unable to achieve what, as its realistic form attests, it sets out to do: to provide a convincing picture of Australia as a whole. The problem lies in White's attitude to Australia. It is difficult to see why White chose to set his first novel in a place for which he clearly has so little sympathy. One suspects that he is drawing on his childhood memories of a beloved landscape rather than making use of the period he spent as a jackaroo on sheep stations between public schools and Cambridge (Peter Wolfe notes that the novel uses materials from the White family station, 'Belltrees').[21] In this period, his abhorrence of grazier life was established. White returned to Australia after Cheltenham seeking a broader experience out of which to write than that which his education had afforded him. *Happy Valley* is in part simply a place outside England to which a young writer had turned, hoping to escape the limits of his background. It is an exotic and unpleasant locale, rather like Graham Greene's Mexico in *The Lawless Roads* (1939), in which White sets his conventional characters and action hoping that they will look more interesting by association.

In *Happy Valley*, in spite of passages which affirm the splendours of the country, there is no deeply felt influence of the landscape on the inhabitants; the town is merely a scab on the face of the earth. White draws attention through his loquacious and portentous narrator to the absence of any organic connection between human inhabitant and place. The landscape is generally uninspiring; the architecture is ugly and ephemeral; the populace is bland and, in small ways, malicious. White's lack of sympathy with the Australian society he depicts is nowhere more in evidence than in his depiction of the conspiracy of jealous housewives who spy on Hagan. These women represent in their joylessness and envy the moral norm of the town. Instead of the characters of the realistic novel, fully particularised yet representative of those forces in society that make for change, White gives us stereotypes and caricatures, exaggerated cartoons of the qualities he finds most widespread and repugnant in Australia.

In the course of the novel, White's centre of interest shifts perceptibly from the valley and the lives of its inhabitants to a metaphysical vagary: Life itself. Oliver and Alys seem at first to be prepared to pitch themselves against the hideous constraints of Happy Valley life. They are defeated, however, not by the place but by what Oliver – and apparently White himself – see as some bias towards disorder in the scheme of things. Happy Valley becomes less a town than a symbol for the wretchedness of life. At times, it is difficult to avoid the conclusion that White chose the place for its very nastiness in order to objectify his bleak vision of the human lot.

Part of the problem lies in a conflict between White's moral concern and his apparent distaste for physicality. The moral concern is manifest in the novel's sketchy and heavily biased presentation of a number of opposed responses to life: the self-sacrificial resignation of Hilda Halliday, the equanimity of the Chinese characters, Sidney's ambivalent urge towards sensual life, Oliver's and Aly's life denial, the detachment of the boy, Rodney Halliday. Among these unappealing alternatives we are supposed somehow to choose how life should be approached. Although the narrator is eager to nudge us at various times towards one or another of these moral possibilities, the novel itself does not come down unequivocally in favour of any one.

White's distaste is manifest in the narrator's sympathy with Oliver Halliday who must bear the main part of the burden of the novel's ambivalent quest for fullness of life. For a time the horrifying detachment he displays during the still-birth which opens the novel gives way to a tentative commitment to joy which alone promises escape from the miserable constraints of the place. But Oliver and Alys surrender to a narrow moralism and fail to take their chance to escape from Happy Valley. This retreat from flux, change, possibility is endorsed not only by the narrator whose judgements are generally indistinguishable from Oliver's but also by the shape of the novel. The corpse of Ernest Moriarty blocks all roads, except that of suicide, that might lead out of Happy Valley.

There is, of course, the escape of Sidney and Hagan to Queensland, but there is every reason to expect that their journey towards a less constrained form of life will be no better fated than that of Starlight and his gang from a much earlier Australian 'happy valley' in Rolf Boldrewood's *Robbery Under Arms* (1888). It remains doubtful whether Sidney, the romantic heroine, and her outback hero will produce anything beyond sex-war and sex-disgust. There is no escape from Happy Valley for the brave or for the timid. Oliver and Alys at the end of the novel drive towards neither intensity of living nor sexual fulfillment. Protected, like their crockery, against breakage, change, movement they carry their Happy Valleys with them.

Given the novel's pervading sense of entrapment, it is significant that, despite the plethora of lovers in *Happy Valley*, White is unable to offer us any enactment of successful sexual love. The short-lived affair between Oliver and Alys is intellectualised and half-hearted, its transports coyly described and unconvincing. Despite the presence of Lawrence brooding over the novel's uncertainties, White is unable to depict sexuality as a redemptive human encounter. However much White might want to see sexuality as a Lawrentian opening of the individual towards a full acceptance of life, he cannot *show* it as such. Hence the inability of White's lovers to escape from their Happy Valleys and find the intensity of living they desire.

There is a second reason for White's inability to confine himself to a realistic treatment of Australia. He is clearly unhappy with the range of social types it offers and with its lack of social life in the sense of the meeting of 'civilised' minds. The novel's only 'polished mind[s]' Oliver Halliday and Alys Browne, are spurious in their intellectuality.[22] Even so, like the boy Rodney, they become

outcasts in a community where indifference is the norm and out-
right brutality not uncommon. *Happy Valley* offers us comic scenes
of low life, the bar scenes and the race meeting, but White has not
yet mastered the mannered satire of colonial social life at which he
will prove adept in his later novels.

White has attempted in the realist manner to encompass a whole
society, but he lacks a grasp of the dynamic nature of social life.
'At Happy Valley', the narrator obligingly informs us, 'man was by
inclination static'.[23] The problem does not lie in Australian society
which at no stage of that country's history since 1788 could be
described as 'static'. The problem lies in White's response to a
society which fails to provide him with the 'civilised surroundings'
which at this stage of his career he considers essential to the
business of writing. White sees Happy Valley as static because he
cannot interest himself in Australian social life and has chosen
to focus the whole society through an unattractive microcosm. In
other words, *Happy Valley* is less an Australian novel than an English
novel set, like so many novels by young Englishmen in the thirties,
in a foreign land. As White notes in *Flaws in the Glass*, he finished
Happy Valley in St. Jean-de-Luz 'because everybody wrote some of
whatever it was abroad'.[24]

Happy Valley has none of the expansiveness of realism, none of
the reluctance we find in Tolstoy to close life within the circle
of aesthetic form. Yet the novel lacks Jamesian concentration;
the details are not all worked into the overall design. The novel
clatters with its borrowings from Eliot: Prufrockian voices and
clumsy versions of the objective correlative. Its interest lies in
what it shows of White's ambitions, his determination to draw on
the full range of the genre and the language, and in what it shows
of the uncertainties that are giving rise to formal problems, those
jarrings of unassimilated influences.

In its central confusion of purpose, *Happy Valley* is very much a
1930s novel. It is a novel written by a young man clearly overshadowed by the modernists of the twenties who perfected techniques
for exploring the inner world of consciousness and for expressing
the contents of the unconscious. At the same time, *Happy Valley*
displays a characteristically thirties suspicion of unchecked subjectivism. Oliver Halliday, like the hero of Edward Upward's *Journey
to the Border*, is eager to escape the circle of himself and find
some fruitful connection with reality. Similarly, White is eager
to tame the more extreme tendencies of modernism by setting

them in an essentially realistic novel. White wants to show that
health and wholeness are found by engaging with reality, if not
in the usual thirties manner by political commitment, then by a
Lawentian commitment to passionate sexual love. But he cannot
convince.

The Living and the Dead

In *Flaws in the Glass* White disparagingly describes himself in the
late thirties as 'chas[ing] after a fashionable style' and as 'paying
lipservice to the fashionable radical views.'[25] We may gain hints
of this would-be fashionable White from several sources. In the
Summer 1938 number of *New Verse* White published a poem, 'The
House Behind the Barricades', which, in its nervous depiction of
the engulfment of the private by the public world, is entirely
representative of the period. The poem describes the threat of
violent political action to a wilfully self-enclosed consciousness
content to feast upon images of a more sensuous and leisurely past
('Desert now the halls where we ate peaches in their season').[26]
In the poem's apocalyptic conclusion, the time-bomb of present
political urgency ticks away the dying moments of a world in which
the individual could still look inward, ignoring 'the actual plane'.

White's style is intended to be as fashionable as his politics. The
opening Audenesque imperative, 'Desert now', is echoed on the
facing page by the opening lines of two poems by Geoffrey Grigson:
'Watch, please' and 'Complete the natural history'.[27] Auden is also
behind White's line, 'that one with the torn eye, the one with the
revolving conscience', with its particularising demonstrative pronoun and its yoking of abstraction and concreteness in the closing
image. Above all, the poem's determination to drag a reluctant
young bourgeois towards political commitment is characteristic in
tone and ideological stance of the Auden group who dominated
the decade and the magazine *New Verse*.

White has come a long way from the pale Housman imitations
of *The Ploughman*. He has shucked off his belated Georgianism,
his preference for images of nature over those of modern urban
life and the wistful air of adolescent melancholy that hangs over
the early poems. He has put behind him his Housman-like habit
of considering death *sub specie aeternitatis* and made it immediate,
realistic, the provenance of contemporary politics. He has replaced

his youthful, Housman-inspired attraction to nostalgic pastoral and the metaphysical pessimism of adolescence with a thirties prejudice against wilful self-enclosure within sensibility. The White we glimpse behind 'The House Behind the Barricades' is not quite up to date, but he thinks he is, or very nearly.

Yet in spite of its Audenesque gestures, 'The House Behind the Barricades' adopts by and large the style that dominated the generation immediately prior to that of the Auden decade. Its long, hesitant sentences, its choice of a nerveless and exhausted sensibility as narrator, its use of the objective correlative – all point to the fatal influence of 'Prufrock'.[28] White's determination to toss his belated Prufrock into the sordidness of the actual bespeaks his desire to be up to date, yet the poem shows an essential uncertainty about which fashionable style the poet ought to be chasing after. 'The House Behind the Barricades' shows us less a young writer determined to make himself over in the image of the prevailing fashion than one unable to decide *which* style is suited to his needs as a writer.

We find these same stylistic indecisions in White's second published novel, *The Living and the Dead*. Despite White's stated aversion to the novel and granting its minor status in his oeuvre, *The Living and the Dead* is crucial to an understanding of his development as a novelist precisely because of its confusion of purpose.[29]

Although not published until 1941, *The Living and the Dead* is more properly a thirties novel than *Happy Valley*. The mood of disillusion with the favourite alternative moral and social orders of the thirties that we find in *The Living and the Dead* places the novel at the close of the decade. Like Auden's 'September 1, 1939' and Orwell's 'Inside the Whale' (1940), White's novel judges the enthusiasms, idealisms and dreams of the decade from the outside. But White is more nostalgic than either Auden or Orwell, for whom the leftist posturings of thirties bourgeois intellectuals have been thoroughly exposed by the shabby close of a 'low, dishonest' decade.[30] The centre of moral concern in *The Living and the Dead* – a sense of the spiritual bankruptcy of the English bourgeoisie and the 'civilisation' for which it had once stood coupled with a search for alternatives – is at the heart of the thirties dilemma.

Given the time of its writing, it seems odd that *The Living and the Dead* should show so unmistakably the influence, both texturally and structurally, of Eliot, Joyce, Woolf and Lawrence. By 'a fashionable style' White means chiefly, as far as his writing is concerned, the techniques of modernism. The chief stylistic influence on the novel is Eliot. Elyot Standish – the Christian name is a giveaway – like the speaker of 'Gerontion', is a 'dry brain' conscious of belonging to a rotten and fragmented civilisation, who waits with Tiresian indifference for improbable signs of new growth.[31]

There is, however, a curious rightness in White's choice of a master influence given the period, 1939–41, in which *The Living and the Dead* was written. The novel records the precise moment at which the dreams of the thirties broke up as a whole civilisation seemed on the point of being swept forever down the gutter of history. What had seemed serious and mature now looked merely silly and shoddy. The communist lamb was lying down with the Nazi tiger. Auden and Isherwood had bolted for New York. White himself dallied in bars not far from the one in which Auden wrote 'September 1, 1939', the requiem for a decade. He even considered staying in New York. The moment of commitment to the business of defeating fascism had not yet arrived. The tone of weariness and disgust that is so insistent in *The Living and the Dead* – the tone that recalls *The Hollow Men* and *Mauberley* – is appropriate to this bankrupt society.

The high modernist flourishes of White's prose style in *The Living and the Dead* seem very outdated in 1941. He eschews the manner of the documentary, the eye-witness account, the journal or the factual record. He avoids also the cool, clipped, understated style that Orwell and Isherwood took over from Hemingway. By the late thirties this style, according to Cyril Connolly, had become so dominant and so exasperating that in *Enemies of Promise* he spliced together quotations from Hemingway, Isherwood and Orwell to make a typical prose passage for 1938.[32] White, however, is not merely avoiding the colloquial manner in favour of the 'mandarin' line preferred by Connolly: the elevated style, long sentences and the concentration on upper class sensibilities that we find in Aldous Huxley and Virginia Woolf. White does not confine his attention as, by and large, they do to an upper-class milieu. The social range of the novel extends from the working class to the shabby lower regions of the upper middle class. Moreover, *The Living and the Dead*, like 'The House Behind the Barricades', offers a criticism of self-regarding bourgeois sensibilities. The young novelist is anxious to convince his reader that he is on the side of political engagement.

However, if we define 'mandarin' as difficult and linguistically sophisticated rather than merely upper-class prose, *The Living and the Dead* belongs in this line. White's particular concern in the novel is to reconcile the historical seriousness his thirties conscience forces on him with a modernist method.

After the experiments with modernist style in *Happy Valley*, *The Living and the Dead* seems assured in its drawings on Eliot, Joyce and Woolf. White has learned from Joyce, for instance, to present entire sections of the narrative in terms of the sensibility, though not necessarily directly through the eyes, of a particular character. In these sections external events and things are steeped in subjectivity. In the symbolist manner environment suggests states of soul. Moreover, the style in these sections serves the same end. The narrative voice loses impartiality and becomes caught up by the sensibility it is registering.

White has also learned, chiefly perhaps from Woolf, to subjectivise time not merely by having his narrator announce, as in *Happy Valley*, that time is not always measurable by the clock but by focusing the action through the consciousness of each of the characters and by paying careful attention to the effects he is achieving at the level of the phrase. Connie Tiarks's fall from the mulberry tree is particularly well handled. By couching the fall in one long spiralling sentence composed of a series of phrases, spaced to measure Elyot's breaths and packed with sibilants and participles to register his horrified response, White allows Connie to crash less through the air than through the fascinated attention of her watcher:

> That was before she began, it happened at first slowly, her fingers slipping as surely as a fruit off its twig, her dress the downward flare that brushed his face, he saw, the rushing was the white dress, the head that tumbled with the sickness of a fruit, her voice stretched out in air.[33]

At times, it is true, the novel's modernist debts are, in Malcolm Lowry's words, 'maldigested and baleful'.[34] We find in a less polished form the same choice of image, the same phrasing, even the same recoil from physicality, that we find in early Eliot: '[o]nce as a child he [Elyot] had stuck a caterpillar with a pin, watched the writhing and a green liquid' (140). Similarly, the staked dog that Eden Standish and Joe Barnett find on the beach reminds us of the corpse of a dog which Stephen Dedalus notices while walking on a beach in *Ulysses*. To compare Joyce's dogsbody with White's is to be impressed by White's penchant for overloading his symbols. Not only must Joe's little terrier stand for the whole, wounded world; it must also be offered to us without a touch of humour, without, for instance, Joyce's genital-sniffing live dog who reminds us that life frisks on in the midst of death.[35] For all the obsessive concern in *The Living and the Dead* with 'the substance of things', the novelist seems curiously unconcerned with things in themselves (58). We never gain the sense, as we do in Lawrence, of the discrete, particular existence of things, whether a lobster on tip-toe or a woman combing her hair in the sun.

Allowing for these local failures in assimilating influences, *The Living and the Dead* is a major step forward in terms of its narrative organisation: the shape of the novel is governed less by the desire to trace a sequence of events than by the desire to register the impact of events on consciousness. In *Happy Valley* White relied on external action. In *The Living and the Dead* the entire action is contained within the retrospection of the central character, Elyot Standish, who thinks back over various events, jumbling their chronological order according to the importance he attaches to them subjectively – all this after leaving the station at which he has seen his sister, Eden, off to the Spanish war. This does not mean that the whole action is focused through the consciousness of Elyot. His enclosed sensibility does, however, frame the whole so that we view a disintegrating civilisation through a consciousness which cultivates a pose of detachment from its corruptions but which offers no way out. Elyot, like the speaker of 'The House Behind the Barricades', hears the call of actual suffering and senses a substantial world outside the boundaries of his cultivated and inward-looking sensibility. But like so many other young middle-class intellectuals in the thirties Elyot cannot break past class and education to touch 'the actual plane'.

Despite its employment of modernist strategies and techniques, however, *The Living and the Dead* retains an omniscient narrator who all too frequently blunders into the narrative, nudging the reader towards the appropriate moral judgements. Moreover, despite being organised around chunks of consciousness that intersect without actually touching one another, the novel retains an uncompromised sense of the characters as inescapably social beings. Behind the novel's confidently modernist surface we may find traces of the traditional realistic form of the bourgeois novel.

Framed by Elyot Standish's retrospection is a *Familienroman* in which
the Standishes are representative figures of the English middle class
in its period of decline.

In a manner characteristic of much thirties writing, White is trying to find a balance between the private and public worlds. Hence
his modernist techniques, which reinforce the private bias, must
reach a *modus vivendi* with the social bias of the novel. Although
the novel is framed by an intensely private sensibility, its form is
intended as a critique of solipsism. We are invited to view through
the 'dead' eyes of Elyot Standish the attractiveness of the more
open forms of living to which he cannot commit himself. In other
words, although Elyot seems, like Prufrock or Stephen Dedalus, to
be a sensibility in escape from the nightmare of history, he has
much more in common with those heroes of thirties novels like
Journey to the Border who are trying to shake themselves out of their
neurotic self-regard into the 'real' world of historical activity.

White's response to the modern world in *The Living and the
Dead* is of the thirties in that it is does not explicitly rest on a
nostalgia for an ideal of wholeness located in the past as did Eliot's,
Lawrence's and Pound's. The novel suggests that the condition of
the civilisation it describes is historically caused and may be altered
by the commitment of individuals to – the terms are admittedly
vague – life, love, socialism. The novel is not in any sense Marxist. It
does, however, see the working class as a source of hope by contrast
to a debilitated bourgeoisie. Such a viewpoint was common enough
among young bourgeois writers during the thirties. But White's
novel discloses an apparently unconscious authorial preference
for those sections of the working class that retain some link to
the old, vital and organic way of life of the English peasantry. Here
White's ideological bias seems closer to Lawrence's than to the
leftist English writers of the thirties, although organicist nostalgia
was common in the thirties, even among the Auden group.

White differs most signally from Eliot, Joyce and Woolf in the
characteristically thirties form of didacticism found in the novel.
The formal expression of this didacticism is found in White's
determination to place at the novel's moral centre an idealised
proletarian figure who takes his stand in favour of life by volunteer-
ing to fight for the Spanish Loyalists. White apparently feels obliged
by the pressure of the times to identify 'life' with the working man
(again, there is a Lawrentian bias in the terms). Joe Barnett embodies a species of proletarian piety whose comedy is unintentional.

Moreover, as an example of proletarian activism Joe could only be of comfort to the threatened exploiting classes. Not only is he the sort of quality-conscious producer of artifacts favoured by William Morris, as distinct from the alienated industrial worker, he also does his revolutionising safely outside Britain.

The Living and the Dead, in short, is sympathetic with but not wholeheartedly committed to the working class as a means of escape from the deadness of contemporary civilisation. This uncertainty on White's part ought to be reassuring. Authorial doubt prevents politically interested art from turning into propaganda. Yet the equivocations in the novel do not proceed from any real complexity of political insight. There is none of that doubleness of vision we find in Marvell's odes or Yeats's political poems. We are not, in any case, led to expect complex insight by the novel's title so much as fully resolved vision. The authoritativeness of the title is calculated to cow us. It promises an apocalyptic division of a whole civilisation into a secular version of the damned and the saved.

Clearly the novel *is* seeking some fullness of life to which it might commit its energies, a fullness in which working-class values, however vaguely understood, must have some part. But what part? And what precisely is meant by the term 'Life' with which White bullies us? There is a presumption in the use of this term which reminds us of another thirties Jeremiah, F. R. Leavis, who, at least, knows what he means by the word.[36] But White, because he is not sure, allows the novel's centre of interest to slip away into vagueness, obfuscation and sentimentality.

White's problem with his working-class characters is a characteristically thirties one: his political sentiments clash with his ineradicable bourgeoisness. The mood of the novel recalls Auden's equivocations throughout the thirties about the Marxist conviction that the future lies with the working class. In a burst of enthusiasm for the Spanish left and righteous hatred of fascism Auden penned the line he later deleted from *Spain* which condones 'the necessary murder'.[37] Auden felt that bourgeois liberal culture was doomed and that socialism was inevitable and probably salutary, but he could not suppress doubts about the desirability of its application to a society whose 'decadent' freedom he enthusiastically enjoyed. He could not altogether slough off the liberal culture that made the individual rather than the collective the ultimate repository of value.

White is writing at a time when the faith of English writers in communism had been undermined by the events of the late thirties and early forties. White himself had never been attracted to Marxism, yet he evidently feels, as late as 1941 when bourgeois individualism was coming back into vogue, that intellectuals had a moral obligation to identify with the oppressed. He also feels that in the working class is to be found a source of value unavailable elsewhere in a collapsing civilisation, even if he is more influenced in this respect by nostalgia for beloved family servants than by ideology. Like Auden, White is not interested in the specifics of how to change the civilisation revealed to be rotten. Like Auden also, his equivocations express themselves in his writing by a tendency to sheer away from the central problems posed by apocalyptic thought, not towards Freud or Marx as Auden does, but towards a Lawrentian faith in things and in sexual love.

The choice the novel offers us is a moral one in the Lawrentian sense that we are required to choose among various responses to life. We are confronted with the ugliness and fragmentation that White sees in modern life and are required to take sides: we must choose between the living-dead, all those who have retreated in the face of life's possibilities, and those who seek 'an intenser form of living' (379). As William Walsh puts it, the novel 'dramatises the distinction which Lawrence made between life and existence'.[38]

The novel offers a choice, however, not between real life and mere existence but one between mere existence and real death. *The Living and the Dead* perverts the Lawrentian vision it seems by its title to have adopted. For Lawrence the absence of God forces human beings to find religious meaning in life itself, particularly in sexual love. There is a morbidity in White's treatment of sexuality that allows him brilliantly to present the parody of love performed by Elyot and Muriel but prevents his giving 'life' to the love-making of Joe and Eden. For these two, love leads only to death. Joe leaves the living-death of England not with his lover in search of more life – a Lawrentian solution – but for the lonely battlefields of a war whose meaning he has failed to grasp. He dies for a set of symbols: 'the *apparent* fact of Spain' recorded in the newspapers (288, my emphasis). Eden's love for Joe fails to overcome her feeling that the world lacks substance. She sees the world as '[a] cold star' (334). She sees their love-making merely as an attempt to infuse into 'the dying body of the world' their living acts and convictions (334). After their night together which fails to warm her into life she flees from a tinkers' camp '[a]s if someone had lived here too fully' (353). Her decision to follow Joe to Spain is a form of suicide. It is prompted by the message that spring brings her of the necessity for the individual organism to submit to the obscure purposes of the larger design, that is, by dying. The novel is more than half in love with the death it promises to oppose.

The word 'world' in *The Living and the Dead* comes to mean not so much the world of social relations – the usual sphere of the novelist – but the material world itself, understood in some Manichaean sense. We are presented in the midst of the general decay of a culture with a single point of value: the love between a working-class man and a disenchanted bourgeois woman. Far from redeeming the deadness, however, this love serves only to underline its pervasiveness. Death insinuates its presence all too easily into even the most intimate moments of love. The recoil from materiality and sexuality is too strongly felt in *The Living and the Dead* to allow the body to provide access to fullness of life. The novel cannot settle on a way out of the living-death it delineates with mingled fascination and horror. The problem lies in the novel's confusion about whether what it opposes is the condition of the world at a given historical moment or is simply the world itself, the world of things that pass.

This indecision on White's part leads not only to a confusion of purpose but also to a suspicion in the novel about the value of its own endeavour. The novel consigns among the dead all those who offer the symbol of a thing or an emotion rather than the reality: the dealers in words, gestures, abstractions. At the same time, the novel converts the world it deals with from something real – a complex and ever-changing whole composed of material facts, social relations and private thoughts – into something abstract: a dying piece of matter adrift in space onto which man is thrown.

What is most germane in this novel to White's subsequent development as a novelist is his consciousness that the central problem he faces formally is that of reconciling his moral seriousness with his intensely self-conscious preoccupation with language. *The Living and the Dead* locates the source of its own formal problems in the impasse reached by the civilisation it describes. The English language, as White sees it in this novel, has been infected by the inability of English culture to connect action and meaning, word and thing, gesture and emotion. This corruption of the word is felt ubiquitously: the newspapers translate the deaths in Spain or China into empty abstractions; the inn at which Joe and Eden spend the night fails to provide the 'Hovis' it advertises, reminding Eden of the gap between sign and referent. The novel, seeking substance rather than sign, is thwarted wherever it turns within English life. By the late thirties England has become for White as much as Elyot Standish, an 'elaborate charade that meant something once, a long time ago. When the figures, the gestures were related to enthusiasms' (228). In a culture where aridity has become so pervasive, there can be no place for the writer who seeks to point the way back to desired simplicities. The solution, as White found after the war, was to relocate his nostalgia and revivify his writing by returning to Australia.

2

Pastoral and Apocalypse

The Post-War Context

Graham Greene in *Stamboul Train* (1932) introduces a comic Edwardian novelist, Q. C. Savory, lingering into the modern world railing against Joyce, Lawrence, and 'morbid introspection'.[1] In the early thirties young novelists serious about their craft were obliged to show themselves acquainted with the experiments of modernism. Not to do so invited the kind of ridicule that Greene directs at Savory. Two decades later the literary fashion had swung so sharply away from modernism that contemporary novelists were more likely to become the butt of ridicule by embracing modernism than by opposing it.

In John Wain's *Hurry On Down* (1953) a comic modernist novelist is introduced to complement Greene's ridiculous Edwardian one. Wain's Edwin Froulish is a caricature of the modernist novelist as Savory is a caricature of the Edwardian one, and the comic quality in both rests upon their having misjudged the tenor of their ages. Edwin Froulish, with his addiction to flashbacks, stream-of-consciousness, word play, punning, absurdly allegorical plots, symbolism, symphonic structure, and his dislike of realism and conventional characterisation, is as out of place in the English literary scene of the fifties as Q.C. Savory was in that of the thirties. Wain's cure for Froulish, by way of a disgruntled character, is 'a course of Thackery'.[2]

In the late 1930s Patrick White was part of the contemporary English literary scene, however peripheral and minor he may have been in it. By the late 1950s his writing had taken a wholly different direction from contemporary English writing. The only English writer of the period with whom he might fruitfully be compared is Malcolm Lowry who had also chosen self-exile from a literary scene

to which he felt antagonistic. There is, however, merit in comparing
White's post-war fiction written in Australia to the English fiction
with which it is contemporary. White shares some significant common features with the English writers of the period. He too is a
traditionalist, at odds with the modern world and showing at times
a strong preference for the conventions of the Victorian novel.
Unlike the English writers, however, he uses a variety of stylistic
conventions in his writing rather than a single dominant style. The
links of his post-war fiction to nineteenth-century realism are clear,
but the realist elements exist inside a frame that places conflicting
stylistic tendencies side by side.

Voss was published in 1957. Among English novels it is contemporary with Kingsley Amis's *I Like It Here* (1958), John Braine's
Room at the Top (1957), William Golding's *Pincher Martin* (1956),
L. P. Hartley's *The Hireling* (1957), Iris Murdoch's *The Bell* (1958),
Anthony Powell's *At Lady Molly's* (1957), Angus Wilson's *The Middle
Age of Mrs Eliot* (1958), and C. P. Snow's *The Conscience of the Rich*
(1958). There has been considerable critical dispute about the
merits of this body of fiction. Several American critics have condemned post-war English novelists for their traditionalism and for
their reluctance to employ modernist techniques.[3] English novelists
and critics have defended the traditionalism of the contemporary
English novel on the grounds that the interest of English novelists
in character and plot, Victorian as it may seem, reflects social
realities in England.[4] Malcolm Bradbury has claimed that there
are in fact modernist orientations in the post-war English novel if
only one looks hard enough.[5] By and large English writers have
accepted the American charge of dullness in the English novel
and in English society, but have expressed satisfaction with a
society that lacks the dangers and bizarreness of American society.[6]
American reality, being 'incredible', justifies the frenzy distortions,
and outrageousness of American writing; English society, being
homogeneous, orderly, and traditional, is more properly reflected
in a restrained fictional manner.[7]

The English mood is summed up by the disgruntled hero of
Amis's *I Like It Here* who dislikes 'abroad' and likes London,
although he wishes it were still the London of the eighteenth
century. Amis' preference for the eighteenth century is sympto-
matic of a general mood of nostalgia that pervades the post-war
English scene. Sometimes the preference is for the Edwardian
period, sometimes for Victorianism or the Augustans – whatever

the age nostalgia deferred to, the same dissatisfaction with the modern world and its characteristic literary modes may be dis- covered beneath the rhetoric. The mood is one of regression, the desire to deny the dissatisfactions of the present by fixing the attention on some less troubling past. It is a mood reflected in the stories of Elizabeth Bowen, particularly those in *The Demon Lover* (1945) which trace the decline of the English middle class in the interwar period and which mourn its vanished assurance. It is a mood of longing for childhood reflected not only in Bowen's stories but also in the manifesto of the 'Angry Young Man', John Osborne's *Look Back in Anger* (1956), where Jimmy Porter prefers Edwardian colonels and nursery games to the angst of living in 'the American Age'. Margaret Drabble, in a passage which stands in stark opposition to 'The Prodigal Son' where White speaks of the desirability of learning to write, as it were, from scratch, sums up the English mood in a 1963 radio interview:

> I don't want to write an experimental novel to be read by people in fifty years, who will say, ah, well, yes, she foresaw what was coming. I'm just not interested. I'd rather be at the end of a dying tradition, which I admire, than at the beginning of a tradition which I deplore.[8]

Lowry had the English novel of the 1940s and 50s in mind when he observed that '[n]othing indeed can be more unlike the actual experience of life than the average novelist's realistic portrait of a character'.[9] The Wells-Gallsworthy notion of char- acter as something fixed, predictable, mechanically determined by class and background – this is what Lowry means by 'the average novelist's realistic portrait of a character'. In the fifties, C. P. Snow was producing characters according to this model as though 'reality' had remained static since the Edwardian period, as though surrealism, expressionism, fascism, the bombing of civilian populations – all the monstrous historical events and extreme artistic movements of this century – had not exploded the orderly social world of 1910. Snow's nostalgia for the Edwardian age is characteristic. Hearing stories of the lost Edwardian world, Lewis Eliot, Snow's autobiographical hero, is swept away by 'the imaginary land which exists just before one's childhood. Often as I heard them I felt something like homesick – homesick for a time before I was born.'[10] This is a nostalgia not merely for a prior age but for a mythical world confused with the paradise of childhood. It represents what Hermann Hesse called 'the worst and most deadly of all dreams'.[11]

The attempt to exclude the extreme, the disruptive, the radically private from the novel, the avoidance of technical difficulty, the attention to common-place lives, the emphasis on realism, moderation, clarity, reasonableness – all this has been seen as merely a swing of the pendulum of modern British fiction, a necessary corrective to the strategies of modernism which had become not avant-garde but predictable by the end of the war.[12] Yet the English literary scene in the fifties remains an impoverished and nerveless milieu, however reasonable may seem its objections to the cultural scene it superseded. Bloomsbury mandarins may have ignored the lives of working- and lower-middle-class Englishmen, but they were aware of, and often politically and morally involved in, a world they rightly felt to be disintegrating.

The English novelists of the 1950s do not confront the great violences of twentieth-century life. We do not feel in their novels, as we feel in *Voss* or *Under the Volcano*, that uncompromising search for appropriate 'design-governing postures', by which to represent a world given over to its own destruction. Malcolm Bradbury has singled out Lowry as an English writer who is exceptional in this regard. White is the other notable exception. White and Lowry are the inheritors both of high modernism and of the 1930s stress on history. Moreover, each extended *both* these movements into the post-war period, adjusting these formative influences on their early fiction to the new conditions that obtained in the aftermath of war. While most post-war English novelists (William Golding is a notable exception) looked back to a more settled order in the past, Lowry and White responded to the shock of the Nazi horrors and the bankruptcy of liberal humanism in the face of those horrors and to the triumphant spread of an affluent mass culture. The formal adventurousness of their writing shows how spurious is the claim that by the fifties modernism had become a 'stylistic backlog'.[13]

By retreating to Castle Hill, White did not isolate himself from the main literary and historical trends of his time any more than Lowry did by retreating to the beach at Dollarton, British Columbia, where between 1939 and 1947 he wrote *Under the Volcano*. White's work after 1947 engages with an historical experience that threatens to negate the idea of history itself. Lowry apart, this cannot be said of any English novelist in the fifties unless, like Malcolm Bradbury, we consider Samuel Beckett an English writer.[14] While English fiction was attempting to connect itself to the less demanding world that existed before 1914, White was placing the captivating images of that world inside a frame that recognised how irrevocably it had become part of the past. *Voss* is not merely an historical novel set in the mid-nineteenth-century; its structure allows White to set side-by-side different interpretations of the world and different literary kinds. The idyll, the pastoral, those forms which emphasise wholeness, continuity and simplicity, are set against apocalyptic forms which stress disruption and discontinuity. Like *Under the Volcano* – itself a palimpsest of twentieth-century literary styles – White's post-war fiction contains a mixture of seemingly antagonistic elements. This stylistic mixing is White's chief means of responding *formally* to the violences and disruptions of his time.

The Aunt's Story

White began writing *The Aunt's Story* in London after demobilisation. The novel was completed in Australia on his return there in 1947. It is White's favourite among his novels and a crucial work in terms of his development as a novelist. Formally and stylistically, the novel looks back to White's experiments with modernism in *The Living and the Dead*. But the modernist tendencies are included within a new frame. The controlling consciousness of the novel, Theodora Goodman, is not a sophisticated urban consciousness, as is Elyot Standish. She is a simple person, but one whose mind is capable of encompassing great human truths. She is also part of the Australian world but separate from it, one of the alienated figures who will allow him in his post-war fiction to bring a richness of texture, theme and style to an experience he finds generally barren and unsympathetic.

It is the social scene not the landscape of Australia with which White finds himself at odds. The land is accepting of outsiders. In the opening section of *The Aunt's Story* the land is more receptive to the 'dark verse' of the exotic names bestowed by the squatters on their homesteads than it is to the squatters themselves.[15] Their lives are the stuff of prose. It is the land that smoulders, that possesses depth; on the lips of the white Australians even the rich suggestiveness of 'Meroë' is lost. Theodora Goodman, however, is not mired in the prosy stuff of their world. Her mornings thrill with the songs of 'bulbuls', thrushes made poetic by a Persian name. Theodora, who responds to the poetic possibilities of words, is the medium by which White returns to his remembered Australia: not the exotic Australia of *Happy Valley* but the pastoral Australia of his boyhood. He returns to an Australia before the great splintering of modernity has entered its closed world.

This return links him to a number of post-war English writers for whom the shapes of nostalgia were those of childhood and of the period immediately before the First World War. White's nostalgia, however, has a harder edge than theirs: it is an aesthetic strategy rather than the result of having reached an ideological impasse. White does not retreat into the mythical order that supposedly remained intact until 1914. Nor does he ignore modernist advances in fictional form.

In *The Aunt's Story* White has made creative capital out of his ambivalence about fictional form and the suitability of Australia to the kind of fiction he admires. He has built the novel on a recognition that the epic forms appropriate to unbroken societies such as that of pre-war, rural Australia are not appropriate to modern experience which, by its very nature, is a broken one. The first section of the novel set in Australia before 1914 employs the myth of an unspoiled order to gain a vantage point from which to trace the movement towards disorder of modern history and continues, with certain equivocations, the traditional and mimetic tendencies present in *Happy Valley*. The middle section of the novel, set in between-the-wars Europe, wholly submits to the modernist impulses with which we found White struggling to come to terms in *The Living and the Dead*. In the final section of the novel White achieves, for the first time, a balance between the main conflicting impulses in his fiction.

In *Happy Valley*, the symbolist tendencies in White's writing were focused on his depiction of Sidney Furlow, while the realist ones were concentrated on Clem Hagan the coarse, extroverted foreman. White was unable to distance himself from an oppressive sense of the 'ordinariness' of Australian life as Sidney Furlow was unable to ward off the aggressive intentions of Hagan. The rough and outward aspects of Australian life carry off the enclosed, feminine world of sensibility as the novel closes. In *The Aunt's Story* White's central concentration is on Theodora's long odyssey into the self. The extrovert world of the red outback male – Frank

Parrott standing in here for Hagan – finally has little seductive power for Theodora.

The chief advantage of concentrating on a single sympathetic consciousness is the unifying perspective such a method allows, especially in the Meroë section of the novel. The symbolism no longer seems like an exercise in technique by a novice author as it does in the earlier novels. We discover Theodora as a sensibility of infinite subtlety and responsiveness through the novel's symbols: the red eye of the little hawk, the grub in the rose, the filigree ball. Even very minor characters such as the Man who was Given his Dinner are invested with a strange, rich life in the novel because we meet them through the endless, delicate reverberations to which they give rise in Theodora's mind. Form, idiom, style, symbolism all develop organically around the controlling centre of Theodora's consciousness.

The formal unity and simplicity of the 'Meroë' section are entirely fitting to the period and the place, Edwardian Australian society. White deliberately stresses the unity of the life by his style and selection of imagery. With notable economy, White encompasses the range of social types afforded by the place. The country houses nourish red- or hatchet-faced farmers preoccupied with sheep and acres. Civilisation in such a milieu means race meetings and, at its most grand, vice-regal visits. Pearl Brawne marks White's first descent into the Sydney *demi-monde*. She is one of those sexual misfits or victims for whom White has an instinctive sympathy and who provide access to a declassed milieu which White will people with the eccentrics and visionaries he favours. For all its narrowness this is a society that presents to the view no uncertainties about where it is headed, no metaphysical anxieties, no inner antagonisms. It is a life lived on the surface by limited but credible characters who sense no abysm within the self. It is a thoroughly materialistic and self-confident world.

Yet the uncertainties are there, although they are never permitted to take centre stage. They become more apparent as the First World War approaches. At intervals the report of a murder or a suicide disturbs the calm, dull routine of colonial life: Mr. Buchanan, the owner of Audley prior to the Parrotts, shoots himself; Jack Frost, the pastry cook, kills his wife and three little daughters before committing suicide; Theodora toys with the thought of killing her mother. Such events are deliberately understated: made unreal by being reported second-hand; made fabulous by the addition of a mistress who bathed in milk; or made ridiculous by the nursery-rhyme name of the infanticide. It is as though the convention of tragedy which allows the artist to contain and give form to the violent and terrifying aspects of life cannot exist in such a world except as its comic obverse, farce. When old Mrs Goodman dies at last Theodora hurtles down the stairs to stand on the back porch unsure whether she must act out a tragedy or a farce. How can she bring home to her decent, suburban neighbour, Mr Love, that real death exists outside the columns in the newspapers from which source he informs her in neighbourly fashion of 'a vile murder in Cremorne'? (123) Death is incidental to this busy, orderly world.

Australian pre-war life presents a facade which denies the possibility that uncontrollable forces might erupt into daily life. Despite the pretensions of the squatters and their wives to being a colonial landed gentry, this is a bourgeois world whose virtues are the bourgeois ones of reliability and constraint and whose notion of character rests upon a static bourgeois notion of personality as the manifestation of class and possessions. White has perfectly adapted the form of 'Meroë' to the life of the place. The foreground is almost entirely lacking in events. We learn of the monstrous and shapeless impulses of life only via gossip or as reported speech. History, the narrative of events 'in serial form', occurs outside Australia as Europe lurches towards war (83). White has made us feel in these opening chapters the static quality of pre-1914 life, its emptiness which, like the filigree ball, waits to be filled with apocalyptic fire.

We view this solid-seeming world through the eyes of a personality that even in this opening section is fragmenting. We feel that we are in the world of the *Bildungsroman*, the novel of development, because of the increasing persuasiveness of Theodora's insights into the world around her. Theodora is by far the most sensitive and receptive consciousness White has yet conceived. She registers external events, however slight their apparent consequence, with a minute responsiveness. Moreover we are persuaded that she grows through suffering towards a wisdom stored up in what one of the epigraphs to the novel calls 'that solitary land of the individual experience' to which we are given privileged access. However, we are able to measure her maturation only by her own subjective standards, by the power of her insights to convince us. Theodora moves not towards reconciliation with the community and the adjustment of her private world to the demands of external reality but towards a more and more radical isolation. It is true that we build up a picture of a palpable social and physical world in which Theodora has her being, a world constantly confirmed by the narrator. Yet this world exists alongside a separate and eccentric view of its contours gradually established in Theodora's mind.

In *The Aunt's Story*, rural Australia is filtered through a sensibility that possesses the subtlety and spaciousness of one of James's or Woolf's female characters. By focusing the life of the place through such a consciousness – one more interested in the symbolist properties of names than in the objects to which they refer, more interested in the shapes which the mind confers on matter than in outward forms or mere facts – White has arrived at a means of framing an experience he finds lacking in the qualities he wishes to explore in his fiction: richness of texture, depth, the poetic possibilities of life.

In the first section of *The Aunt's Story*, we recognise a sharply present world of things, detailed and diverse, that is independent of Theodora's perception, yet increasingly Theodora does not meet and accede to the demands of the 'real' world. As Theodora's contact with the external world becomes more tenuous, the society around her becomes more and more materialistic. Her father, George, who shares with her an interest in spiritual odysseys is bought out by his squatter neighbours. His own odysseys to Europe are financed by the sale of his paddocks until the last remnant of the land that had supported his gentility is sold to the arriviste brewer who marries Una Russell. Thus the tenuous link between the colonial squatter and the English landed aristocracy is finally severed. The bourgeois world swallows the old order. From genteel to commercial, from stable to energetic, from ordered to incoherent – everywhere the Australia of 'Meroë' lapses from fixed, pseudo-aristocratic forms into the ugliness and vulgarity of the modern world.

This movement of decline is registered in the novel not only by the progressive alienation of Theodora Goodman from a world whose banality oppresses her but also by the formal movement of the writing away from the epic towards the ironic mode. By focusing the novel's concern with the Homeric theme of voyaging through Theodora Goodman, White is able simultaneously to evoke the two senses of 'epic' Georg Lukács outlines in *The Theory of the Novel*: in the Homeric age before the dawn of philosophy humans were at home in the world; in the modern world, after the metaphysical spheres have been broken, humans must go in search of meaning through a world no longer adequate to 'the soul's inner demand . . . for wholeness'.[16] In 'Meroë' the Homeric allusions at first serve to establish the stability of the grazier world as Theodora, already nostalgically, views it. This world is unbroken, limited but whole.

Theodora herself is destined to embark on the modern odyssey 'from which there [is] no return': the journey into the self once the fatal rift between inner and outer has been discovered (82). Sensing this, in a passage rich with Homeric suggestion, Theodora grasps that her mother, like Penelope, is fated never to embark: '[h]er world had always been enclosed by walls, her Ithaca' (p. 82). Theodora, however, must leave this intact world because, between her mother's time and her own, the genteel way of life that had made it possible has broken down.

At Meroë George Goodman read the *Odyssey* and invested the life of the house with an epic quality. In the between-the-wars Europe in which Theodora seeks adventure in the second section of the novel 'the ghosts of Homer and St. Paul and Tolstoy wait[ ] for the crash' (133). The forms which correspond to the great phases of European civilisation – the epic form of the heroic phase, the call to inwardness of Pauline Christianity, the realist epic – have suffered a decline into a modern world represented by the garish Mrs Rapallo whose pomp is that of clowns and circuses. Adventuress (in the vulgar sense), imposter, American – Mrs Rapallo is the vulture feeding on the past of Europe. While Theodora adventures in search of meaning, Mrs. Rapallo adventures in search of bric-à-brac.

What strikes us most forcefully in reading 'Jardin Exotique' is not the radicalness of the content – the decay of European civilisation was a hackneyed theme by 1948 – but the sheer assurance of the writing. In the middle section of the novel the prose dramatises the break-up it records in the world of events at the same time working out an appropriate idiom in which to convey what is now apparent in Theodora as incipient schizophrenia. The prose style, in its endless crystalline bifurcations, submits to, rather than seeks to contain, the fragmentation of the content. White has exactly calculated a response at the level of form and style to that, 'great fragmentation of maturity' to which Henry Miller refers in the epigraph to this section of the novel.

In 'Jardin Exotique' White attenuates the connection between 'the personal' and 'the universal' in order to give expression to the full complexity of the relations between consciousness and history. Theodora's disintegration as a personality is not *caused* by historical events. The bearing of external tensions on her inner illness is tenuous at best. We are aware of two parallel movements of collapse, and that outside Theodora's skull is conveyed with far less particularity than that within. White's prose has become a fluid vehicle that slips effortlessly between the subjective and the objective worlds so that we are often not quite sure which we are in.

At the conclusion of the 'Meroë' section, Theodora had come to accept that '[t]here is no lifeline to other lives' (125). This acceptance does not enrich her inner life. It 'hollow[s] her out' (125). Henceforth, she will have to rely on her imagination to invent the others who will serve in lieu of relationships. In the course of her wanderings through Europe a qualitative leap in isolation occurs so that Theodora loses contact not only with people but also with the physical world itself. Now she must walk through a surprising and fragmented world.

In Europe she enters reluctantly into the age of symbols in which, all substance having disappeared from the world of things, the objects of that world can serve only as equivalents for states of soul. The memory of the simple world of childhood and Australia where the roses were real and fleshy cannot sustain her. This phase of symbols is replaced by one in which Theodora's mind is still more radically at odds with the world she inhabits. By the time she finds herself in the Hôtel du Midi the *jardin exotique*, which has the outlines of the garden at Meroë, is 'untouchable' (134). Its living objects have been frozen, made abstract by the mind, and are 'static' (134).

The objects in the *jardin exotique* are symbolic in an abstract and chilling sense: they no longer participate in a fruitful union between the mind and the world of things. Yet the garden is not wholly bereft of the presence of the mind. Its 'pink and yellow mouths, coldly tear[ ] at cloth or draw[ ] blood' (134). Theodora's subjective life has spilled into the garden. Hence the distorted, exaggerated quality of the flowers. Although Theodora has withdrawn from nature, the grotesque forms of her inner life force themselves upon the world of things. Her soul in torment twists the world to its own shapes.

In expressionism White has found the mode perfectly suited to 'Jardin Exotique'. The violent distortions of expressionism allow him to give form to Theodora's radically disoriented perception of the world. Realism would be inappropriate as a means of embodying Theodora's way of seeing. Nor would symbolism, of the kind he employs in *The Living and The Dead*, be appropriate. White wants a strategy which allows him to treat objects not as correlatives *for* emotion but as expressions *of* emotion. Expressionism, with its violence and its distortions is ideally suited to delineating Theodora's rending apart of subject and object.

At the same time, expressionism allows White to embody his own acutely negative response to European civilisation in the late thirties in a manner that realism could not match. As Walter Sokel has observed of the German context: 'a largely negative attitude to society leads away from realistic observation to exaggeration, distortion, shrillness, and abstractness, qualities which reappear in Expressionism.'[17] White's visits to Germany as a young man were evidently influential, as were Lowry's. Both took away with them strategies and perspectives which were to appear much later in their development as novelists, in the German section of *Riders in the Chariot* as much as in *Under the Volcano*. Expressionism is a marked quality in White's style. It is noticeable in his chromatic effects, his penchant for distortion and for close-ups of anguished faces (very like those in Francis Bacon's portraits), his obsession with fragmentation and extreme individuality. His transcendentalism, his contempt for the bourgeoisie, his antagonistic view of the modern age, the gothic strain in his writing – all agree with central stresses of expressionism.

There were expressionist tendencies in *The Living and The Dead*, but in the middle section of *The Aunt's Story* expressionism has become a central strategy of style. This is most notable in the violence that suddenly appears as Theodora's perception of the world becomes fearful and distorted: 'she could not escape too soon from the closed room, retreating from the jaws of roses, avoiding the brown door, of which the brass teeth bristled to consume the last shreds of personality' (133). The extreme violence of these fantasies links them to the savagely expressive works of Munch and Kirchner: 'That is all very well, and true, Monsieur Durand, Theodora would have said, but you forget how you bared your teeth one morning in the glass, and wondered whether their desperation would bite, or whether your tongue, branching suddenly and peculiarly from your mouth, might not be uprooted by the hand like any other fungus' (225).

One of White's finest pieces of caricature is the description of Mrs Rapallo making her entrance which has not only the violence and distortion but also the jerky sense of line, the chromatic expressivity, and the cluttered composition we find in expressionist paintings:

> She was put together painfully, rashly, ritually, crimson over purple. Her eye glittered, but her breath was grey. Under her great hat, on which a bird had settled years before, spreading its meteoric tail in a landscape of pansies, mignonette, butterflies, and shells, her face shrieked with the inspired clowns, peered through the branches of mascara at objects she could not see, and sniffed through thin nostrils at many original smells. (149)

The organisation of this little scene is deliberately painterly. We see Mrs. Rapallo from the outside as a bizarre organisation of details, shifting forms, and colours, moving through space. The expressionist style in which this scene is presented is set against other, more nostalgic, painterly styles employed in the novel. General Sokolnikov's picture of himself lying with his shirt open, waiting for tea while peasants manhandle a cow outside his window, for instance, suggests nineteenth-century realism (168).

It is hardly surprising that White took from his German experience in the thirties a vivid sense not only of the enormity of the political events of the time but also of the extreme formal strategies by which modernist artists have sought to express those enormities. How safe and simple pre-1914 Australia must have seemed from the perspective of the 1940s, and we can feel White's nostalgia for the simple forms of Australian pastoral life along with his revulsion at the banality of Australian suburbia in the 1950s in 'The Prodigal Son'. What is surprising is that White should stress in *Riders in the Chariot* the similarities rather than the differences between post-war suburban Australia and the nightmare of Germany in the thirties. The crucifixion of the Jew, Himmelfarb, in a Sydney factory yard is meant to remind us that the human propensity for cruelty is universal. We should expect that White would find the hectic and fragmented forms of expressionism appropriate to the treatment of a disintegrating Europe but not to a homogeneous Australia in which 'the great millenium of dissolution, the epoch of ideas', has not yet arrived (160). In *The Aunt's Story* this is in fact the case: in Australia life is lived on the outside, in

Europe real life is all on the inside, inseparable from the sickness of the soul which twists the actual world into the shapes of its illness.

This is the Europe Theodora prepares to leave at the end of 'Jardin Exotique'. As the section closes the Hôtel du Midi and its cast of derelict, between-the-wars characters, who are partly real, partly figments of Theodora's imagination, are consumed on the bonfire of their own lusts and illusions. This is White's mode of expressing the final heave of an exhausted Europe into the great rending down process of the Second World War, as the Consul's death in *Under the Volcano* is Lowry's. Both novels straddle the war years and dramatise the historical debacle of the time. Both internalise the events they describe: take them out of history and throw them into the psyche of an individual whose suffering is representative. Each has a central character whose consciousness is richer and more expansive than that of other characters, yet is also flawed. At the close of 'Jardin Exotique' Theodora Goodman leaves behind the corrupted forms of a Europe that has lost all contact with the meanings that once lay behind its habitual symbols.

Theodora puts behind her the Europe of *The Living and The Dead*: the world of 'metal hieroglyphs' that point to no meanings (246). She resists the call of a Greek innocence represented by Katina Pavlou, the loveliest of her creations, as White resisted the appeal of Greece after the war. She is overcome by 'an immeasurable longing to read the expression on the flat yellow face of stone' (246). In other words, she is returning to Australia. Yet Theodora Goodman leaves Europe in possession of a sensibility of immense complexity and creative power. Hers is a fragmented and isolated consciousness, yet out of her inner life she is able to create visions.

This is necessary if White is to return to Australia and create there, not in Europe, the rich and self-conscious art of which he has by now proved himself a master. Theodora has learnt the trick that will henceforth sustain White as an 'Australian' writer: the trick of giving independent life to one's illusions, of allowing the mind to fill the 'real' world with its own inventions. This is the meaning of her letter to the Parrotts; 'the time has come at last to return to Abyssinia' (250–1). For there were always two Meroës: the first is that of the sour earth of a new country; the second is the land where names have the pure meaning of musical notes which is not in Australia, of course, nor in Africa, but in the imagination.

In the final section of *The Aunt's Story*, 'Holstius', White disentangles the outside world from the world of Theodora's consciousness. White's familiar, intrusive narrator makes a comeback, and we find his presence especially disconcerting after his withdrawal during the 'Jardin Exotique' sequence. The narrator's primary purpose is to heap scorn on the normal world from which Theodora has withdrawn and to bludgeon us into siding with Theodora against the pettiness, the small-mindedness and the cruelty of the 'normal'. It is difficult not to object to this narrative bullying. We may concur with the narrator's evident repugnance for the Frank Parrott who complacently consigns his sister-in-law to a 'home', but should we feel obliged to condemn Frank because he enjoys his breakfast? However, White's narrative stance in this final section of the novel is not the result of an authorial failure of nerve after the rigours of 'Meroë'.

In this brief section, White establishes the narrative method on which he will build his subsequent novels. For all its obvious limitations it will prove a remarkably flexible instrument. Into the final stage of the unfolding of Theodora's odyssey White has cunningly inserted a vignette of Australian squatter life. Here, in sharp contrast to the expressionist distortions of 'Jardin Exotique', the normal aspects of life are exaggerated with genuine comic effect. The Parrotts are deliberately wicked caricatures of ordinary life, but they are not at all distorted. We see them warming their posteriors, plotting how to dispose of Theodora and eating their breakfasts. The very solidity of their world is emphasised so that we find all the more shocking the unbearable loneliness of the aunt who asks: '[w]hy . . . is this world, which is so tangible in appearance, so difficult to hold?' (266). This method of setting normal social life against the life of isolates and eccentrics will find its completion in *Voss* and *Riders in the Chariot*. In *Voss*, the journey of the expedition into the interior of the continent, another symbolic journey into the self, is interspersed with comic scenes of bourgeois life in Sydney. White in his post-war fiction approaches from a new direction the thirties problem of finding some method by which both the inner world of subjectivity and the outer world of social activity can be given expression in the same text.

The narrative method that makes its appearance in 'Holstius' represents a major breakthrough in White's fictional development. In the first two sections of the novel White pushes to their extreme stylistic expressions the opposed modes by which the two worlds, that of inwardness and that of social experience, are given form in fiction. In the third section a single, slender bridge between the two worlds is suggested by the child, Lou Parrott, who inhabits her parents' world of cheerfully extroverted normality yet who sympathises with Theodora's wholly inward world. Lou anticipates Laura Trevelyan in *Voss* as a link between radically alternative worlds. By exaggerating the distance between the social and the psychological, White has found a way out of the impasse reached by English writers in the thirties who felt obliged to show their commitment to history but who could not abandon sensibility. White is able to employ in the same text both the strategies of realist prose fiction and those strategies derived from symbolism and to deal with history without using journalistic kinds of discourse.

The two worlds are, in the words of Holstius who is himself one of Theodora's illusions, the 'irreconcilable halves' of human experience: reality and illusion which constantly trick one another into assuming fresh shapes (272). The Parrotts' solid-seeming, extroverted life cannot dissolve Theodora's wholly inward life. Nor can Theodora deny the substantiality of their world merely by tearing up her tickets home and by repudiating her name (names for Theodora have always tended to betray the spiritual possibilities of words by fastening them to things).

Paul Klee observed during the First World War that 'the more horrifying the world becomes . . . the more art becomes abstract; while a world at peace produces realism in art'.[18] The organisation of *The Aunt's Story* neatly illustrates this remark. Unlike the German Expressionists after the First War, White after the Second was able to return to a land at peace, a land whose complacent air of certainty, whose faith in the materialistic, cried out for realistic treatment. In *The Aunt's Story* war-threatened Europe is treated abstractly while peaceful Australia is treated realistically. Yet Theodora carries her own war inside her, and her return to Australia suggests a means by which White's apocalyptic modernism will be accommodated to the Australian scene. White will set in Australia the figure of the outcast, the mad person, the visionary who seeks a unity that transcends the fragmentation and banality White associates with the common world.

The Tree of Man

'Pastoral Masks a Conflict'.

William Empson

The eventual result of White's return to Australia in 1947, as Guy Innes had promised the young novelist in London, was to bring '"the colours . . . flooding back onto [his] palette"'.[19] The immediate result, however, was a lengthy period of creative self-doubt during which the novelist cultivated his garden, raising flowers, vegetables, dogs and goats.[20] *The Tree of Man* issued from this period of uncertainty in which White found himself outcast from the European milieu which he had known before the war. The novel marks a new direction in White's writing and conveys both the satisfactions and frustrations of living at Castle Hill and being once again in Australia.

Towards the end of *The Tree of Man* Stan Parker attends a production of *Hamlet* in Sydney. Watching the play, the old man ponders his own unresolved life and his lifelong difficulties in discovering the meanings of words:

> Was this Hamlet, he asked, coming and going throughout the play, a white, a rather thin man in black? That we have been waiting for. Is this our Hamlet? With poor knees. The words that he had read, and was remembering, tried to convince the old man. Once he had known an old horse called Hamlet, a bay, no, an old brown gelding, a light draught, that belonged to an old cove, Furneval was it, or Furness? who would drive into the village for groceries, flicking at the flies on Hamlet with the whip. That was one Hamlet. Or standing in the feed shed, in that trench coat that he had hung on to after the war, for years, till it became green, the buttons had dropped off, and it was separated from its origin, but that morning, or in fact many mornings, as he mixed the good bran and chaff, the real Hamlet floated towards an explanation, or was it fresh bewilderment?[21]

The style of the passage has a tentativeness which encourages us to take at face value the preference White states in 'The Prodigal Son' for simplicity and humility as an artist and as a man. In spite of A. D. Hope's notorious judgement that *The Tree of Man* is 'illiterate verbal sludge', the predominant style of the novel has a simple directness that is quite absent in *The Living and The Dead* or *The Aunt's Story*.[22] Much of the difficulty posed by White's mature prose style derives from the pervasive use of sentence fragments. This may irritate readers who like prose fiction to obey the rules of composition handbooks, but it scarcely makes for a reading experience as demanding as that required by the novels of Joyce, Woolf or Faulkner. The sentence fragments in the passage above serve as a notation of the consciousness of the characters and do not require the reader to follow the stream of *subconscious* thought. As interior monologue the passage is less demanding than much of the writing in *Happy Valley*.

Moreover, the narrator does not hesitate to ascribe a moral essence to the man; the epithet 'good' which modifies 'bran and chaff' serves not only to evoke the simple pastoral virtues which would naturally appeal to the old man but also to indicate the narrator's endorsement of Stan's bucolic values. It is as though, his nerve having failed after the uncompromising demands *The Aunt's Story* made on the reader, White contritely offers us a humbled narrator and an uneducated and unsophisticated central consciousness. In place of intellectuals and madwomen we are given Stan Parker, a simple man who cannot 'interpret' the literary *Hamlet* because his mind runs after 'the old brown gelding'.

The gelding is the most unlikely conceivable embodiment of the name Hamlet and thus suggests the point at which Australian life is most divorced from literature. Furthermore, the horse is owned by 'an old cove' whose own half-remembered name contains an obscure literary joke: H. H. Furness and F. J. Furnivall were nineteenth-century scholars whose fields included Shakespeare studies, philology and bibliography. The joke further establishes the incongruousness of European literary forms in the Australian context. Shakespeare has declined from the living dramatist, to a canon of holy scripts attended by pedants 'flicking at' metaphorical flies, to a neutered horse in outback Australia. It would seem, then, that White considers Australian life inimical to a high literary mode, and Australian landscape as a 'Great . . . Emptiness' in which civilisation can make its appearance only in the form of grotesquely located relics from a richer past, the occasion for irony.[23]

Such a view would account for White's apparent decision to abandon the rendering of complex sensibilities: White is frustrated by what he sees as the oppressive ordinariness of Australia and is writing out of that boredom and frustration. Yet the reader's overwhelming impression in reading the novel is not that White is bored with the life he treats but that his interest and involvement have been quickened. Reading *The Tree of Man* one feels that White has at last achieved what he so anxiously wanted to achieve in *The Living and The Dead*: a direct, passionate and morally serious rendering of lived actuality.

In *The Tree of Man* we find for the first time in White's writing the possibility of human integration into the natural world. The novel enacts the lives of the Parkers in its slow curve, its evocation of seasonal growth and decay. Their life together grows, achieves its brief perfection, and withers following the same organic pattern as Amy's rose bush. Even death is part of this circular process. As the novel closes, Stan's grandson, recalling his dead grandfather, walks through the bush-filled gulley that is all that remains of the virgin land Stan cleared in the beginning. As he walks he puts out 'shoots of green thought' and the novel ends with the triumphant assertion of circularity: 'in the end, there was no end' (499).

This celebration of organic process allows a reconciliation, however short-lived, between 'inner' and 'outer'. Even Stan's initial desecration of the bush with the axe and fire makes him part of the world he changes. Stan at this stage has the purely representative inner life of essential Man and he meets Nature at its most pristine and, as the Biblical echoes make clear, Edenic. The opening of the novel offers us a vision of prelapsarian simplicities, of a life before the inevitable decline of civilisation into gesture, abstraction, the separation of inner and outer, life and language. Evoking this idyll, the prose aspires to a state of simplicity. Words possess only their barest, denotative function, yet precisely because there is such an equivalence between words and the few, fundamental objects they denote – tree, axe, man, dog, fire – the words achieve the epic, incantatory and universal qualities of Biblical narrative: Stan is *the* man; Amy is *the* woman. White, it would seem, has found in the pristineness and simplicity of his beloved pre-1914 rural Australia, the connection he has so long sought between words and things, events and meanings.

There are, then, two irreconcilable views of Australia in whose terms the novel might be read: Australia as fundamentally impoverished and inadequate for a novelist seeking depth in characterisation and poetic intensity in style; Australia as a place whose pristineness makes possible an essential connection between humans, nature and language. To some extent these two views correspond to White's divided experience of Australia: his visits as a child to the rural properties of the White brothers which were a source of idyllic memories and evoked his most glowing descriptions of the Australian landscape; his experience of encroaching suburbia on his return to Australia after the Second World War which was a source of irritation and evoked the contempt which characterises so many of his remarks about modern Australia. These opposed views are suggested in the ambivalent responses to Australia in 'The Prodigal Son'.

The genesis of *The Tree of Man* as White puts it in the essay, lay in his dissatisfaction with what he saw as the ordinariness, the banality, and the ugliness of Australian life – 'the exaltation of the "average"'.[24] Yet, in the process of writing the novel White found new 'avenues for endless exploration', by which he means exploration not only of Australia but also of the business of novel-writing.[25] 'The Prodigal Son' discloses an irresolution on White's part about the material that has given shape to *The Tree of Man*. Such irresolutions thwarted his desire to achieve formal unity in his first two novels. In the post-war novels, however, White is more aware of, and more in control of, his own divided allegiances. He sets out to draw on two opposed tendencies in his previous fiction which we may loosely call realism and symbolism. The two tendencies and their problematic relation to one another are sketched in 'The Prodigal Son':

> Because the void I had to fill was so immense, I wanted to try to suggest in this book every possible aspect of life, through the lives of an ordinary man and woman. But at the same time I wanted to discover the extraordinary behind the ordinary, the mystery and the poetry which alone could make bearable the lives of such people, and incidentally, my own life since my return.[26]

White proposes, then, in the realist manner exhaustively to treat ordinary life. At the same time he seeks in the symbolist manner to discover 'the mystery and the poetry' which lie 'behind' the ordinary. His intention is to bring together what Harry Levin calls 'reality' and 'richness'.[27] In *The Tree of Man* White sets out to find some means of reconciling the conflicting claims of imaginative and realistic writing by attempting to discover in the common experience of his countrymen and women aesthetic richness and spiritual depth.

When White tells us that only 'the mystery and the poetry' made bearable his life in Australia we glimpse the distance he puts between life as it is (the 'ordinary') and art (the 'extraordinary'). By using 'poetry' as a synonym for whatever is more than ordinary, White intimates that the opposition may be grasped in literary terms. Effectively, White has smuggled the techniques of symbolism into the realistic epic. White's conception of character does not rest on the assumption that identity is manufactured in a mechanical fashion by history, class and environment. These 'externals' are granted their shaping influence; nature, in particular, etches itself into the psyches of White's characters. Yet White throws those of his characters who count into symbolic fires in order to see what remains after all the socially given components of character have been rendered down: pure essence or pure absence. His visionary characters tend to seek a core of selfhood which is prior to society, nature and language. The rest of his characters, those whose identity rests upon externals, simply dissolve.

The richness of *The Tree of Man* is apparent in the way White has attended to the texture of the writing. This is not merely a matter of the prose style, which is mannered at times. Rather, it has to do with the organisation of the novel into a series of painterly 'scenes'. Within each of these scenes there may be action, but there is little in the way of narrative progression. Our experience of reading the novel as a 'story' is interrupted as we become aware of the pictorial quality of the writing.

The novel opens with a canvas of pioneer life: here is the untouched bush, and here in the centre is a little clearing where the man is building his make-shift house. The newly-wed Amy Parker looks back on the ramshackle place in which she has lived as 'a shining scene, with painted houses under the blowing trees, with the carts full of polished cans in which the farmers put the milk, . . . with blue smoke from morning fires' (21). We are presented with peasant studies of Amy in the Realist manner: Amy gathering mulberries or milking:

> She sat with the bucket between her strong legs, her buttocks overlapping the little sawn-off block she had always used as a milking stool. What saved her from appearing ludicrous was the harmoniousness of her rather massive form beside the formal cow'. (229)

The scene in which Ray Parker pursues an unknown girl through a park at night is in an expressionist style. By emphasising the

angularity of the shapes and the sharp contrasts between white
and black, White foregrounds the briefly glimpsed face of the girl
'with its blurry, moon-geography' (393). The narrative focuses our
perspective not through Ray's eyes but from a point behind him
so that the effect of the writing is to create a pictorial image. We
recognise Ray as an alienated and threatening figure in an urban
study, someone on the outside staring down passages or streets into
lighted windows or open doors that will not give him entry.

A crucial 'scene' is that in which Stan Parker rescues Madeleine from the burning house, Glastonbury. Here the house is
a spatial representation of Stan's mind. White draws attention
to the symbolic quality of the fire more explicitly than he does
with the flood. It soon becomes clear that the purpose of the
fire is to destroy more than trees, houses and the vanity of the
men who fight it. It attacks the very fabric of socially approved
reality. The fire consumes identity to the extent that it depends
upon the assurance of having a fixed place in an ordered social
world, a place signified by possessions: 'each man remembered his
house . . . which until now he had considered solid, and all those
objects he had accumulated, and without which he would not have
been himself' (173).

The fire threatens the very heart of the community. The men
who ride from the fire to Durilgai 'to be in the centre at least'
find only the signpost, the post office, and the store (174). Here
they find intact the absolute minimum of the communal means
of exchanging messages and goods. The men are allowed to fall
back on this centre because its vunerability has been so thoroughly
exposed. Their sense of identity which rests on their place in a
social order' is only as 'solid' as the possessions which uphold
it. They will move no further in the direction which threatens
dissolution of personality. Stan Parker, unlike the other men, is
prepared to move beyond the framework of the community. Stan
'worship[s]' the fire precisely because it promises to render down
the socially constructed part of himself (178).

Amy's nudge sends Stan into the burning house so that he might
rescue her romantic fantasies of Madeleine, but Stan obeys a private
compulsion. The house 'open[s]' itself to him with the implied
promise that it contains possibilities, sensual and otherwise, which
he has been unable to realize in his life so far with Amy (178). He
abandons the ordinary world, and with it his wife, with a line that
neatly parodies the manly understatement of the Australian 'bloke'

convention: "'I'll have a go'" (179). Thus sloughing off his everyday persona, he steps into a 'houseful of poetry' where Hamlet and Madeleine wait for him in the eternal rooms (179).

Inside the house objects have become part of a symbolic landscape, and Stan must struggle to separate the actual from the poetic nature of his mission. His problem is to advance not only temporally and physically into the house but also into the self, into interior space. For a moment, he is overwhelmed by the symbolism. Time is 'becalmed in the passages'; the cupboards are clogged with the detritus of the past (179). He stands becalmed among these timeless and impenetrable passages until snatched back into 'a desperate situation' (180). Now his ordinariness is oppressive to him. He is the working man in his 'cloddish boots' standing at a loss in a room where mirrors and furniture are designed to reflect the importance of their owners. He remembers that he is the common man come to rescue the trapped, upper-class girl and is nervous that his clumsy words will spoil their introduction. In mounting towards the purity of the upper rooms, he is again engulfed by the mysterious quality of his mission. The fire has burnt the solid Victorian furniture; it has shivelled up the 'prettiness' of upper-bourgeois life; it has exposed the secrets of the rich.

The fixed, normal world in which identity rests securely on class and possessions has been consumed. All objects are now 'without reflections'; they do not give back to the viewer evidence of his place in the world (180). Stan steps over the hank of hair that once supported vanity and breaks into 'the heart of the house' where his consummation ('climax') waits (180–1). He meets not a solid woman but an embodiment of poetry, Madeleine. The fire has entirely swallowed the ordinary world. The 'papier-mâché globe that the girls used to learn the capitals from' has gone 'up in a puff' (p. 181).

Madeleine, then, is the imprisoned princess, Rapunzel, who waits in her tower with her long hair flowing. She is Stan's trapped vision of poetic possibility waiting to be released. One could readily apply a Jungian reading to this scene. Stan confronts in the figure of Madeleine his *anima*, the veiled woman, with whom he must effect a *coniunctio oppositorum* in the alchemical flames of transmutation.[28] However, although she appears to Stan to be composed of shimmering fire and although, like Hamlet's Ophelia, she affects a touch of madness, Madeleine is a woman waiting to be rescued: that is, restored to the actual world. Madeleine is a bourgeois princess and Stan a very proletarian knight. They must negotiate the doors that separate the classes before passing through the fire into the solid world.

The introduction of the class theme restores a realistic element to the narrative. The language they must use, which encodes the class barriers that divide them, almost betrays Madeleine into referring to 'the servants' staircase' (182). This, in any case, is closed to them: the rooms in which the maids have been 'contained' lead only to 'dead ends' (182). Stan Parker and Madeleine cannot return to the 'real' world as lady and proletarian. They are forced to grapple with one another as man and woman.

Madeleine and Stan, like Sidney Furlow and Clem Hagan and like Eden Standish and Joe Barnett, are sexually stirred by the distance between the classes. The upper-class woman of sensibility, beauty and constraint waits to be ravished by the no-less-willing working man. In White's two early novels this attraction found its appropriate, if unlikely, expression in the sexual act. In both cases, White clearly intended us to see this leap across the classes as essentially healthy, though whether for social, sexual or psychological reasons was not quite clear. In both cases also, White's attitude towards this union was ambivalent. His sexual politics of healing were in conflict with his ideological instincts: hence the association with the death principle of the love between Eden and Joe.

In *The Tree of Man*, White neatly sidesteps his ambivalences. He shifts the terms of the union from those of sex and class to purely symbolic ones. Stan and Madeleine are joined only when they put aside desire. Not their flesh but their bones meet (language which looks forward to the depictions of the violently unworldly lovers in *Voss*). Thus the sexual aspects of the marriage of opposites are swallowed by the symbolism. As the twined lovers descend the staircase the inessential fleshly beauty of Madeleine is discarded while her essential, inner beauty – the poetic core Stan has projected onto the girl – is appropriated by the man. Stan emerges from the fire, if not purified into a final shape, at least refined. He has discovered a selfhood more fundamental than that which is offered to the world as personality. He has uncovered the poetry so long imprisoned within him. The empty husk of Madeleine is cast aside on the grass, 'dry retching' out of her own nothingness (184).

For a moment in the midst of the fire the immense distance between the classes is negated, but White does not trouble himself or us by attempting to show lovers from antagonistic classes struggling towards health and wholeness in a sterile social order. Stan and Madeleine return to their former lives, once again separated by the endless space between the classes. They were allowed to meet not as human beings but as trembling symbols winding down a Jungian staircase. After thus being turned into symbols they are simply dumped back into reality and into their familiar roles as socialite and cow-cockie.

Nevertheless, Stan has made off with something of permanent value. He has stolen out of the rich butcher's house the spiritual essence of gentility to which the colonial upper orders aspire. He has grasped the sense of beauty that supposedly makes leisure, wealth and refinement 'genteel'. In literary terms the Australian common man has broken out of the prisonhouse of realism. The outback proletarian hero has ransacked the country house – admittedly an imitation – of the old order and made off not only with the beautiful daughter but also with the rarefied consciousness that has traditionally belonged to the leisured upper classes.

Stan does not, of course, 'make off' with Madeleine. He returns to his prosaic world wherein he is irrevocably married not to 'richness' but to 'reality'. Yet the symbolism in the fire scene belongs not to Madeleine but to Stan. The objects in the burning house are charged with emotion and significance that have their origins in Stan's consciousness. In *Happy Valley* the working man, Hagan, was attracted to the beautiful Sidney Furlow but could not enter her inner world. In *The Tree of Man* the inwardness belongs to the crude, inarticulate farmer. Madeleine's beauty and the sense of spirituality suggested by her formal perfection are qualities that reside in Stan's mind. She herself returns to a 'reality' infinitely more squalid, vulgar, and empty than Stan's life with Amy. In this scene White stakes his claim to the conventional matter of Australian realism and asserts his right to do with it as he will. In this sense 'reality' and 'richness' have joined at the level of style and narrative stance. The techniques of symbolism have been applied to the traditional matter of realism.

Voss

Three years before *Voss* was published in 1957 the narrator of Iris Murdoch's *Under the Net* remarks that 'the present age was not one in which it was possible to write an epic'.[29] It may not have been

possible in England, evidently it was in Australia. *Voss* is White's
most important novel, one of the key novels to be written since
the war. It is at once his most Australian novel and that which
secures his status as an international modernist novelist. It is a
national epic which looks back to the nineteenth-century realist
novel and forward to the metafictional novels of post-colonialism
of Wilson Harris, Salman Rushdie and Peter Carey. It is an epic
in the sense that it tells the tale of a people, it dramatises their
beginnings and projects possible futures. It employs heroes and
involves great undertakings. It is an epic also in the sense that it
combines elements from everywhere imaginable – realism, allegory,
mysticism, heresy – and makes a new kind of whole out of that
mixture. The question is, how are these disparate elements made
to cohere?

Formally, *Voss* gives the appearance of being two radically different kinds of novels placed uneasily side by side. The first deals
realistically with the rise of a bourgeois family. The Bonners, having
put behind their lowly origins, are cheerfully new-rich. We follow
their further rise, through the marriage of their daughter, Belle,
into the colonial version of the landed gentry. Their niece, Laura
Trevelyan, knocks the family a rung or two back down the social
ladder by adopting an illegitimate child and by accepting a position
as a school-teacher. However, by virtue of her role as midwife to the
colony's tiny cultural élite, she promises a rise more glorious, if less
tangible, than her cousin's. In this milieu the star of the bourgeoisie
is on the ascendant. This 'novel' deals with a social world which it
pictures as aggressively worldly and extrovert. Its favourite mode
is comedy of manners, its preferred narrative stance involves an
intrusive contempt for its characters.

The second 'novel' deals allegorically with Voss's expedition into
the heart of the country. The members of the expedition are meant
to be seen not only as characters but also as types in a religious
scheme. They make up a single allegorical figure, 'Man', as he
journeys not through the physical world but into the self. Here
the conventions of class are parodied and inverted. The characters
cannot assert their identity by what they own. They are obliged to
confront one another with their essential selves. Here the style is
high, tortuous and dense; the narrator's favourite stance is that of
a detached wisdom signalled by the gnomic sayings he drops into
the narrative.

To gauge the difference between these two tendencies within

the 'novel' I shall examine two representative passages. In the first passage the narrator describes the Bonners' house in Sydney.

> The comforts, both material and spiritual, so conveniently confused in comfortable minds, inspired the merchant's residence. Of solid stone, this had stood unshaken hitherto. As a house it was not so much magnificent as eminently suitable, and sometimes, by pure chance, even appeared imaginative, in spite of the plethora of formal, shiny shrubs, the laurels, for instance, and the camellias that Uncle had planted in the beginning. The science of horticulture had failed to exorcize the spirit of the place. The wands and fronds of native things intruded still, paperbarks and various gums, of mysterious hot scents, and attentive silences: shadowy trees that, paradoxically, enticed the eyes away from an excess of substance. Moreover, the accents of poetry were constantly creeping in through the throats of doves, and sometimes young ladies might be seen, sampling strawberries from the netted beds, or engaged in needlework in a little latticed summer house, or playing croquet with the military, but later, in the afternoon, when the hoops made long shadows on the crisp grass.[30]

In this passage the narrator's contempt for the world he describes is oppressive. The narrator forces his judgements on us. We find his presence too strident, too much at the forefront. It is as though White does not trust us to arrive at the correct attitude towards the Bonners' world. Hence, rather than let the material speak for itself, he mediates it jealously through his censorious narrator. In the first sentence we are told that 'comfortable minds' confuse material and spiritual comforts. The sole function of the parenthesis in the sentence is to allow the narrator to consign the Bonners, along with all those guilty of the cosy materialism of the colonial bourgeoisie, to the lowest circle of White's Hell: the circle of the spiritually slothful. The insistent irony in the passage is designed to hector the reader into accepting an underlying distinction between the spiritually torpid and the spiritually adventurous. The adverb, 'conveniently', displays a school-masterly sarcasm intended to bully us into accepting what is after all a contestable judgement. Why should a house not be designed with comfort in mind?

All this lobbying by the narrator detracts from the essential gracefulness of the sentence. If we remove the authorial intrusion the sentence makes its point with elegance and wit. The verb, 'inspired', with its suggestion of poetic afflatus is masterly. At once, we grasp the vantage point from which the narrator's thunder bolts are being hurled. The muses who inspire the Bonners' world are not the nine of poetry but the pasteboard saints of the fallen modern world. The echo of a saccharine, middle-class piety ('all the comforts of home') is set delicately against the echo of a vanished order in which Apollo's muses inspired far other worlds than these.

The rhetoric of the passage is governed by an underlying distinction between the bourgeois complacency described and some vague, poetic intensity of life which is alluded to but not stated. This distinction allows the narrator to measure the Bonners' world against a richer, but unspecified, mode of living. Allowing that the house has been built of 'solid stone', the narrator immediately hints at some threat to its solidity: 'had stood unshaken hitherto'. What is in store: earthquake, bulldozers, apocalypse? We are not told, but we gather that for all its appearance of permanence the house of Edmund Bonner is built on sand. The narrator turns his attention to the too-easy task of deflating the Bonners' social pretensions by the parodic use of real estate terminology: 'as a house it was not so much magnificent as eminently suitable'.

Behind the narrator's contempt for Bonner's circumspection we may detect White's contempt as a grazier's son for the commercial middle classes. Although White publicly repudiated the politics of his class during the sixties and seventies in favour of the Australian Labour Party, his disdain for the new-rich is more aristocratic than socialist. White's genteel but inverted snobbery approves of ladies who masquerade as cooks but never bourgeois who masquerade as ladies (compare White's amused description of the Athenian ladies of the old aristocracy who pride themselves on their cooking and cultivate postmen with his vindictive description of Lady Kerr in *Flaws in the Glass*).[31] We may also detect behind the narrator's jibes at Edmund Bonner, White's recognition that in the bourgeois fear of beauty and display lies a fundamental challenge to aestheticism. Like Katherine Mansfield in puritan, provincial, turn-of-the-century New Zealand, White longs in the colonial cultural wilderness for unashamed artifice.[32]

The narrator objects to the substantiality of the Bonners' world, to its limited, formal, self-containment. Against their world he sets a suggested rather than a stated way of life which is mysterious,

sensuous, poetic, spiritual. Just as he seems about to draw in more
precise detail the richer world he proffers, the tone shifts. The
'accents of poetry' that creep into the garden bring with them not
the 'spirit of the place' but an altogether debased type of poetry.
This poetry speaks not through the authentic warblings of native
fauna but through the throats of imported birds. With the doves
come young ladies engaged in appropriate mid-Victorian recrea-
tions: needlework or 'sampling strawberries from the netted beds'.
The poetry that is to be heard in Edmund Bonner's garden is a pale,
safe variety. Its sweets, contained by 'nets', are soft-centred. It is the
kind of poetry, conventional and limited, that Ralph Angus recalls
with slight nostalgia when discussing with Turner the altogether
dangerous poetry of Frank Le Mesurier. The poetry of the Bonners'
garden poses no threat to the world that Angus, the Bonners and
even the flotsam Turner 'know': that is, the world of conventional
acceptance. Le Mesurier's poems are designed purposely 'to blow
the world up' (251).

The second passage I shall examine describes a sunrise during
the wet season in the interior of the continent:

> About the same hour, Voss went to the mouth of the cave. If
> he was shivering, in spite of the grey blanket in which he had
> prudently wrapped himself, it was not through diffidence, but
> because each morning is, like the creative act, the first. So
> he cracked his fingerjoints, and waited. The rain was with-
> drawn temporarily into the great shapelessness, but a tingling
> of moisture suggestd [sic] the presence of an earth that might
> absorb further punishment. First, an animal somewhere in the
> darkness was forced to part with its life. Then the grey was let
> loose to creep on subtle pads, from branch to branch, over
> rocks, slithering in native coils upon the surface of the waters.
> A protoplast of mist was slowly born, and moored unwillingly by
> invisible wires. There it was, gently tugging. The creator sighed,
> and there arose a contented little breeze, even from the mouth
> of the cave. Now, liquid light was allowed to pour from great
> receptacles. The infinitely pure, white light might have remained
> the masterpiece of creation, if fire had not suddenly broken out.
> For the sun was rising, in spite of immersion. It was challenging
> water, and the light of dawn, which is water of another kind. In
> the struggle that followed, the hissing and dowsing, the sun was
> spinning, swimming, sinking, drowned, its livid face a globe of

water, for the rain had been brought down again, and there was, it appeared, but a single element. (277)

In this passage the intrusive narrator has been reined in. The writing achieves its effects through the use of myth, Biblical allusion and imagery. The experience of reading this piece of description is altogether different from that of reading the first passage. We read the first piece chronologically, guided through linear time by a narrative voice eager to tell us who the villains are. The second piece reveals layers of meaning one within the other. We are not hurried along on the surface of the narrative but are forced inward.

On the literal level White describes a sunset as seen by Voss on a rainy day. By focusing what we see through Voss's eyes, White suggests the scope of the man's egotism. Voss regards his mind as the origin of all motion in the world. The sunrise is *his* 'creative act' and when he sighs a breeze is sent out into the expectant world. Behind Voss's arrogance lies the post-romantic conviction that the mind is the active partner in the marriage into which it enters with the outside world. In the rising sun scene Voss tests the limits of this notion. He makes the scene dependent on his mind not only for its life, colour and form but also for its very existence. Voss creates the world anew and the great scene is utterly dependent on what he puts into it. The 'masterpiece' of his creative powers is the addition to the dull scene of an 'infinitely pure, white light'. This light spills not from the rising sun but from Voss's mind. Such light is to be found nowhere in nature. This moment of absolute creative self-assertion gives way as the sun struggles upward and Voss's nerve apparently fails. Given Voss's failure to hold up the world created out of his imagination, we are left with the actual world.

Through the piece White threads a complex pattern of allusions. Most obvious are the allusions to Genesis 1: i–iv. Before the creation, the author of Genesis tells us, 'the earth was without form, and void; and darkness was upon the face of the deep'. In his role as creator Voss confronts 'a great shapelessness', and watches the light of dawn move 'upon the surface of the waters'. Voss's 'infinitely pure, white light' recalls the light which issued from the original divine fiat. Voss, then, usurps the creative role of deity. This becomes something of a habit with him. Later he comes to see the sunsets as celebrations of his own 'divine munificence' (330). In the passage that describes the sunrise, then, White uses Biblical allusions to suggest the way in which Voss egotistically views the world.

There are, however, troubling complexities in White's use of allusion in this passage. Unlike the God of Genesis whom he emulates, Voss botches the world he makes. More troublingly, the Genesis account is not the only myth of origins alluded to in the passage. The allusions to Genesis are complicated by allusions to Plato. There are Platonic suggestions in the cave itself. Voss is like the man in Plato's myth who stumbles out of the dark cave in which the mass of humanity is confined into the light of the real. Voss is even referred to as 'the superior being in his cave' (277). The obvious Platonic allusion is to *Timaeus*. In Plato's version of beginnings the demiurge fashions a rational cosmos out of the original chaos of the elements. Plato is more conscious of the problems of imperfection and limitation than is the author of Genesis. He attempts to account for these problems by his notion that the demiurge allowed inferior ministers to copy the perfect original he himself had made. This account seems to explain the shortcomings in Voss's version of creation. Voss is simply an inadequate copier. The Platonic myth seems more closely to agree with Voss's version of the creation than does the Genesis myth. For Plato the world was created not out of nothing as in Genesis but out of a primordial chaos. This would seem to explain White's use of the word 'shapelessness'. There is, moreover, a Platonic ring to the word 'receptacles'. In *Timaeus* Plato suggests that the demiurge used a containing vessel, a cup or receptacle, as the nurse or matrix of becoming.[33]

However, we cannot merely substitute Plato's version of beginnings for that of Genesis. Although Plato allows for an element of necessity and imperfection in creation, he nowhere suggests that the created world was formed by malice. There are such suggestions in White's account, and their function in the narrative is disturbing.

For Voss to create is to punish. He senses the earth concealed in the great shapelessness as a presence 'that might absorb further punishment'. The primal act in Voss's version of the origin of things is not the giving but the taking of life. He hears somewhere in the darkness an animal being murdered. The use of the passive mood ('was forced to part with its life') points to a malign purpose working behind the creative process. Thus the greyness that displaces the darkness is 'let loose' upon the as-yet-formless waters. This greyness, being a mixture of light and darkness, chaos and form, ought to be the stage through which the world passes into its finished state. Yet Voss sees it as some malignant thing that 'creep[s]' and 'slither[s]'. The imagery suggests a view of the creative process as the loosing of brute violences upon the world. The world described in the passage never emerges, as does the world in Genesis, into a clear distinction between light and darkness. Its final state is a mixture of light and darkness in which the former is dominant. Suffering and incompletion are the conditions of this world as it is. To be a creature is to be controlled by unseen forces ('moored unwillingly by invisible wires').

White, then, does not merely allude to the myth of origins in Genesis in order to place us inside Voss's skull in a dramatic and economical fashion. He gives us two distinct versions of beginnings, then cunningly undermines both. At this point the allusions are no longer an economical means of revealing Voss's consciousness. The attention of the reader is overly concentrated on the allusions themselves. Had White wished merely to deflate Voss's pretensions to divinity, a simpler handling of the allusions would have been far more effective. The passage refuses to make its rhetorical point in a straightforward manner: Voss imitates Jehovah and falls short. White seems less concerned to reveal character than to overwhelm us with the sheer allusiveness of the writing.

The chief problem in coming to terms with the passage is the way in which the writing is so overtly concerned with how it shall be read. The writing resists our attempts to make sense, to order, to give coherence, to extract meanings. Yet we are tantalised with the prospect of meaning somewhere below the slippery surface of the narrative. We are tempted, teased, puzzled, sent off on wild goose chases – but we are never quite illuminated. As soon as we feel we have grasped the meaning of the piece, some new allusion is insinuated into the writing, confusing what has gone before.

If we are to grasp what White is doing with his manner of writing, we must work through, not around, the tribulations to which he subjects us as readers. Our difficulties in reading are not the result of uncertainty of purpose on White's part. White deliberately slows down our passage through the narrative. We are forced to participate in the process by which the passage generates meaning. Like Voss watching the sunrise, and, of course, like White himself, we build up meanings out of texts. The passage not only invites interpretation, it is itself an exercise in hermeneutics in which Voss, with obscure and subversive purpose, interprets Plato and Genesis. Moreover, by its sly inversions of orthodox readings of the Bible and by its intimations of hidden meanings, the writing invites subversive reading. The writing colludes with Voss's subversive habits of thought.

In order to address these problems we must backtrack, looking at the passage in terms of a third level of allusion which is intimated rather than stated and which partly relies for our recognition on our noticing the clues towards such a reading scattered through the novel as a whole.

Watching the sun rise, Voss is first aware of a 'liquid light' which precedes the fiery emergence of the sun. There is an implied distinction between Voss's 'infinitely pure, white light' and the ordinary light of day, a distinction which is not at all present in Genesis. The God of Genesis makes light as part of nature. Voss seeks a pure, undivided light which is outside nature, not something created along with grass and trees and animals but a transcendent principle which is superior to and opposed to creaturely things. Voss's light is 'infinitely pure', undivided and uncontaminated by the mixture of light and darkness which is found in nature. This light has much in common with the Gnostic world of light, the undivided world of purely spiritual being. Voss, in fact, consistently sees himself in Gnostic terms: as one struggling out of multiplicity into unity, out of matter into spirit.

By 'Gnostic' I mean the specific beliefs of the various Christian heresies rather than the Jewish Gnostic thought which Colin Roderick discusses in relation to *Riders in the Chariot*.[34] Voss is pre-eminently a 'heretic' against orthodox Christianity, and his specific beliefs – dualism, antinomianism, spiritual election, opposition to Jehovah – would have made him immediately recognisable as a Gnostic to the Church Fathers. The chief differences between the Jewish and the Christian varieties of Gnostic thought lie in the more extreme dualism of the latter along with their predilection for 'blasphemous' interpretation of Biblical texts and their habit of treating their systems as truths revealed to initiates rather than fictions which stand in metaphorical relation to an inscrutable Deity.

As a truly spiritual man, Voss considers himself an 'alien' in a world in which matter and spirit are fatally mixed to the advantage of the former. In the division of the expedition into 'oil' and 'water', the earthy men and the elect, Voss is pre-eminently the elected one. Like the Gnostics, Voss lays claim to a 'knowledge that comes with sovereignty over every province of illusion' (Frank Le Mesurier hears Voss make this claim telepathically shortly before the leader blasphemously intones his own divinity: '"I am I am I am . . . "' (246). Like the Gnostics, Voss is a God-opposer. He pits himself against the God of conventional Christianity. Like the Gnostics also he has a taste for subversive readings of Christian narratives, as Palfreyman finds to his discomfiture. In Voss's view, the hero is not the Christian underdog but the rebel against divine omnipotence and conventional religion. As the expedition moves into the desert even Voss's followers are persuaded by his delusion to see him as a Gnostic version of the Godhead. Thus they cease to 'question why the supreme power [by which they understand Voss] should be divided in two' (264).

What is the purpose of this Gnostic material in *Voss?* No doubt it touches upon White's eclectic religious interests. White was very knowledgeable about esoterica and mysticism generally.[35] This, however, is not to our purpose here. The question is not what is White's own attitude towards this material but what is the function of Voss's heretical attitudes in the novel? In the first place they serve to make Voss's character more extreme. Not only does the German have pretensions to divinity, he also has a personal animosity towards the God of the orthodox. This extravagant egotism in Voss's character and the introduction of a subversive subtext into the parts of the novel that deal with Voss serve to exaggerate the main opposition on which the novel is built: that between the normality and materialism of Sydney bourgeois life and the violence and extremity of life in the interior of the continent.

White keeps apart the two main directions in *Voss* – towards a parodic version of traditional realism on the one hand and towards a modernist species of allegory on the other hand – because he wishes to examine their adequacy to a central problem for the novel: what conventions or forms will serve in the business of making fictions out of Australia; how shall the continent be 'read'? For the Australia which he confronts in *Voss* is not yet a world. It is a circle whose circumference is ungauged, on the edge of which huddles a tiny outpost of Englishmen and women clinging to the conventions of 'home'. In their understanding the continent is a blankness waiting to be written on. For White, to read this place in terms of the models provided by the traditional novel, particularly by the Victorian novel with which the action of *Voss* is contemporaneous, is to imitate the imitators: the huddling English. The colonial social world is one in which the fixity, hierarchy and air of permanence of the Victorian class structure can appear only as travesties. White is determined in *Voss* to question this structure in terms of the worlds it excludes and cannot comprehend and to encourage in his reader subversive reading habits which will undermine that structure. In a sense, the reader of *Voss* is obliged to reenact Voss's journey away from the controlling structures of orthodox versions of 'reality' into the chaotic heart of the country and of the text itself. The subtext of Gnostic allusion White has worked into his novel carries the reader along with Voss into an interpretative enigma.

It was necessary for White to make as opposed as possible the worlds of Voss and Mr. Bonner. These worlds are competing interpretations of Australia. Each is a totality, something complete within itself, that claims to 'contain' the continent (the suggestive pun is Richard Poirier's with American novelists in mind).[36] The merchant 'contains' the country as a totality of material facts and things, a whole that can be mapped, carved up and turned to profit. Voss 'contains' the continent as a metaphysical totality, a pure idea which his will imposes on reality. '"The map? . . . I will first make it"', he tells Mr. Bonner (19). Both views rest on self-serving notions of perception. Each sees only what suits his purpose: Voss sees only the architecture of matter; the merchant sees only its flesh. The problem is, whose eye is sufficiently encompassing to see the continent as a whole without excluding whatever fails to fit neatly into his system?

White has created in Voss a figure who chooses the most extreme isolation of mind open to him: radical exile from the community and rejection of its materialistic vision of the land. Unlike 'ordinary' Australians, Voss refuses to settle for no more than a small square of the country's face. While merchants like Bonner set up stone monuments to an unattainable permanence on the fertile periphery of the country, Voss is determined to pit the vastness and ugliness of his own nature (Laura describes him thus in the course of their queer courtship [p. 83]) against the identical qualities he expects to find in the central deserts. While squatters like Sanderson and even small-holders like Judd attempt to enclose themselves within their acres, Voss is determined to contain within the compass of his skull the entire resistent continent.

In this endeavour the barren heart of the continent will prove both collaborator and reward. The deserts of the interior confirm Voss's heretical bias against matter. Their absence of the sensuous will encourage the spirit to attempt the infinite. Only when the spirit (in Voss's terms 'spirit' may be equated with either genius or will) has become as limitless as the Godhead it has toppled will it prove equal to the metaphysical possibilities of the continent. The scope of Voss's daring is thus commensurate to his task: the making of a version of Australia out of the bare bones of the country that is agreeable to visionaries rather than farmers and merchants. If Voss is to supplant the curtailed interpretation of Australia of squatter and merchant he must first dispatch their comfortable deity. Orthodox, materialistic Christianity serves the purposes of those who read in the scrutable face of their God approval of their proprietary and utilitarian conception of the world. The world to them is not a text to be read in search of metaphysical disclosures but a topography to be mapped, divided and farmed. Nature to them is not a book between whose lines are intercalated moral lessons and anagogues but a blank slate which, once inscribed with the cartographer's co-ordinates, offers commercial opportunities.

Such a megalomania as Voss's does not hesitate to wrestle with divinity. Although Voss sees his personal metaphysical struggle in Gnostic terms, he, unlike the original Gnostics, is locked in battle not with a still potent Jehovah but with the deity of the colonial bourgeoisie who is merely a windbag full of platitudes. This unworthy opponent must be done away with not because He retains the power to terrify, but because He supports the structure of conventions that holds together a thoroughly materialistic society. This God throws an unendurable limit around the imagination.

Like Stan Parker, though from a different angle, Voss assaults the barriers to the free play of the imagination that go with the English system of classes as established in the colony. Stan makes off from the blazing house of gentility with the essence of poetry, leaving the absurd, imitative edifice to collapse. Voss's notions of the scope of the imagination are rooted in the German romanticism which teaches him to disdain burgher conventions and burgher materialism. He makes off with the only redeemable part of the bourgeois world through which he stalks his contemptuous way en route to the interior and his own fires: Laura Trevelyan. Laura is the passive, female germinative principle fertilised by his male, creative will: she brings forth the colony's infant culture. Stan Parker was at a loss what he should do with the poetry he grasped momentarily in the burning Glastonbury. The embodiment of that poetry, Madeleine, was too inconsequential to be fertilised by his richer but uncrystallised imagination. Voss not only clears a space for the imagination in Australia, he also settles it. Frank Le Mesurier with his 'mad' poems that lack an audience and Laura Trevelyan with her tiny 'salon' set about the business of cultivating the garden of vision Voss marks out in the wilderness of colonial philistinism. Laura's protégé, Willie Pringle, discusses with her as the novel closes how the artist might overcome the 'inherent mediocrity' of Australians as a people (441).

Voss is not an artist himself. He is, however, 'genius': the inspired visionary of romantic theory whose faithfulness to the ideas of transcendence and unity offers an escape from the alienation of living in a fallen bourgeois world. Voss sets out on his expedition confident that Man (meaning Voss himself) can occupy the space vacated by the Christian deity, recapture his lost essence, and thus render his life meaningful. He fails, but he leaves behind him those who will assert vision, transcendence and beauty against Australian materialism. The Gnostic allusions that play around Voss reinforce these romantic themes. They make him more extreme, but do not make him wholly unattractive as a character. Rather like the Byronic anti-hero or Melville's Ahab (who also has Gnostic sympathies),[37] he is flawed, doomed, yet commanding as a presence, captivating even. His monomaniacal pitching of himself against God allows complex ironies to surround him: his pretensions are overweening; he has clown-like qualities; but he is never merely ridiculous. He fails in his efforts to deify the self, but failure does not wholly dispel the fateful glamour of the attempt. Ambivalences about the value of the German's romantic posturings are locked into the novel.

Voss offers us not so much an 'interpretation' of Australia as a denial of the possibility of ever arriving at any final interpretation of Australia, of the world or of literary texts. The expedition is thwarted in its desire to inscribe its legend on the country by the discovery everywhere of writing: of messages, languages, inscriptions that resist decipherment. A definitive interpretation of the cave drawings or the Aboriginal dialects or the meaning of the comet is as unlikely as the key to the Revelation of St John on which Palfreyman's uncle is working. The new world is discovered as a palimpsest of meanings already written in the minds of its discoverers, which they impose on the existing order of meanings of those already there. Homer may serve to chock a table leg in Brendan Boyle's shack, but his writing surrounds the expedition.

Voss is the epic of the broken modern world in which there can be no homecoming. It is also the epic of Australia, because Australia, for White, is both the 'modern' world – fallen away from any contact with the transcendent, adrift, rootless, antithetical to the imagination – and also a visionary realm of imaginative possibility associated with childhood and the earthly paradise. It is the unavoidable object of his restless, ambivalent gaze.

3

The Artist and Suburbia

In *Flaws in the Glass* White describes his response to Australia in the periods before and immediately after the War:

> As I could not come to terms with the inhabitants, either then, or again on returning to Australia after World War II, I found consolation in the landscape. The ideal Australia I visualised during any exile and which drew me back, was always, I realise, a landscape without figures.[1]

In his novels of the sixties, *Riders in the Chariot, The Solid Mandala* and *The Vivisector*, White peoples the Australian landscape and moves towards a reluctant accommodation with the figures in the landscape.

In this period White encompasses more and more areas of Australian social life, including the suburban world to which he has consistently shown a strong aversion. The attitude of distance and disdain remains, yet the stance adopted by the artist figures within the novels towards this most representative form of Australian life undergoes a significant change. A complicity is acknowledged between the romantic-modernist figure of the artist and the common forms of social life on which he draws.

At the same time the metaphysical strain in White's writing becomes more prominent. The religious intensity of the novels is no longer a function of a dominant character as it is in *Voss*; it is dispersed through the novels and made structural by the use of controlling symbols like the chariot in *Riders* or the marbles/mandalas in *The Solid Mandala*. White pushes the novel form further towards religious allegory than he did in either *The Tree of Man* or *Voss*, where the realistic notion of character had already been complicated by symbolism and allegory.

By putting such a weight of symbolism onto Stan Parker in the burning house scene in *The Tree of Man*, White signalled a new tendency towards allegory in his writing. *The Tree of Man* is not, however, allegorical in the way that *Riders in the Chariot* and *The Solid Mandala* are. Stan Parker's credibility is not prejudiced by his association with Adam Kadmon or Christ or the holy fool archetype. The allegorical bias in the two later novels threatens at times to subordinate the credibility of the characters to an overtly symbolic design: the symbolism becomes abstract rather than organic.

This allegorical tendency has exhausted itself by the time *The Vivisector* appears. Moreover, while accepting that there are allegorical tendencies in *Riders* and *The Solid Mandala*, we need to be careful about identifying White's own point of view too closely with that of any character or group of characters or with some overall 'vision' abstractable from the novels. White's catankerous attitude towards various features of contemporary life is often made evident in the novels, but the narrative viewpoint is too shifting, ambivalent and unstable to be identified with any single authorial 'vision'.

Riders in the Chariot and *The Solid Mandala* raise acutely the problem of the function of religious thought in White's novels. Some critics see the religious ideas and images in the novels proceeding from a coherent authorial position. White's own statements in essays and interviews about the importance of religion to him personally have encouraged his religiously oriented interpreters.[2] The religious impulse is clearly one he holds to be at the centre of the human condition, involving a great but perplexing truth that his novels dare to confront directly in a sceptical age. Moreover, religion is one of the central values, along with art and love, which he considers to be denigrated in his homeland.

Nevertheless, accepting that religion has an important place in White's fiction, two crucial questions remain to be answered by those who seek to abstract a single religious viewpoint from the novels: is there any discernible consistency among the various religious positions that are to be found in the fiction; is religious allegory compatible with the novel form; is the pursuit of the author's 'vision' a proper interpretive approach?

Riders in the Chariot

Riders in the Chariot invites allegorical interpretation. The central event in the novel is the 'crucifixion' of an elderly Jew, Mordecai Himmelfarb, who sees himself as the long promised Messiah of his race. Other characters in the novel correspond to the major protagonists of Christ's passion. Miss Hare and Mrs Godbold, like the Biblical Marys, tend the body of the man they regard as a saviour after his Deposition. An aboriginal painter, Alf Dubbo, assumes the role of Peter denying his master, in this case to the conductor on the bus to Sarsaparilla.[3] There is even a Judas figure in the person of Harry Rosetree, an apostate Jew who hangs himself in remorse for his part in the death of Himmelfarb.[4] Not surprisingly, given the web of Christian imagery in the novel, at least one critic has described *Riders in the Chariot* as a religious allegory that recreates the main events of the Christian story in modern Australia.[5]

Colin Roderick, however, suggests that *Riders in the Chariot* is 'an exercise in medieval Jewish mysticism – its purity marred, to all appearance, by the alien imposition of the central drama of Christian dogma'.[6] Roderick describes *Riders in the Chariot* as 'a sustained metaphysical allegory' in which the author clearly sympathises with the esoteric doctrine on which the novel is built.[7] The problem is, exactly which species of religious allegory does the book belong to? Is it Christian or Jewish, orthodox or heterodox? Or does it embody a pantheistic form of nature mysticism?

Critical approaches which see the novel as a religious allegory associate White's point of view with those of the visionary characters in the novel, particularly Himmelfarb's. The common problem, to which they offer different solutions, is to decide whether the Christian parallels of Himmelfarb's 'crucifixion' outweigh the Jewish mysticism he espouses.

Leonie Kramer, on the other hand, argues in a provocative article that White *attacks* the mysticism embraced by his four visionaries. Kramer challenges the 'critical orthodoxy that sees him as an exponent of mysticism'.[8] She describes the chariot itself as a 'stubbornly unconvincing' symbol whose remoteness from the real world and the sufferings of the visionaries is deliberately emphasised by White.[9] According to Kramer, the four riders are not united by their common vision of a chariot that symbolises the transcendental. On the contrary, it is 'a projection of their delusions'. Kramer, however, is no less assertive in her attempt to pin down White's point of view than the 'critical orthodoxy' she opposes: 'In fact, his fiction heads in the opposite direction from transcendentalism, towards an assertion of secular humanism'.[10]

Critics have produced evidence from the text of *Riders in the Chariot* in support of arguments claiming on the one hand that White is endorsing mysticisms of various kinds and, on the other hand, that he is presenting a 'critique' of mysticism. Clearly, all the critics cannot be correct.

White's point of view is always ambiguous and often self-contradictory. Alan Lawson suggests that the point of view in White's novels 'is capable of changing within a single sentence, and often'.[11] There is a need, then, to explain what Kramer calls 'the function of ambiguity in the novel',[12] but it is not necessary to trace the author's constantly changing, ambivalent viewpoint through every sentence in the novel. The notion that a single, consistent religious (or secular) point of view shapes every event and symbol within the novel to a unified purpose is neither sustainable nor critically useful. Rather, we should follow G. A. Wilkes who urges that the characters' beliefs and moments of inspiration should be treated as 'myths' of which the novelist avails himself.[13] Religious vision in the novel serves as a kind of myth, an informing structure, which is surrounded by ambivalence. The interpretive difficulties the novel poses derive from the complex ironies that play around the 'myths' adopted by the main characters. This is not to say that White mocks religious vision, merely that he has not written a tract, the purpose of which is to endorse some particular variety of religious opinion.

The central problem we face in interpreting *Riders in the Chariot* (and this applies to the religious material in White's work generally) is not White's attitude to mysticism *per se*, but the way in which the various religious ideas held by the characters are disposed in the overall economy of the novel. The most fruitful way to approach the religious ideas in the novel is through the four main characters who variously embody those ideas. Our task as readers is to gauge the exact degree of irony and sympathy with which the narrator invests them at particular moments in the narrative.

*   *   *

Mary Hare has been described as a 'nature mystic who experiences a sense of union, not simply communion, with natural objects and creatures'.[14] Certainly, she believes that she is able to lose her identity at times by merging with the divinity she holds to be immanent in the natural world. But, if the novel endorses the notion that God is immanent 'in every veined leaf', Mary's closeness to nature should lead her to the complete identification with Him she seeks (67). In fact, her original, naive conception of nature is challenged in the course of the novel by her own experience and by the viewpoints of other characters. Specifically, her implicit trust in the essential goodness of the world is undermined by the apparently unmotivated malevolence of Mesdames Flack and Jolley and, later, by the transcendentalism of Himmelfarb, her friend and fellow visionary, who sees the material world as a place of suffering and spiritual entrapment.

Mary not only refuses to acknowledge that any force other than goodness operates in nature, but is filled with pride in her own spiritual awareness. Her arrogance arises from her belief that she is innately spiritually superior to other people and that she will be illuminated by virtue of her election. Convinced that she '*know[s]*' (39), while her father is tormented by partial knowledge, she comes 'to expect of life some ultimate revelation' (26). 'The Ladies' present a direct threat to Mary's happy conviction that, while human nature contains a large measure of 'ugliness and weakness' (35), the natural world of trees, animals, water, even rocks is a mirror image of her own uncomplicated goodness.

This optimistic view of the world can only be preserved in isolation from human contact. Such human contact as is forced on her, with family and servants, only increases her distaste for people in general. Rejected for her ugliness and simplicity, she retreats into a private world in which she is largely happy. Understandably, she finds it impossible to like, far less love, human beings.

Mrs Jolley, the housekeeper Mary invites to Xanadu, sees herself as the embodiment of social virtue, a mother of some means (undisclosed), whose children all own cars. She is a petty, malicious bully who justifies her persecution of Miss Hare in terms of her unassailable faith in conventional, lower-middle-class materialistic values. She attacks Mary as an isolate and an eccentric. More importantly, she challenges Mary's trust in universal goodness with a conventional notion of good and evil that has all the formidable weight of church-going, brick-bungalow suburbia behind it.

Mary's horrified reaction to Mrs Jolley's 'pink cake' makes explicit her increasingly irrational obsession with the problem of 'evil'. On the apparently innocent cake the housekeeper has inscribed: '*For a Bad Girl*' (66). At this point Mary senses 'some danger to the incorporeal, the more significant part of her' (66). Although it is not clear whether Mrs Jolley is being deliberately malicious or merely facetious, Mary accepts the accusation at face value. She now becomes afraid that Mrs Jolley has guessed the secret of her elect, inner life by occult means and is forced to question for the first time her view of the world and herself. She is even confronted by aspects of experience – the predatory nature of wild creatures, and her obscure part in the death of a beloved pet goat – that call into question her detachment of an authentic, inner self from the confusion and 'evil' of the outside world.

At first she associates this newly discovered presence of evil in herself with a previously unacknowledged 'human element' (90). That is to say, she recognises that she possesses a measure of self-importance and the ability to participate in the dishonesties and petty cruelties of social interactions along with other human beings. Thus she attempts to preserve from contamination the spiritual part in herself, that part of her which enjoys an immediate relationship with the natural world. Because the natural world is all she has as a child, and nearly all as an adult, she comes to believe that it is wholly good and charged with an indwelling spiritual presence. She discovers in her relationships with trees and animals not merely a substitute for, but an alternative to, the human relationships of trust and warmth she is denied: 'On these she would expend her great but pitiable love' (19).

By separating the force of 'evil' from the 'incorporeal, the more significant part of her', Mary seeks to maintain her faith in the inviolability of that goodness which she believes to be immanent in the world. But she has substituted for her original naive trust in universal goodness a dualistic vision that makes her increasingly paranoiac. She comes to see Mrs Jolley not merely as a nasty, pathetic human being, but as a diabolical agent ('medium', [86]) of Mrs Flack who is herself more than human, an intangible, pervasive force of evil. Mary ignores the complex motivating forces of guilt, loneliness and frustrated sexuality in both women by reducing them to stereotypes.[15] In so doing she attempts to uphold at least part of her simplistic view of the world by projecting 'evil' and complexity away from the essence of herself.

Mrs Jolley and Mrs Flack suspect a sexual relationship between Himmelfarb and Mary Hare. When Mrs Jolley describes the Jew as 'dirty' and suggests that 'things' have been going on in the orchard, Mary is incensed (331). The truth is that the lonely spinster, overjoyed to find herself treated as a human being, has begun to see herself as a 'woman'. At one point, holding Himmelfarb's hand she finds her body 'elongated into . . . shapes of love and music' (340). She turns to her companion hoping to find that he shares her fantasy that her limbs were 'so long and lovely, and her conical white breasts not so cold as they had been taught to behave . . . ' (340).

In her relationship with Himmelfarb Mary Hare discovers a sense of spiritual communion. But she also finds herself subject to very human, if tentative, desires for sexual union. Mrs Jolley awakens the memories of envy and shy sexual desire that Mary has so long repressed. She also calls into question Mary's notion of her own spiritual superiority, her elect inner life which compensates for her many rebuffs by society. Mrs Jolley wheedles out Mary's secret conviction that she is spiritually superior. From her secure position as a pillar of suburban society she proclaims the inner life of her mistress 'evil' and 'sick': '"Who is not wicked and evil, waiting for chariots at sunset, as if they was taxis?"' (97). But Mary's reaction to Mrs Jolley's attacks is increasingly paranoiac not merely because her housekeeper exposes and cheapens her esoteric, inner life but also because Mrs Jolley threatens Mary's whole view of nature and self.

Mary comes to see Mrs Flack as a superhuman and ubiquitous force of evil watching her from her lounge, even 'directing' her (330). Evil, which she had been able to ignore before the arrival of her housekeeper is now a powerful and general presence infiltrating the natural world of Xanadu and her own, previously inviolable, self: '"Then I am offal, offal! Green, putrefying, out of old, starved sheep. Worse, worse!"' (331). She now sees the world in the grip of a 'conspiracy of evil minds', in the face of which only the 'loving-kindness' she has experienced with the other three riders can offer salvation (335).

Miss Hare is curiously 'fascinated by bad' for one with such a faith in goodness (330). But her theory of goodness is threatened by Himmelfarb's supposedly complementary vision as well as by Mrs Jolley's materialism. In their dialogue beneath the plum tree, Miss Hare attempts to express her touching faith in nature in the hope that this sympathetic person will accept her version of truth: '"how can we look out from under this tree, and not know that all is good?"' (172). But the Jew has experienced too much of the evil in the world to be convinced. Above all, he insists on the need for redemption from sin. At first Miss Hare is unable to accept this notion of sin because her experience of evil has been less extreme than his. She concedes that some people are possessed by evil, presumably Mesdames Flack and Jolley, but cannot ascribe more than a limited reality to that evil: '"it burns itself out"' (172). She refuses to allow that the chariot symbolises redemption from the material world as it does for Himmelfarb.

Mary invites Himmelfarb to Xanadu because she trusts that he will see 'the essential mystery and glory' beneath the crumbling facade, the spiritual reality within the decaying body, but he sees the reality, not her myth (105). He is overwhelmed by its 'desolation' so that momentarily Mary considers that he too is merely a materialist (338). The Jew, of course, is no more a materialist than Miss Hare. For him, however, 'mystery and glory' reside *beyond* the world of matter.

Mary had hoped to experience 'some ultimate revelation' through her relationship with the natural world. But she is so drawn to Himmelfarb, the one man who treats her as a human being, that she comes to accept a view of the world similar to his own: 'I think you mentioned . . . that we were links in some chain. I am convinced myself that there are two chains. Matched against each other. If Mrs Jolley and Mrs Flack were the only two links in theirs, then, of course, we should have nothing to fear. *But!*' (343). Mary has substituted a dualistic view of the world for her original belief in natural goodness and divine immanence.

The threat of evil that has come to obsess her culminates in the fire at Himmelfarb's house. Mary enters the burning house hoping to rescue her friend and receive there the revelation she has been expecting so long, but she is not granted any visionary moment. Instead she imagines she sees the burning body of the Jew and is convinced that evil has triumphed. Himmelfarb, however, has been removed before the fire and Mary is able to lie at his feet as he lies dying in Mrs Godbold's shed. There, at last, she believes that she has 'entered that state of complete union which her nature had never yet achieved' (491). She is not, however, granted any 'ultimate revelation', nor does her soul achieve complete union with divinity. She discovers peace in the belief that the 'heavenly spirit' of the man she has worshipped has painlessly 'entered her' (492).

Only now is Miss Hare liberated from the 'demons' of repressed sexual energy that have tormented her since Mrs Jolley brought them to the surface of her mind. Mrs Jolley had guessed the secret of Mary's coy sexual desire and her pathetic need to be treated as a *woman*. Sexually repressed and withered herself, the housekeeper had branded the innocent relationship between the two outcasts 'dirty' (331). Now Mary knows herself to be fully accepted by Himmelfarb, her thwarted sexuality, once accepted, becomes the least part of their relationship. The memories of her humiliation at the ball and her envy of the beautiful Miss Antill, are at last banished: 'And all the dancing demons fled out, in peacock feathers, with a tinkling of the fitful little mirrors set in the stuff of their cunning thighs' (492).

Mary Hare's version of truth meets Himmelfarb's beneath the plum tree in the garden at Xanadu. While she sees only the goodness of the natural world, the Jew has a vision of the chaos of all generation precipitated by his memory of the fire raid at Friedensdorf. In terms of the Jewish Gnosticism that deeply influences his thinking, he sees souls being sent down from their original, purely spiritual home protesting at their incarnation in the forms of plants, stones, animals, and human beings. The material world is likened to a 'chafing-dish' of fire designed to purify the souls and prepare them for their return to the spiritual realm whence they originated (174). Himmelfarb sees his own role in this process as that in which Hezekiah, David and Akiba failed: to redeem the 'lost sparks' of divinity imprisoned in the material world (345).

Himmelfarb submits to his mock crucifixion in the factory yard at Sarsaparilla because he sees this violent 'joke' on the part of his workmates as the vindication of his messianic role. On the Jacaranda-tree he hopes to redeem not only himself and his race but also those splintered pieces of divinity which are the only redeemable part of the world. For a moment he becomes so detached from the taunts of the xenophobic mob that he believes he has been given the sign he has been expecting: 'So, he raised his head. And was conscious of a stillness and clarity . . . at the centre of which his God was reflected' (464). But he must come down again, 'unsteady at the level of reality to which he had been returned' (468). Above all, Himmelfarb does not redeem the world or even himself as he had hoped: 'Very quietly Himmelfarb left the factory in which it had not been accorded to him to expiate the sins of the world' (469).

As Himmelfarb lies dying in Mrs Godbold's shed he confronts those figures from his past life he had failed to love sufficiently. He discovers that his relationships with other people must be relived and understood even at this late stage. He must expiate his failure to love others not by turning from the world and its inhabitants in pursuit of mystical revelation but by coming to terms with his purely human failings. So he contends first with his father, Moshe. As a young man Himmelfarb had been filled with disgust at the sight of his father, drunk in the company of a gentile and two prostitutes. On that occasion he failed to forgive, although guilty himself of the same sins and receiving his father's generous support. They are brought together only now that Himmelfarb realizes that he himself is 'at the point of failure' (479), where previously he had been arrogant enough to despise that worldly Jew, his father, for his apostasy.

Secondly Himmelfarb returns to his life with Reha, his wife. The scope of his vision does not excuse his failure of the woman who had loved him. He had cut himself off from Reha not through intellectual but through spiritual pride. His marriage had signalled a choice on his part to move away from his dedication to the intellect in favour not only of the Jewishness he shared with her but of his belief in his own election, his special role in the divine plan, a notion originally inspired in him by his mother and her fanatical sisters. But this very belief in his role as messiah of his race cuts him from from his homely, Jewish wife, as Stan Parker's visions cut him off from Amy: "'You!" she cried, choking, it seemed, with desperate blood. "Much will be made clear to you! But to us, the ordinary ones?"' (158). Himmelfarb is unable to comfort his distraught wife because he accepts her division of men into the elect and ordinary, a division that promises him absolute knowledge and her only ignorance.

Himmelfarb is so completely dedicated to his private inner vision that he can dismiss the sufferings of the external world as passing details in a vast design, the material world itself as illusion. But this inwardness cuts him off from ordinary people who are subject to doubt and suffering without the consolation of a vision of transcendence. Himmelfarb's mystical preoccupations lead him to consign his wife among the transitory material things and relationships he must put behind him.

Finally, Himmelfarb appears to achieve that long-awaited state of complete detachment, of equanimity, that justifies all the pain he has seen and experienced as a man: 'By that light, even the most pitiable or monstrous incidents experienced by human understanding were justified, it seemed, as their statuary stood grouped together on the plain he was about to leave' (492). The conclusion, of course, is Himmelfarb's. The reader does not follow him beyond the world into the purely spiritual reality he seems about to embrace. Moreover, it is not clear whether Himmelfarb is moving entirely beyond matter and doubt or whether he is merely returning in his mind to the conviction and warmth of his mother-dominated childhood:

> Again, he was the Man Kadmon, descending from the Tree of Light to take the Bride. Trembling with white, holding the cup in her chapped hands, she advanced to stand beneath the *Chuppah*. So they were brought together in the smell of all primordial velvets. This, explained the cousins and aunts, is at last the *Shecchinah*, whom you have carried all these years under your left breast. As he received her, she bent and kissed the wound in his hand. Then they were truly one. (483)

The *Shecchinah*, previously described by Himmelfarb as the creative love of God or the lost sparks imprisoned in the world, is now identified with the wife he has loved through the years. He achieves his aim of becoming Adam Kadmon, not by redeeming the whole world, but by returning to the scene of his wedding, by becoming one with the wife he has failed in the past. The lesson Himmelfarb learns at this point was known all along by his wife, but he never thought to ask her while she lived: 'she sensed the distance between aspiration and the possibility of achievement, and she was unable to do anything to help him' (157).

Ruth Godbold, the washerwoman of Sarsaparilla, is the least isolated and inward-looking of the four visionaries. Her early background is rural, poor, fundamentalist. Her Christianity is fervent, simple and joyous. Despite the suffering she has seen, particularly the death of her younger brother, and the hardships she has borne, her view of the world remains optimistic.

Mrs Godbold's evangelism is often embarrassingly demonstrative. She offers to pray for Miss Hare who simply cannot see any point in Christianity or prayer, at least in the forms practised by the Christians she has known. As Alf Dubbo lies drunk and bleeding from tuberculosis on the floor of Mrs Khalil's brothel, Mrs

Godbold expectantly asks him if he is a Christian. She confesses
to Himmelfarb, the Jew, her terrible secret, that her husband,
Tom, 'has never been saved' (249). Her constant desire to 'save'
her husband is suggestive of the same spiritual arrogance that
mars Himmelfarb and even Miss Hare. Moreover, her unsolicited
concern so irritates Tom himself that she serves only to hasten
his disintegration by reminding him of his own hopelessness. Tom
Godbold is tormented by his evangelistic, hymn-singing, pious,
charitable wife whose goodness and forgivingness are a constant
unstated reproach: 'Ruth Joyner suspected that what she had done
in innocence was bringing out the worst in people' (298).

Ruth sets out to rescue Tom from Mrs Khalil's brothel in her
favourite role of long-suffering Christian wife. She sees her expedition as an 'errand of love' (309). But she discovers a reality more
complex than she had expected. Even the whores are searching
for 'Love . . . like anybody else' (311). Mrs Godbold discovers love
where she had expected lust, degradation and sin. Her own previous notion of love is undermined by her experience in the brothel
and shown to be limited.

J. F. Burrows suggests that after the brothel scene the narrator
proceeds to 'canonize' Mrs Godbold.[16] It is a mistake, however, to
assume that White regards Mrs Godbold as Mary Hare does, as 'the
most positive evidence of good' (72). The narrator's attitude to her
is generally ambivalent. Her charity, her humility, her acceptance
of outcasts and eccentrics are clearly positive virtues in contrast to
the xenophobic suspicion of outsiders, the mean-mindedness and
malignancy of Mesdames Flack and Jolley. But her conception of
Christianity is simplistic and sentimental; her expression of it is
often unconsciously humorous: '"But Tom", she would say, in her
gentle, serious, infuriating voice, "the Re-Birth, I think it is lovely"'
(259). Moreover, her charitable impulses lead her to interfere in
the spiritual as well as the material affairs of others. She is always
offering succour from her inexhaustible storehouse of grace and
shank-bones.

Ruth Godbold does change in the course of the novel. As a young
girl on the boat to Australia she is 'released' one night from her
body. Her soul hovers in the vastness 'until recognizing that the
rollers were folded into one another, and the stars were fragments
of the one light' (270). At this stage she sees all matter as the
manifestation of a beneficient divinity. Her position is sharply
different from that of Himmelfarb who sees the world in the grip

of darkness and even evil. Much later Mrs Godbold comes to see herself as 'the infinite quiver' shooting her 'arrows [children] at the face of darkness' (549). The events of her life, particularly the crucifixion of Himmelfarb, lead her to believe in the presence of a force of darkness operating in the world.

Alf Dubbo, the Aboriginal painter, like Mary Hare, is 'often hopeful of arriving eventually at understanding' (384). He hopes that his vision will complete itself 'through revelation', but he expects that art, not mystical illumination, will be the medium of his redemption (385). Dubbo's vision of infinity is more tentative, less obsessive, than Himmelfarb's or even Mrs Godbold's because his art depends on the material world for metaphors with which to express his vague aspirations to transcendence: 'where other men might have prayed for grace, he proceeded to stare at what could be his only proof of an Absolute, at the same time, in its soaring blues and commentary of blacks, his act of faith' (387).

Dubbo's 'proof of an Absolute' is the spirit that moves in him during the creative act. But the work itself expresses a contradiction between the longing for transcendence signified by the 'soaring blues' and the painter's acknowledgement of doubt, complexity, pain expressed by the 'blacks'. In an ambitious moment he determines to 'clothe the formless form of God' (397). But the wings of the Angel of the Lord he paints in a later work point to the difficulty of expressing the infinite through the material medium of art: 'He could at least admire the feathery texture of the angel's wings as a problem overcome, while forgetting that a little boy on a molten morning had held a live cockatoo in his hands, and opened its feathers to look at their roots, and become involved in a mystery of down. Later perhaps, falling asleep, or waking, it might occur to the man how he had understood to render the essence of divinity' (404).

This reliance upon the external world does not prevent the painter from retreating within the closed circle of himself. His art is a communication with himself alone, a means of expressing his visions and aspirations in 'hieroglyphs' that must remain inaccessible to others (384). He feels guilty, even dirty, after revealing this private world to Humphrey Mortimer, the art critic. At times Dubbo feels able to cut himself off completely from the external world and those in it because he believes presumptuously that he can find all the images he needs for his art inside himself: 'Everything is inside of me, waiting for me to understand it' (380). But as he matures he comes to acknowledge the force of the contradiction in his art. He restates his intention of painting the chariot thus: 'he would now transcribe the Frenchman's limited composition into his own terms of motion, and forms partly transcendental, partly evolved from his struggle with daily becoming, and experience of suffering' (385).

Dubbo's creativity thrives amid sleaziness, disorder, life in its most primitive and energetic forms. During his stay at the dump he is able to paint the obsessive souls of men inside their corrupt bodies. At Hannah's place he uncovers treasure even in his own vomit and concedes a limited perfection to the sterile union of Hannah, the prostitute, and Norm, the drag-queen. His inner world is able to transform physical decadence in the world outside into images of truth as he sees it.

Like Mary Hare, Dubbo is unable to grasp the attraction of Christianity. As a child he is saved from 'savagery' by the Reverend Timothy Caulderon and his sister. But their 'Great Experiment' is unsuccessful (352). Alf simply cannot visualise Jesus Christ and is unable to accept any 'truth' which does not appeal to his imagination. He is aware too that both his guardians use their religion to avoid coming to terms with their failures in life. With the exception of Mrs Godbold, the Christians Alf meets are hypocritical or self-deceiving. In later life a park bench prophet informs Dubbo that the Lord is about to return to trample the evil doers. Dubbo is distressed because those to whom the Lord is about to deal out justice have provided him with aid, lodging and even friendship.

Dubbo can only see Christ as a lifeless wooden god, not a suffering man. Accordingly, he cannot connect the Christian myth with his own experience of suffering. The victim of untreated tuberculosis and syphilis, Dubbo attempts to dissociate his diseased body from his creativity as he tries to dissociate the visions expressed in his art from the material world that provides him with his metaphors. He sees his sickness and his creativity as 'the two poles . . . of his being'; the one furtive and destroying, the other regenerative (383–4). So his life and art contain a series of contradictions which he is unable to resolve. He even recognises a duality in the outside world between those moments 'when the sun deceives with gold' by allowing the world to meet his creative expectations, and the 'actual colours, of grey-brown' (383).

The gap between the actual world outside his head and his vision closes as he watches the crucifixion of Himmelfarb. Instead of the bare Jacaranda tree, 'the painter [is] made to visualize the divine tree in its intensity of blue' (460). Now he is totally committed to the world inside himself rather than that outside. So he fails to aid the Jew to whom he owes allegiance as fellow visionary and friend. Finally, he is alienated from the world and those in it not by his race, but by what he sees as his artistic integrity: 'Now Dubbo knew that he would never, never act, that he would dream, and suffer, and express some of that suffering in paint – but was, in the end powerless. In his innocence, he blamed his darker skin' (461). As a man he suffers, as a visionary he dreams of escaping from suffering. As an artist he can only express that suffering in paint. He cannot act to alleviate it.

In the figure of the crucified Jew he sees an image of all the suffering in the world. The meaning of Christ's willing sacrifice which has hitherto eluded him, now becomes clear in terms of the event he is witnessing: 'As he watched, the colour flowed through the veins of the cold, childhood Christ' (463). He is, however, unable to set down in paint the ideal of 'detached, contemplative suffering' he sees in the crucified Himmelfarb.

The formal problem of expressing the infinite in the limited medium of paint can only be solved by infusing the colours that symbolise transcendence with the knowledge learned from his own suffering. As he paints his conception of the Deposition, his own body moves swiftly towards death. At last Dubbo sets out to paint the chariot itself, 'to restate his conception of the chariot' (513). He transfers 'the effulgence of his spirit onto canvas' (514). But the gold of transcendence in his chariot painting is finally his own blood. The material world forces itself into the closed world of the painting: 'The sharp pain poured in crimson tones into the limited space of the room, and overflowed. It poured and overflowed his hands. These were gilded, he was forced to observe, with his own blood' (515).

*   *   *

Each of the four visionaries is an outcast from society, Himmelfarb because he is Jewish, Mary Hare because she is mad and ugly, Mrs Godbold because she is poor, and Dubbo because he is black. Each develops a personal, inner version of reality in preference to the

narrow view adopted by those ordinary people who reject and
persecute them. In so doing they limit their responses to the world
outside them, although they discover an inner richness denied to
their persecutors. All come dangerously close to Eustace Cleugh's
refusal to 'believe in anything outside the closed circle of himself'
(35). Himmelfarb surpasses Eustace in this respect. Yet they are
preserved from the dryness and solipsism of Eustace Cleugh by
their common ability to love others, at least each other. Only this
ability separates them from the introversion of the Reverend Timothy Caulderon who becomes 'walled up . . . in his own ineffectuality
and lovelessness' (364). Each has to learn to love without reserve
slowly and painfully in the course of many failures.

Each of the visionaries claims to have intimations of spiritual
reality, but these intimations do not add up to a single vision of
Truth shared by all. Each has to learn to open himself or herself
to other interpretations of truth. In doing so they distinguish
themselves from Mrs Flack who also claims to see things 'as they
really are' (446). Mrs Flack proclaims that 'the truth is what a
decent person knows by instinct' (42). The truth, however, is
difficult to see from any angle. Only by modifying their visions
in the light of what they learn from each other and from their own
experiences do the four visionaries avoid falling into Mrs Flack's
dogmatism.

The novel, then, does not endorse any particular religious position, but rather explores the religious instinct itself as it is variously
understood by four individuals. Each of the four has to learn to
accept the complexity of experience and to refrain from attempting to impose his or her vision on experience. Their occasional,
inconclusive glimpses of a divine purpose operating in the world do
not cancel out their doubts or differences. Nor do those glimpses
serve to explain the sufferings they experience in terms of some
divine plan. In the end their intimations of a Great Design are
no more satisfactory than Mrs Hare's limp explanation to her
daughter: '"Only our Father in Heaven will be able to tell my pet
why He made her as He did"' (23). Similarly, the last cry of the
lady from Czernowitz, about to enter the gas chamber, calls into
question Himmelfarb's belief that in the light of the divine purpose
all the suffering in the world is justified.

> 'God show us!' shrieked the lady from Czernowitz. 'Just this
> once! At least!'. (204)

Thus the allegorical tendencies in the novel are controlled by an authorial reserve that is ironical, but not mocking. White maintains a necessary distance from his visionary characters and from their visions of transcendent meaning, and it is this distance that allows such diverse and contradictory interpretations of the meaning of his work to proliferate.

The Solid Mandala

The Solid Mandala lacks the bewildering complexities as well as the epic proportions of *Voss* and *Riders in the Chariot*. Several critics and reviewers have noted that, while the scope of the novel is less ambitious, the tone is more humane than in White's previous novels.[17] The characters and action are less extreme. Nevertheless, the meaning and the stature of the novel remain elusive. The disagreement with which *The Solid Mandala* was greeted by reviewers and critics bears witness to this.[18] There has been no consensus about the meaning of the novel at all. As with *Riders in the Chariot*, a number of contradictory allegorical interpretations which see the novel as embodying Christian or Eastern mysticism or Jungian psychology have been advanced.[19]

According to Thelma Herring, Arthur Brown is both human and divine. He 'can apprehend ultimate reality . . . and in the end, divinity is seen to be immanent in him'.[20] Although Herring suggests that White fails to present Arthur coherently as a character, she has no doubts about the success of his presentation as a symbol. By becoming a mandala, Arthur is identified with the inner meaning of the novel itself. A. P. Riemer sees *The Solid Mandala* as a Jungian allegory in which the human qualities of the characters clash with their function as archetypes.[21] Riemer considers that Arthur's humanity only serves to prevent his achieving the symbolic apotheosis with which White ultimately sympathizes. But Riemer is less concerned with the characters, even as purely symbolic figures, than with the explicitly Jungian archetypes employed by the novelist. Arthur's marbles, or solid mandalas, according to Riemer, illustrate two notions central to Jung's theories: the quaternity and the alchemic philosopher's stone. The knotted taw which Arthur loses represents the hermetic *rotundum* containing the secrets of the universe. Arthur's loss of this marble signals his failure to become the demiurge and unlock these secrets. More recently, in a book-length critical study of White's work, to which White himself took strong exception, David Tacey has also elaborated a Jungian reading.[22]

Patricia Morley is anxious to refute Riemer's contention that *The Solid Mandala* endorses the Jungian notion that the modern mandalic experience contains not God but man at its centre.[23] However, she also sees the novel as an allegory, but one shaped by a vision that is Christian, orthodox and essentially mystical.[24] Waldo and Arthur Brown 'embody man's flesh and spirit', but the novel demonstrates the interdependence and unity of these two attributes.[25] According to Morley, White's God is both transcendent to, and immanent in, the world.[26]

Allegorical interpretations force readers to respond to the novel according to whether or not they accept the systems of belief which, supposedly, it endorses. Each of the critics above refers to a specific variety of religious (or quasi-religious in the case of Jungian psychology) thought as a means of making sense of the novel. Each maintains that White himself is committed to the religious system he or she discovers in the novel. However, the contradictions that emerge among these critics call into question the assumption that White has left signposts in the novel which point to a coherent religious viewpoint, which makes sense of all the events in the novel, and which constitutes White's own 'vision'. Allegory as a form depends upon there being some coherent viewpoint which can be extracted from the text. By this standard *The Solid Mandala* is a failure because its doctrinal core is impossible to identify. By the same standard, however, it succeeds as a *novel*, a form which by its nature is dramatic and exploratory rather than didactic and closed.

Nevertheless, the many esoteric allusions in *The Solid Mandala* do encourage the view that a specific system of religious meaning serves as structuring centre in the novel. The complex ironies of *Voss* were brought to bear primarily on the characters within the novel. In *Riders in the Chariot* the structure of religious symbolism was becoming intrusive, although White still appeared to be working primarily through his characters rather than through an imposed structure of meaning. In *The Solid Mandala* White *seems* to have moved closer to allegory proper. The novel is full of religious and esoteric allusions. At times it is difficult not to agree with Thelma Herring that: '[a]ny difficulty one may experience in perceiving White's meaning is inherent in his theme: he has never been at such pains to give his readers clues, not only through the titles of the books that Arthur reads but also through the definition of "mandala" that he finds in an encyclopaedia'.[27]

The Solid Mandala does not, however, argue a case or embody a doctrine. The 'clues' do not point to a system of belief with which the reader can sympathise only 'on grounds that are extraneous to the novel'.[28] Rather, it *tests* the validity of the models by which its characters interpret their experiences. Thus it reflects ironically on those its critics employ to interpret its meaning. White is playing another obscure and sardonic game, leading his determined exegetes up the garden path into a familiar interpretive maze.

The novel's spiritual themes are focused through a visionary simpleton, Arthur Brown, twin brother of Waldo, a Whitean intellectual and dry stick who looks back to Elyot Standish in *The Living and the Dead*. Part of the problem of forming a coherent picture of Arthur, of deciding how we are to respond to him, arises from White's technique of presenting him through the perspectives of other characters. These perspectives, even where sympathetic, cast an ironic light on Arthur's spiritual quest. There is a disparity between the public persona, Arthur the 'dill', and the perceptive and sensitive private person within. The question is, to what extent does the narrative allow the reader to 'see behind the words'[29] of Arthur Brown into the hidden, authentic self, which Arthur himself describes as 'the part that matters' (29)?

Arthur himself believes in a dualism between the spiritual part of himself that moves towards some final insight and the body in which the spirit is enclosed: 'Then Arthur realized Dad would never know, any more than Waldo. It was himself who was, and would remain, the keeper of mandalas, who must guess their final secret through touch and light . . . . His body might topple, but only his body, as he submitted the marble in his pocket to his frenzy of discovery' (240). By concentrating on his mandalas, Arthur hopes eventually to understand 'All' (200). At crucial points in his life he seems to be granted at least a partial insight into the ultimate secret. As a child he is taken to *Götterdämmerung*: 'Who and where were the gods? He could not have told, but *knew*, in his flooded depths' (217, my italics). In the mandala dance he performs for Mrs Poulter he offers his prayers not to abstract gods in the conventional attitudes of religion, but to what he '*knew* from light or silences' (265, my italics). He communicates to the dying Mr Feinstein a knowledge that Dulcie considers 'let[s] in God; (278).

Can we accept the view of Dulcie and Arthur himself that Arthur possesses a special insight into reality? Does the novel wholeheartedly endorse Arthur's insights? If so, the meaning of *The Solid Mandala* is expressed by those gnomic utterances which Arthur invests with oracular conviction: '*God* . . . is a kind of sort of *rock* crystal' (87); 'the world is another mandala' (245).

Such an approach ignores the ways in which Arthur's visions are undercut in the course of the novel. The simultaneous presentation of Arthur as an overgrown child who loves cars, service stations and ju-jubes and as one of 'God's fools' is somehow discordant.[30] Arthur's delight in the lollies and grease guns at the Speedex Service Station may be a permissable modern quality of visionary simpletons, but it also invests Arthur as a character with that familiar Whitean reserve – the lifting of an eyebrow, the angle of which is always difficult to gauge precisely.

More important, the reader cannot help feeling that Arthur's craving for spiritual fulfilment arises from a need to find some compensation for the pleasures of everyday life which he is denied. White's description of Arthur, derelict, alone and half mad, peering through the Feinsteins's window into a world of comfort and belonging from which he is excluded is moving precisely because that world is attractive and real. Although R. F. Brissenden maintains that: 'Arthur's world is one of warmth, sunshine and easy love,' Arthur's visions can never make him happy or end his isolation.[31]

At times White uses Arthur's simplicity for comic effect. Arthur's rhetorical question addressed to Mrs Poulter, '"I expect women are pretty attached to their breasts"' (256), plays on the gap between the spiritual understanding which he aspires to achieve with her, and the sexual undertones of the relationship which neither will acknowledge. In fact, a repressed sexuality underlies most of Arthur's relationships.

Waldo and Arthur both court Dulcie, the former repelled by, the latter consciously unaware of, the sexual implications of their wooing. Waiting to see the pregnant Dulcie '[Arthur's] thighs would quiver in anticipation of blissfully joyful union with his love' (275). Immediately before the mandala-dance, White evokes the frustrated sexual yearnings of both Arthur and Mrs Poulter in a scene that is all the more powerful for its understatement. Mrs Poulter describes a fantasy in which the social and sexual needs her husband, Bill, had never satisfied find their fulfilment through the mediation of a stranger who recognises that she is 'different' (264).

Her protestations that she 'love[s] Bill' only serve to reinforce the impression that her sexual potential has never found an adequate outlet (264).

Arthur, for his part, asks to touch her hair which Mrs Poulter has allowed to flow free in the manner of a lover. In so doing she discovers an image of the passions and needs underlying the apparently innocent surface of their relationship.

Arthur trusts that Mrs Poulter will intuitively understand the meaning of his dance, will *see* that he is a visionary rather than a mere simpleton, but the state of mind suggested by her reactions does not support his trust. Mrs Poulter looks at the ground and plays with her hair because she is embarrassed by this shambling man of whom she is nevertheless fond. The 'vision' that Arthur believes she tries to avoid ('throw . . . off') is not so much his own illumined inner vision of truth at last communicated to another person as the sight of this large, physically awkward man (266). Above all, the dance is described with a humour, a pathos and a lightness of touch that raises a question about how seriously we are take the heavily Jungian symbolism.

> 'I'm going to dance a mandala for you, Mrs Poulter,' he said . . . .
>
> He knew she was preparing to laugh, but wouldn't, because she had grown fond of him.
>
> 'The mandala?' she said, soberly enough. 'I never heard of a dance called that. Not any of the modern ones.'
>
> He did not attempt to explain, because he felt he would make her see. (265)

The reader's response to Arthur is further complicated by suggestions of homosexuality and incest. When Waldo accuses Arthur of being a 'big fat helpless female' he points to a certain effeminacy in both twins and an under-current in their relationship that deeply disturbs him (230). Discovering Waldo decked out in Anne Brown's decayed dress, Arthur recognises 'some such translation in himself of his brother's personality' (291). The novel does not condemn either twin for his sexual ambivalence, but we are made aware that the complex descriptions of their acts and relationships concocted by the twins serve to avoid confronting the underlying force of sexual energy.

Waldo's pretensions to spiritual celibacy only serve to draw attention to his closeted sexuality. White's treatment of the ways in which Waldo describes his own motives and emotions to himself and the force of unspent desire that manifests itself in his relationships is both moving and funny. Waldo disguises his attraction for Wally Pugh, which finds its only outlet in an 'inebriating' embrace, by affecting a disdain for the pudgy and inept boy (128). In a similar way, he describes to himself his 'prim and virginal' approaches to Bill Poulter as an attempt to improve his taciturn and illiterate neighbour by providing him with books (142). His intention to convert Bill into a literary companion recalls his earlier hope to achieve the same with Dulcie Feinstein. In both cases his fear of sexual surrender, which shows itself as distaste and arrogance, is abstracted, made literary, and hence sterilised.

All these hints surface in Waldo's act of transvestitism: 'When he was finally and fully arranged, bony, palpitating, plucked, it was no longer Waldo Brown, in spite of the birthmark above his left collarbone .... She could afford to breathe indulgently, magnificent down to the last hair in her moustache, and allowing for the spectacles' (193). Waldo's bizarre act is both a surrender to his repressed homosexuality and a nostalgic self identification with his mother whose aristocratic sensibility he continues to admire. But he fails to achieve the 'satisfactory image of himself' he covets.[32] He is confronted by the cleavage between all his unconvincing personae – clerk, mother, writer – and the aging, ridiculous man perceived by the world and reflected ruthlessly by the mirror.

Arthur also refuses to allow that actual events call into question his subjective interpretations of their meaning. In the passage dealing with their incest, White sets their desire for a spiritual communion and a return to the mythical innocence of childhood that overwhelms and consoles them during the act itself against their promised awakening to the daylight world and its judgement: 'As they lay in the vast bed time was swooping in waves of waves of yellow fluctuating light, or grass. The yellow friction finally revived their flesh. They seemed to flow together as they had, once or twice, in memory or sleep. They were promised a sticky morning, of yellow down, of old yellowed wormy quinces' (209).

Arthur's self-recriminations are not entirely groundless. He informs Waldo that he hates himself at times because he can 'see' himself (207). In respect of his spiritual aspirations and his desire to love others better Arthur is rightly 'conscious of the distance between his desire and perfect satisfaction' (262). Morley maintains that this 'perfect satisfaction' is achieved when White associates Arthur with Christ in the final section of the novel.[33] However, the constant reminders of Arthur's repressed sexuality and the self-delusion they suggest, together with the state of mental derangement to which he is finally reduced, should cause us to question whether White intends his reader to make such an association uncritically. It is Mrs Poulter who makes the association after the collapse of her own faith in Jesus: 'And He released His hands from the nails. And fell down, in a thwack of canvas, a cloud of dust' (303). Christ's sudden, theatrical fall from His cross is the pivotal point of Mrs Poulter's 'private Armageddon', as Morley notes.[34] Her plaster-cast Jesus, representing a sentimental religiosity, collapses when she is faced by a major, personal crisis. In the place of Christ, the convenient 'myth' of which she has availed herself, she now puts Arthur Brown.

Attempts to formulate Mrs Poulter's statements beyond this point into a coherent theological position fail to allow for the ambiguities in the text.[35] Her confession to Arthur: 'I believe in you,' merely begs the question (311). Does White intend us to identify Arthur with Christ as Mrs Poulter does, or is Arthur merely a repository for the sexual and maternal drives she has repressed or diverted throughout a lifetime?

> 'I believe in you, Arthur.'
> So she did, *this man and child*, since her God was brought crashing down. (311, my italics)

Above all there is the problem of deciding whether or not Arthur is in part responsible for Waldo's death as he believes himself to be: 'When Arthur saw the murder he had committed on his brother he began to try to throw him off . . . ' (294). Arthur sees the hatred that Waldo has always directed at all living things. He also sees that he has bred that hatred in his brother apparently by his very existence. He sees himself as 'the getter of pain' (294). Arthur's self accusation cannot simply be dismissed as the delusion of a simpleton. Like Miss Docker in *A Cheery Soul* and Mrs Godbold in *Riders in the Chariot*, Arthur's goodness, in some cases, brings out the worst in others. Waldo and Mrs Allright are both victims of 'the destructive power of good'.[36]

In view of the ambiguities in Arthur's character the impulse to

identify the novel's point of view with his visionary experiences
must be suppressed. The most fruitful avenue of approach to an
understanding of the mystical and esoteric references in the novel
is provided by examining the types of irony that surround them in
their specific contexts rather than by trying to identify their source
in some school of thought outside the novel itself.

The very explicitness of the references raises questions about
White's attitude to the materials on which he draws. The 'clues'
that seem to point to the novel's inner meaning are *too* obvious,
their introduction into the novel *too* artificial from so slippery an
author. At times White's application of Jungian theories can only
be construed as deliberately grotesque parody. Arthur's analysis of
one of his own dreams, for instance, recalls Jung's notion of psychic
rebirth in a bizarre fashion.

> 'I dreamed about you Waldo. You had lumps of Pears soap
> trying to come out of your nostrils. You seemed upset. I
> wonder what it means .'
> Waldo was revolted. He broke a basin.
> 'Perhaps it means,' said Arthur, 'you're afraid of having a
> baby'. (209–10)

Most of the esoteric references in *The Solid Mandala* are linked
to Arthur's quest for spiritual perfection. He associates his four
marbles explicitly with his mystical aspirations after reading a
definition of the mandala in an encyclopaedia. The passage he
reads, which is quoted in the novel, has a striking similarity to
Jung's theories about the mandala.[37] His dream in which a tree
grows out of his thigh (260) is reminiscent of an illustration in
Jung's *Psychology and Alchemy*,[38] drawn from a mediaeval alchemical
manuscript. The passage dealing with the 'hermaphroditic Adam'
with whom Arthur identifies himself, is taken directly from the
same work.[39]

> 'But they would lie together, and the dark bed was all kindness
> all tenderness towards them, the pillowed darkness all feathers.
> Skin was never so velvety by day. Eyelashes plait together in
> darkness. As Venus said, in the old book Arthur came across
> years later: I generate light, and darkness is not of my nature;
> there is nothing better or more venerable than the conjunction
> of myself with my brother.' (229)

Arthur radically misapplies the alchemical symbolism to an actual event with incestuous overtones. Similarly, the sexual implications of Arthur's identification of his brother with the mystical Tiresias inserts a disorienting and bizarre perspective between the myths to which the novel refers and the events it sets up. The importance of the Tiresias myth in the novel relies on the ironic contrast between Waldo's literary identification of himself with the blind soothsayer and the quality that Arthur seizes on: "'How he was changed into a woman for a short time'" (282–3).

White, then, is concerned to explore a conflict between the systems of belief adopted by the characters and their experiences and relationships in the real world. In a similar way, he explores the foreign nature of conventional ideas about man, God and even architecture which the European immigrants attempt to assert in the Australian environment. George Brown sees his escape from Europe as a rejection of the restrictive conventions of class, religion, tradition and myth, but the conventional attitudes which he brings with him to Australia, represented so vividly by his 'classical pediment', show that he remains as trapped by the limitations of nineteenth-century Rationalism as he was by Baptist fundamentalism. The 'impasto of nonconformist guilt' (146) he carries with him mocks his efforts to free himself from the influences of myth 'by way of Intellectual Enlightenment, and the voyage to Australia' (145). Similarly, the rise of the Nazis in Germany adds a hollow ring to the assertive rationalism of Mr Feinstein who prides himself on his liberation from mediaeval Judaism in the stilted and outdated language of nineteenth-century positivism: "'No man today, of any intellectual honesty, could adopt any but a rationalist stand in view of politico-economic developments and the advances in scientific discovery'" (103–4).

The narrow rationalism embraced by Brown and Feinstein quite as much as religion, myth or mysticism sets out to interpret human experience within a rigid framework of assumptions. By setting various interpretations of the world, each restrictive in its own way, one against the other, White avoids committing himself to any of his characters. The novel rejects, above all, rigidity: '[Arthur] had begun to fear for Waldo, for some lack of suppleness in his relationships with other people. There were moments when Waldo was as rigid as a closed cupboard' (243).

In the final section of the novel Mrs Poulter's *Armageddon* draws together her limited understanding of the *Revelation of St John*, guerilla warfare in Asia, the concentration camps, urban crime, and the pain of childbirth: 'All the films, all the telly, all the black-and-white of the papers was turning real, as the great clouds, the great tanks, ground up groaning over Sarsaparilla' (302). The apocalypse that the novel recreates is not an allegorical anticipation of the Second Coming, but the intrusion of reality into Mrs Poulter's consciousness through the protective myths provided by religion and the mass media. The event that precipitates her crisis is the sight of the dogs, Runt and Scruffy, eating the voice box and penis of the dead Waldo. The wasted procreative and communicative potential of Waldo Brown is thus placed in her mind beside televised translations of the war in Vietnam and newspaper accounts of rape and social injustice.

Finally, the novel brings home the inability of human beings to react to actual suffering, actual bullets, actual death because they impose myths, esoteric or banal, between their inviolable sense of self and the world: '"Bill said people had never in history had it so good . . . You couldn't complain. Not with the electric frying-pan . . . not with the phone, and two doctors. And the telly"' (295). Here the myth of Australia as the fortunate country and the related myth of consumerism as the purpose of human existence serve to make all the violences and oppressions of contemporary history unreal, removed.

Thus themes found in the 1938 poem, 'The House Behind the Barricades', are present in the the novel of the 1960s: the gap between consciousness and history, the inability of the individual to feel implicated in or personally responsible for political crimes, the distancing effect of the media by which political images are received. Now, however, White has abandoned the timid Prufrockian consciousness of the 1930s poem, while updating some of the modernist techniques he acquired as a young 'English' writer. The thirties methods and perspectives have been applied to post-war Australian suburbia rather than Europe on the edge of war. The montage technique of modernism and the political urgency of the Auden generation have been taken into an unlikely context, but with rich effect. The richness is achieved by the layering of levels of implication – political, psychological, metaphysical – that have been built into the writing. It is also a function of White's ear for vernacular speech energies which depend for their comic effect on a slight element of exaggeration. The Poulters are comic figures through whom essentially tragic themes can be played out.

They are a means by which all that White learned as an apprentice novelist in the England of the 1930s can be used in a post-war world that is steeped in the particulars of his Australian experience, yet at the same time universal.

*   *   *

In an exploratory and wholly undogmatic sense White can be said to be a 'religious' novelist. What is significant is that the religious sense in his work is connected to his understanding of what it means to be an Australian novelist: it is part of his modernist concern with the effects of re*placing* a tradition – religious as well as literary – in a part of the world where it is profoundly alien.

No-one has so far related the religious dimension of White's writing with his role as an Australian novelist. This involves more than the crude dualism White himself establishes between Australian materialism and visionary experience of elect outsiders: Jews, the mad, the marginalised, and so forth. In practice, the religious sense in his writing and the sets of binary oppositions religious themes have generated there have provided a means of exploring the immensely complex problem of inherited significances in Australia. How are the patterns of meaning and image that are essential to the European high cultural tradition on which White draws to be made meaningful in the context of a new world with its own traditional patterns of significance?

In responding to this problem White has followed a similar path to that of the New Zealand painter, Colin McCahon, perhaps the greatest Australasian painter so far. McCahon began painting as a regional nationalist, deeply interested in the particular referents of New Zealand. He moved on to employ Christian symbolism, then Maori myths and motifs, in his work, continually registering the tragic irony by which these various structures of meaning had become distanced from the situation of contemporary human beings without losing their force or attraction. White, like McCahon, begins his nationalist period by focusing on images of a known, loved and local landscape. He moves on through varieties of Christian and esoteric symbolism from *The Tree of Man* to *The Solid Mandala*. From *Voss* through to *A Fringe of Leaves* he shows a developing interest in Aboriginal religious and cultural beliefs, though these are never integrated into his work as closely as Maori cultural icons have been integrated into the work of New Zealand writers and artists.

In *Voss* the crazed religious heresies of the explorer served White as a means of standing apart from the available interpretations of Australia. In *Riders in the Chariot* various religious paradigms – Christian, Jewish, pantheistic – collide as Himmelfarb hangs on his cross in a Sydney factory yard. But those interpretive systems fail to merge into any single vision of Truth. They remain myths or constructs in whose terms the characters read their experience. Above all, they remain at odds with the everyday Australian world into which they have been introduced. *The Solid Mandala* with its nostalgic celebration of common Australian life uncovers the religious possibilities within the mundane – not in Stan Parker's gob of spittle, but in the cultural traffic of suburbia – and explores the complex relation of dependence between 'visionary' and 'ordinary' experience.

By *The Vivisector* the religious sense is shown to be at home in Australia. Hurtle Duffield, White's ironic yet affectionate version of the 'Great Australian Artist' has a religious sense that embraces the Judaeo-Christian inheritance, but he is inarticulate about that inheritance. He is indifferent to religion as an explicit set of beliefs or values. He *is* articulate about his debts to Australian landscape and even society. More important, his spiritual role as artist and seer exists in a symbiotic relation to the raw, meretricious and seductive Australian world of which, however reluctantly, he is part.

The Vivisector

Bertrand Russell once observed that the world in which we live can be understood as a result of muddle and accident, but if it is the outcome of deliberate purpose, the purpose must have been that of a fiend. The religious sense in White's novels starts from much the same position, although at times it appears to adopt the opposed, apparently insupportable, conclusion that God in fact exists, but is a flawed, possibly even malign being. The God who figures in White's work is not, of course, a 'fiend'. That would imply a singleness of divine purpose that is as alien to White's conception of the Deity as is any singleness of authorial purpose (or 'vision'), to White's practice as a writer. He or She (we shouldn't be too specific about

gender: White sees sexual ambivalence as a fundamental characteristic of creation as well as creativity) is finally inscrutable to humans.
God is known chiefly through those moments of brief illumination
experienced by his visionary characters, his artists, homosexuals
and misfits, but these prove impossible to translate into the terms
of human discourse. Moreover, those epiphanic moments focus on
the physical world as much as they do on the transcendental.

What those moments of illumination demonstrate about the
divine nature are of little comfort to his earnest exegetes of the
various schools of mysticism. The benevolence of the Deity is
erratic at best. Or perhaps his aim is not very good. 'Everyone
can make mistakes, including God,' as White himself puts it in a
1969 conversation.[40]

The Vivisector explores the nature of God as well as the nature
of the artist. It is a hubristic novel, in the tradition of *Moby-Dick*,
over-reaching and full of seemingly contradictory elements ranging
from social satire to metaphysics – a capacious rag-bag of a novel.
It is also a 'romantic' novel, in the hackneyed sense of the word.
Almost every cliché of the romantic artist struggling with his vision
in a fallen world is invoked in the novel. The theme of the artist as
both God-opposer and God-imitator is itself a romantic stereotype.
Nevertheless, Hurtle Duffield is neither an archetype nor a stereotype. The tensions in the novel develop out of the gap between
Hurtle's romantic view of himself as the archetypal artist and the
various alternative perspectives of him we are offered. Hurtle's view
of art continually subjugates external reality to 'vision'. In this
respect his romanticism is as limiting as Himmelfarb's mysticism.

Born into a working-class family, Hurtle's earliest awareness is
characterised by alienation, self-division and a conviction that he
has been gifted with a special insight into the nature of reality. At an
early age he is sold to a wealthy Sydney family who provide him with
all the bourgeois advantages. The Courtneys conveniently embody
all the specious middle-class values against which the increasingly
alienated Hurtle rebels.

The war allows Hurtle to sever himself physically from his adop-
tive family, so that he considers that the slate of the past has been
wiped clean. Amid the horror of the trenches he resolves to
commit his art to 'this physical life'.[41] But he retains his childhood
conviction that 'only [his] thoughts were real' (105). As Nance
Lightfoot, the prostitute, later accusingly remarks, Hurtle does
not even acknowledge that other people exist: '"While you're all

gummed up in the great art mystery, they're alive, and breakun
their necks for love"' (204).

After the war the young artist goes through a period of poverty-
stricken bohemianism in Paris. White seems content to use such a
well worn convention without providing any significant insight into
the types of painterly theories, styles or fashions which influence
his character at this vital stage of his artistic development. The
return of the disillusioned, isolated artist to his native Australia
does not correct this lack. Hurtle is determined to develop his
creativity in terms of the 'vision' he discovers inside himself rather
than by painstakingly mastering the techniques of other artists,
or by identifying himself with any school.[42] By taking up with
the prostitute, Nance Lightfoot, Hurtle becomes even more the
stereotyped, down-and-out artist rejecting both his bourgeois and
his proletarian backgrounds in favour of the 'criminal classes'.

The long period of the painter's middle years is largely ignored.
We leave Hurtle as a struggling young painter contemptuous of
public recognition. We discover him again as a successful, middle-
aged artist, critically acclaimed and financially secure. His public
self is disillusioned, isolated and arrogant. Inwardly, he finds himself spiritually empty. His mind is likened to a 'darkened cabin'
(395). But he hopes, if only in moments of inspiration, that his
inner void might 'blaze eventually with light' (386). In the meantime he receives creative afflatus from the vulgar types he observes
in the street or occasionally condescends to meet, and even from
the putrescence and degeneration of material things. Hurtle feels
he can afford to disdain the common herd who daily submit 'their
blander substance to the acid of his . . . experience' (275).

Hero Pavloussi is his spiritual bride and fellow debauchee. She
is God-obsessed, blasphemous, guilt racked, suicidal and possibly
lesbian. There is much here for both the dissipated, cynical persona
and the hidden illuminate to explore. A number of romantic types
of the artist are suggested during this period. Hurtle is the afflicted
isolate, the truth-teller, the visionary who sees people from above.

As Hurtle moves into old age his desire to create a spiritual child
in Kathy Volkov, his teenage lover, remains unfulfilled. He seeks
then to make his art the definitive comment on his life and to
tie the end to the beginning. His meeting with his sister, Lena
serves to re-establish this long severed link to his lost childhood
but simultaneously breaks the taboo of non-contact. Immediately
afterwards he is 'stroked' by God in His twin aspects of vivisector

and illuminator. Paralysed and apparently senile he sets out to express the essence of his faith: 'the soul itself' (589).

As critics have noted, there are insistent echoes of Romain Rolland, Joyce and White himself.[43] It is inevitable, of course, that yet another portrait of the artist should recall all those previous portraits. Nevertheless, although the novel has been decried for its reliance on Romantic convention and for its platitudes and stereotypes, it is conceded that White manages to pull Duffield out of all the clichés credibly and succeeds, against all the odds, in creating one of his largest characters and 'a major novel'.[44]

Perhaps the most suggestive comment about how we are to respond to the novel is provided by Richard Coe when he asks whether *The Vivisector* may be major not in spite of but *because* of its apparent flaws, its clichés and purple passages:

> with all its faults, its Teutonic solemnity, its overwriting, this *is* a major novel .... But above all, there is the fact that the novel has a theme – not so much a message as a question – and all the platitudes scattered over its surface not only disguise but, in an oblique way, contribute to its real integrity and seriousness of purpose.[45]

The question is, how do all these platitudes contribute to the novel's 'real integrity and seriousness of purpose'? There is a need here to recognise the *deliberateness* of White's strategies, especially his use of romantic clichés. White has moved the conventional elements on which he draws into the foreground of the novel, but the romantic conventions and Jungian archetypes are used satirically. They are a function of the way the central character sees himself as *The Artist* rather than of the way White himself sees artists in general or himself in particular as an artist.

Hurtle's relationship with Nance Lightfoot is a case in point. She is to provide a means of revealing 'through the forms his spirit understood this physical life' (177). Her rolling, fleshy body transports him by analogy to the 'golden paddocks' of boyhood (191). Ironically, he gains the same feeling of power pouring his visions of life into the 'formal vessel' of her body (210) that his father gained through the creation of wealth out of his paddocks.

At times Hurtle even believes that he loves Nance, forgetting his arrogant disregard of her as a person independent of his vision of her. He uses 'the architecture of [her] body' (203) as a vehicle for the expression of that vision in which she is shown to be 'vegetable in form and essence' (207). He regards her as little more than an animal, dissociating his creative self from 'his own animal' that responds to her sexually (218). He values her for what he sees as her very mindlessness: 'it would be terrible, if Nance enjoyed glimmers of sensibility' (220).

After their symbolic marriage night, he escapes from her physical presence that quickly disgusts to protect what she has given which will become his painting, 'Marriage of Light'. The 'only convincing self' which takes over at the easel has nothing in common with the lust-worn prostitute (217). Even his body which has entered hers is an instrument serving to express in paint the focused vision of the mind. Unable to love her adequately, Hurtle recognises 'the great discrepancy between aesthetic truth and sleazy reality' (200). In that polarity Nance occupies the lower half.

Nance herself is aware of Hurtle's inability to love her. But she remains drawn to him, not only sexually, but because she sees him subconsciously as her spiritual complement. Her own aborted spiritual aspirations and unfulfilled sexual desires centre on Hurtle as the dreamt-of young man who will teach her to 'see things as they're supposed to be' (255).

Nance cannot separate sex from associations of pain, violence and cruelty. As a young girl she had been raped by her father on a fishing trip, with the result that sexual penetration became linked in her mind with the struggling fish on the hook and her father's brutal penis. Subconsciously, then, she expects to be abused by the young man in the green overcoat who reminds her of her father. 'Fuckun', her art form and livelihood, is a persistent surrender to the mixture of desire and disgust which she felt towards her first violator. It is also an illustration of the gap between expectation and performance which both goads and disappoints her: '"It's what you never find that keeps you at it"' (236).

Nance is doubly brutalised by Hurtle's treatment of her. Firstly he claims the right to use her body as a repository for his own mental energies, thus denigrating her mind. Secondly, Hurtle's detachment of the authentic, inner self from the urges of the body, reduces her sexuality to the status of a deformity: '[h]e kissed her hare-lip, her disgusting john' (260).

On one level Nance herself sees her vagina as a wound or deformity like her mother's hare-lip. But the attitude of disgust is Hurtle's. His kiss is not an attempt to heal, but an act of exquisite condescension executed by his animal half and savoured, spiritual-ised by his other, creative half. Thelma Herring describes Hurtle's attitude to low life as '*nostalgie de la boue*'.[46] If Hurtle wallows, he does so with a purpose, not merely to indulge himself. Like the mediaeval alchemist he hopes to find his own spiritual perfection in the slime of the slime.[47]

Hurtle's attitude to the natural world is ambivalent. The artist 'operates' on the forms of matter with the same detached violence with which he cauterises Nance on canvas. The rock paintings signal a turning away from physical opulence to the starker reality that Hurtle now discerns beneath appearances. But Hurtle merely swings from one extreme to another, from the celebration of Nance's rolling belly and 'big ripe purple mouth' to the dissection of rocks (201). Like Nance and Rhoda, Sunningdale and the piece of land up the line illustrate the two halves of Hurtle's divided response to the world.

The novel is structured around such dualities. On the one hand, Hurtle experiences a 'rage for physical exertion' while building his shack amid the scrub (226). He indulges and encourages 'that lean animal', his body, while feeling only cynicism for his painting. On the other hand, he soon finds Nance's cornucopia rancid and submits again to his curse or gift. It is not simply that art, like mysticism, is an attempt to transcend the limitations imposed by matter. Hurtle refuses to recognise that his painting requires both the colours and the architecture of nature if he is to express the complexity of experience. Hurtle himself creates the division he perceives in the world.

In the early rock drawings truth avoids him because he sees only one half of a complex reality. They are 'rocks of his mind' created out of what he finds in his own lacerated soul (237). He is himself 'operated on' by what he discovers to be another mental landscape. So he attempts to heal himself 'by adding to their flesh, by disguising their scars, with touches and retouches of paint' (230). Painting over his psychic scars, however, cannot protect him indefinitely from the question that undermines the certainty with which he had previously asserted what was real inside and outside his head: 'But did he, any more than the others, see himself as he truly was?' (242).

Accordingly, Hurtle begins his 'self-portrait with warts' (224). What emerges is not the visionary truth teller, but masks, distor-tions and dishonesties. The ascetic who could forget about his body is no more convincing than the vain 'lyrical onanist' (246). The Doppel-ganger that confronts him in the painting exists in the 'distorting mirror' that is all art (249). Perhaps the difference between White himself as autobiographer and Hurtle, his character, is that White begins the act of writing – fiction or autobiography – with the knowledge that art is always by its nature a distorting mirror. This acknowledgement, indeed, is the enabling condition of all its writing, with its insistent, complex and subtle explorations of the possibilities opened up by these very distortions.

Hurtle's romantic-expressionistic view of the artist had assumed that the hidden, essential self, that is, 'that part of him which, by some special grace, might illuminate a moment of truth', was itself the source of the creative act (210). The self-portrait announces his failure to assert the absolute authority of his creativity. He is confronted by an image of his cruelty, his narcissism and his depravity (259). The painting accuses him of dishonesty in his self conception and, accordingly, untruthfulness in his view of the world. He is forced to admit that he has 'created' what he found not only in Nance but in himself and in the physical world (231).

Hurtle admits his cruelty and dishonesty to himself for the first time. When Rhoda, his hunch-backed sister-by-adoption, had accused him of deliberate maliciousness after his visual rape of her at St Yves de Tregor, Hurtle defended his action to himself in terms of what he had seen, not what he had done. He considered that Rhoda had failed to allow for 'his real intentions' which were to express the true forms of great beauty he had discovered beneath the deformed surface of her body (142). In fact, he had entered her room 'his voice offering unconvincing excuses in advance' (134). He had used Rhoda, as he was later to use Nance and the rocks, as convenient 'empty vessel[s]' into which to pour his visions of the 'truth'.

Central to Hurtle's character is a tension between his tendency to justify or condemn himself out of all proportion to the facts and the belated recognition that he is linked to ordinary people by his very dishonesties and doubts in the face of the elusiveness of 'truth'. White is tilting at the convention of the romantic artist as outsider, criminal, visionary through Hurtle's posturing, but this cliché is not the only object of the novel's irony. *The Vivisector* draws on a variety of conventional materials. In *Voss* European conventions of architecture, art and religion were set against the blank slate of the continent. In *The Vivisector* they are introduced into a burgeoning twentieth-century, urban Australia.

On one level White dramatises the point made by art critic, Robert Hughes, in *The Art of Australia*, where he observes that the rapidly expanding market for Australian painting in the late 1960s signalled nothing more important than did rising production of wool and meat. A nationalistic, culture-consuming middle class had arrived, eager to procure local art, but that, according to Hughes, did not guarantee the production of better paintings.[48] In *The Vivisector* White traces the emergence and consolidation of Australian art in terms of the social patterns of consumption and procurement through three generations. From the arriviste Courtneys investing in a Gainsborough to the grocer Cutbush displaying exotic and unsaleable delicacies in his shop and modern Sydney 'high society' at a concert of classical music the appetite of the Australian middle class for 'culture' is mercilessly satirised.

Jungian archetypes in *The Vivisector* are exposed to an irony similar in tone to that directed at the Australian art industry. In both cases White clearly discovers a core of meaning within a set of conventions that readily attract the spurious. Hurtle is intended to be seen as a genuine artist despite his posturing. Similarly, the mandalic representations and Jungian archetypes that figure in the novel are not dismissed; they are attempts to get close to an acknowledged but elusive spiritual reality. They are not, however, a definitive map of the true spiritual path of the artist or the individual which the novel means us to accept unequivocally as 'true'.

Derek Mahon sees the chandelier in the Courtneys' drawing room at Sunningdale as the same mandalic representation of God that Stan Parker spat out as a 'jewel of spittle' and Arthur Brown found in his glass marbles.[49] White, it is true, invites such identifications: 'he knew all about a chandelier, from perhaps dreaming of it, and only now recognizing his dream' (24). Hurtle recognises in the chandelier a representation of an ideal state 'inside' himself (53). This is the only authentic self from which, he believes, the artistic impulse proceeds. It is also that part of him which allows the visionary-artist to perceive the truth beneath appearances.

Hurtle conceives his struggle towards omniscience as artist and visionary in archetypal terms that exclude his share in common humanity. Even his sexual liaisons are seen as expressions of his visionary quest and his treatment of his lovers can be excused on the grounds that they serve the higher purpose of his search for truth.

Moreover, the clichés of the White 'canon' are invoked in a slyly mocking fashion in the course of the narrative. At one point the novel refers ironically to Voss's epic journey through Hurtle's grandfather who had also attempted to ride to the centre of Australia. Moreover, Harry Courtney mentions a copy of 'the Leichhardt manuscript letters' in his possession (164). In 'The Prodigal Son' White himself speaks of reading 'contemporary accounts of Leichhardt's expeditions' preparatory to writing *Voss*.[50] Voss's 'allegorical' trek has suffered a deflation. Grandpa Duffield, who dreamed of riding to the centre of the continent, is struck down by a seizure on the Parramatta road and his son is forced to pay off the donkey purchased for the epic journey. Harry Courtney's library of Australiana is kept purely as an investment and the Leichhardt manuscript is sold to raise money for the Red Cross. By reading a book from this same library Hurtle passes the test that allows him entry into the bourgeois world and by rejecting Harry's attitudes to art, literature and Australia he establishes himself as an authentic artist.

Even Nance Lightfoot, in drunken mood, reveals spiritual aspirations and, at the same time, suggests a very traditional type: 'I've always been hopin' ter find something of value in the sea . . . A pearl, or somethun. And never found nothun – but a used Frenchie' (188). The whore has been searching for the pearl of great price.[51] The allusion indicates an inner world of spiritual aspiration beneath the coarse outward picture of the whore, but there is a gap between the secret self-image and the person presented to the other. Hurtle's refusal to recognise the sensitive woman beneath the whore calls into question his conviction that his own secret self perceives unflinchingly the truth beneath appearance. Thus his romanticism is satirised not merely as a self-conceit apparently inherent in his personality, but as a limited convention that distorts his response to the world and causes pain to others. At times he is himself sceptical of his belief in the superiority of art to life: 'Art as he had known it, as Maman's little sissy boy, as a priggish, pimply youth, or l'Huissier's know-all pupil, had appeared more desirable, not to say more convincing, than life; when Nance Lightfoot, in her drunkenness, had started raising doubts' (207).

Hurtle Duffield, like all White's visionaries, explores 'the country of the mind' as a world autonomous and real within its own borders.[52] But his exploration is shaped by his own self-conceit. The mental country is landscaped to fit the strictures of his romanticism. Voss advanced into the desert as the man-God of Gnostic myth. Himmelfarb moved into a mental version of the terrain of the Old Testament as the primordial man of cabbalistic myth. Hurtle 'vivisects' himself in the role of 'The Artist'. At the same time he blunders round in the external world adapting people to the requirements of his aesthetic aspirations. He discovers, however, not only that people resent being operated on 'in the name of truth – or art', but that his idealised visions of art and self rest uneasily on very human motivations (462).

Hurtle's guilt after Nance's death continues through the period of his middle years that the novel ignores. But the torment and self-contempt that his relationship with Nance occasioned have not encouraged humility as an artist or reconciliation with humanity. In accepting that his role as an artist causes pain to others and that there is an inevitable measure of dishonesty in his art, Hurtle has embarked on a new movement towards self-deification. He has discovered a link between the artist and God whose work of creation is such an imperfect mirror of His perfection: 'He had never been altogether dishonest: nor yet entirely honest; because that isn't possible. Even saints kid themselves a bit. God or whatever couldn't have been entirely honest in creating the world' (245).

Previously, the artist's innermost core, 'his real and secret life' (94), had been invested with such perfection that the idea of God and religious observances had amounted to so much 'kidding' (147). God, as a transcendent being, was less interesting than the evidence of an absolute reality within himself. At fourteen he had discovered that, in the absence of God, 'he was his own dynamo' (147). When Hurtle discovers his 'dynamo' to be tainted by cruelty, his adolescent atheism and ensuing agnosticism are finally replaced by the petulant pose of Promethean heretic.

Hurtle's new frame of mind is revealed through his conversation with the homosexual grocer, Cutbush, in a Sydney park. The painter asserts his independence of all human contact: 'I am not in need – of anything, or any one' (268). In marked contrast to Himmelfarb's ideal of detached, contemplative suffering, Hurtle's spiritual state could be described as detachment without equanimity. Because he cannot justify the chaos and suffering in the world in terms of a transcendent Absolute severed from, and uncontaminated by, the world, the God in whom he believes must accept responsibility for both halves of his experience. He sees God as the 'Divine Vivisector' and the source of man's creative 'brilliance': "'Yes, I believe in Him . . . Otherwise, how would men come by their cruelty – and their brilliance?'" (269).

Voss discovered that the dichotomy between good and evil was inherent in the scheme of things. By recognising that God too was tragically divided, man could rescue his own divine half from its imprisonment in matter. Hurtle Duffield displays no facility for, nor interest in, such abstruse and dubious metaphysical schemes. His new belief in God answers a need for someone or something to blame for human suffering in physical reality. The type of knowledge to which he refers does not constitute an innate apprehension of spiritual truth which is arrived at by illumination independent of, and opposed to, physical perception.

> Hurtle too knew better than everybody . . . not that he could have explained what he knew: because he saw rather than thought. (108)

Precisely what he sees is hard to pin down. His view of 'reality' is only one among several in the novel and is ironically undercut by those of the other characters. During Hurtle's conversation with Cutbush on the park bench, his disoriented (or heightened from another point of view) perception of the material world is set against the grocer's more prosaic view. To Hurtle the world is no longer 'plain and consistent' but miraculously strange (269). The normally perceived world outside his head threatens to dissolve. On the other hand, the world, as Cutbush naively apprehends it, conforms to the more limited desires of the homosexual grocer.

> 'I'm not married.'
> 'Go on! You don't say! There's time, though!' The grocer glanced towards the other's crutch. (266)

After the encounter, the painter returns, spiritually renewed, to his art leaving the grocer masturbating 'on barren ground' (272). In the painting, 'Lantana Lovers under Moonfire', Hurtle depicts the Divine Destroyer as the moon showering malevolence on the lovers in the form of excrement. '[T]he waves of enlightened evil proliferating from above' reduce the grocer's attempts at evil to those of a child (350).

Hero Pavloussi seeks to be able to believe again in a transcendent God whose perfection will liberate her from her obsessive and guilty depravity. She even insists that her husband, Cosmas, a richly ambiguous God figure, is wholly benevolent in his intentions.[53] But Cosmas, of charitable impulse, is unwilling to accept responsibility for his charges. His drowning of a bagful of cats and desertion of his adopted, Aboriginal daughter, Soso, identifies him in Hurtle's mind with the capricious demiurge against whom he is locked in Promethean struggle.

Ironically, at one point Hero hysterically restates Hurtle's conception of the Divine Vivisector and alludes, in evidence, to the drowning of a bagful of cats by the husband she had revered as a god: '"*Who* is cruel? Greeks? Turks? Man is cruel! . . . God – God is cruel! We are his bagful of cats, aren't we?"' (366).

Seeking to rediscover the lost faith of her youth in a benevolent divinity, Hero drags her lover on a pilgrimage to a Greek island. But the saints and shrines fail to provide a road back to this innocent faith. The mother-superior of the convent they visit is worldly by a necessity Hero refuses to recognise and is unimpressed by the histrionics of a nostalgic tourist too self-indulgent to offer a donation. In the chapel of the saintly hermit they find only a pile of excrement.

'I think we have lost our faith in God because we cannot respect men. They are so disgusting.' (406)

Hero's idea of God is defined in terms of the men she has worshipped: Cosmas and Hurtle. Her desire to find 'a reason and a purpose in this *Dreck* [excrement, i.e., herself]' is an expression of disillusionment, not of hope (408).

Hurtle had entered the affair hoping to find 'a spiritual bride' to rescue him from his emptiness and scepticism. His own and Hero's compulsive sexuality quickly dispatches the illusion. Looking into Hero's eyes during a break from their 'pneumatic' lovemaking, he discovers that 'there were no depths to reach: there were the positions of love' (364). He continues to hope, if only by occasional moments of inspiration, that the void he finds in himself will 'blaze eventually with light' (386). In the meantime, he is forced increasingly to recognise the facts of disease and decay that challenge the body's pleasures and its vanity. But he remains sceptical of Hero's constant anguish over her failure to transcend her depraved desires and of his own occasional intuitions of illumination.

> They were holding in their arms mild dyspepsia, incurable disease, old age, death, worst of all – scepticism. He couldn't suggest to Hero Pavloussi that his paintings alone might survive the debacle, because it wouldn't have been of comfort to her; it was no more than a slight satisfaction to him while his body continued a source of pride. (372)

Hurtle leaves Perialos convinced that he has at last come to terms with himself. While Hero desperately pursues salvation from herself and the world, Hurtle clings to his devils (390). Only his art is finally important to him, and if that is to express what he sees as truth, it must draw on his depravity and scepticism as well as those 'apocalyptic moments' (408). Above all, he refuses to reject the physical world in a search for illumination, or truth, or God. If God exists, He exists as a 'formal necessity' (404). As they are about to leave the island he has an Epiphany watching a small, golden hen. Ironically, he is unable to communicate his discovery to the God-obsessed Hero.

> The golden hen flashed her wings: not in flight; she remained consecrated to this earth even while scurrying through illuminated dust. (409)

For this brief moment Hurtle seems to touch the very core of reality. But do such passages 'underline [White's] dedication to . . . divine immanence' as one critic suggests?[54] For a moment the painter ceases to see the external world as we normally do, as something taken for granted. But he does not discover a reality that transcends the physical world, or even a force immanent in that world. He identifies reality with the physical bondage of the little hen to the earth. The phrase 'illuminated dust' suggests an immanent divine presence only if we ignore a previous treatment of the image: 'To remember that a flight of motes was of the same substance as passive grey domestic dust had always delighted him' (362).

Hurtle is quite aware that the 'grey domestic dust' is transformed into something beautiful, apparently spiritual, by a common physical phenomenon. But, while Hero is horrified to have to find 'a reason and a purpose in this *Dreck*' (408), Hurtle is delighted to allow forms of potential beauty to germinate 'in their natural conditions of flaking plaster, rust deposits, balding plush, and pockets of dust enriched with cobweb' (407–8). For Hurtle, the physical world is the locus of the incarnation of his own 'unregenerate soul', not that of the Incarnation of the Logos (404).

Considerable irony is directed at both Hero and Hurtle. Both have anthropomorphic concepts of God and both are obsessed by their spiritual self-lacerations. Both are attracted to each other by their 'passionate illusions' and both fail to achieve what they had expected from the relationship (528). Moreover, both alienate themselves from others by their self-indulgent concern with the states of their own souls.

Hurtle asserts that, in a world of flux and deception, his creative 'eye' clearly discerns reality. The 'mad eye' which is associated with the vivisectionist's knife, cuts through appearances. His art, then, expresses the 'truth'. Yet the only constants that Hurtle confronts in the world of the novel are ambiguity and inconsistency.

Even on a sexual level, there is hardly one important character in the novel who is not in some way sexually ambiguous. There are hints of a lesbian relationship between Hero and Boo Davenport. In fact, one is never sure whether the latter is frigid or promiscuous. At one point she appears 'in drag'. Caldicott, Cecil Cutbush and possibly Don Lethbridge are homosexual. Kathy Volkov attracts Hurtle originally because of her boyishness. Hurtle himself indulges in paedophilia with Kathy Volkov and contemplates anal-eroticism. As he grows older he begins to develop breasts. Alfreda Courtney is possibly frigid, and even Harry is reduced by his gentleness to 'a big heavy old hairy woman' (103). Only Rhoda, the dwarf, is wholly, cruelly heterosexual. Her fate, as the planchette reveals, is to be a '"*Woman*"!', dreaming of the broad backs of men (121).

Adding to the confusion, White displays a richly extended interest in puns and syntactical ambiguities. The name-punning has been extensively analysed by Morley.[55] Rhoda is rose or rodent. Duffield is du-field (from the country) and, conversely, Courtney is both court-nee (born at court) or, in Rhoda's case, born short. The Pavloussis' chauffeur, who returns Soso to the reservation, is ironically named Sotiri which is Greek for saviour.

After Hurtle's stroke syntactical conventions are for the most part abandoned. Puns and multi-levelled ambiguities convey his fragmented view of the world and his limited ability to express himself. The effect is frequently amusing, if grotesque, for instance: 'I won't . . . Snot my meteor' (579). Morley has suggested that Hurtle is here trying to say that 'snot' is 'not [his] *métier,* meteor',[56] but the meaning at which White hints is ambiguous. Is Hurtle suggesting that he will use the unattractive aspects of the material world ('snot') as a means of expressing the infinite ('meteor') in his art (metier)? Is Morley right when she asserts that Hurtle has become 'man himself . . . a meteor *hurtling* through the cosmos seeking his eternal "HOME," (579)?[57] It is a procrustean effort that renders such syntactical confusion into singular meaning. Whatever the reader is intended to discover in such lines as: 'UTBUS in gold as you floating out' (570), or the final line in the novel, '[t]oo tired too end-less obvi indi – ggoddd' (642), we must allow for the sly, authorial irony that invests Hurtle's character throughout the novel. Critics like Morley have treated such mystifying lines as keys that make the cryptic meaning of the novel finally clear.[58] But the last section of the novel is recalcitrantly ambiguous. Meanings and levels of possible meaning proliferate in almost every sentence. Hurtle's final achievement, artistic and spiritual, is enigmatic by design and should be approached with careful consideration given to the ironies in the passage that precedes it.

Hurtle begins his final painting convinced once again that he has at last abandoned all his illusions and become the tabula rasa to which he has so long aspired. The 'desert' that confronts him describes an inner emptiness, the essential landscape of the soul as well as the virgin ply-board. His intention is both to express the infinite in his painting and to become identified with the infinite. Accordingly, his conviction that 'he was being painted with, and through, and on' shows that he believes that he has achieved his spiritual and artistic goals simultaneously (639).

But only when his 'psychopomp', Kathy Volkov, appears before him does he dare to mix 'the never-yet-attainable blue' (641). Indigo is to be the colour of God, with whom Hurtle now claims 'a longstanding secret relationship' (641). But, just as he is about to apply the symbolic colour to the board, he suffers his second stroke.

Then lifting by the hairs of his scalp to brush the brushhairs bludge on the blessed blue.

Before the tobbling scrawl deadwood splitting splintering the
pricked stars plunge a presumptuous body crashing. *Dumped.*
(642, my italics)

'Before' Hurtle is able to achieve his 'presumptuous' goal of
expressing the infinite in his art, his body is 'dumped'. The
painter fails to express the infinite through the physical medium
of paint. Does Hurtle Duffield, the truth-seeker, then, achieve the
goal of his old age, the discovery of ultimate meaning?

As I see it, painting and religious experience are the same thing,
and what we are all searching for is the understanding and
realization of infinity. (epigraph)

At the very end of his life Hurtle would undoubtedly agree with Ben
Nicholson's epigraph. But to the very end he also continues [t]o
fortify himself against the truth' (638). He resents the 'pertinence'
of Mrs Volkov's letter which conscripts him into a limping army of
suffering elect. His pride is unable to accept that artist, homosexual
grocer and seamstress have all been '*stroked by God*' (637). Although
Hurtle has always maintained that those he portrayed, or vivisected,
in his paintings were shocked by the 'truth' he revealed about
them, he is reluctant to admit the truth of Mrs Volkov's letter.
He himself stands accused by the epigraph from Saint Augustine:
'They love truth when it reveals itself, and they hate it when it
reveals themselves.'

Mrs Volkov's letter horrifies Hurtle as Rhoda's similarly couched
letter had years before. As a young man he had balked at being
'brought closer . . . [to Rhoda] by suffering from something incur-
able . . . ' (181). Now he rejects Mrs Volkov's letter and her 'hor-
ribly illuminating argument' because he does not wish to admit
that art, like a humped back or homosexuality, is an affliction
that unites the artist with all those who suffer in some way (638).
The letters both remind Hurtle that he has something in common
with the ordinary, afflicted human beings he despises and whom he
regularly sacrifices in the name of art.

Hurtle remains neither humble nor charitable as is shown by his
attitude to, and treatment of, Don, Cec and Rhoda, his faithful
admirers and helpers. Moreover, his favourite romantic role of
visionary truth-perceiver encourages his refusal to admit that his
friends and fellow sufferers have inner lives and aspirations of their

own. He fails to love Rhoda, as he failed to love Nance and Hero, because he sees all the women in his life as empty vessels into which he must pour his visions of truth. But he is tormented by occasional recognitions of the distance between his versions of the people he has known and the actual human beings who continually surprise him by disclosing souls as tormented and frequently as percipient as his own.

The 'spiritual self-justification' he pursues through his art is undermined by this essential dishonesty (489). In fact, Hurtle's identification of creativity with illumination, his last and greatest presumption, rests on still more distortions of the truth. His vision of a 'hermetic guide' is a case in point (622). At first we see through Hurtle's eyes: 'he might have paused to indulge, if the perspective of archways and parquet hadn't been flooded with a vision: of a figure, small certainly, but in its formal, golden grace instinctually true to archetype. He was walking giddily, as he hadn't for years, but without illusions or expectations; his great joy was in recognising his psychopomp, so very opportunely descended with "love and thoughts" to give him courage' (621).

However, in one of those narrative switches of perspective at which White is adept this 'embodiment of a spirit' turns into 'an anonymous wrinkled soubrette hurrying in her pink from the LADIES' (621). So 'his Kathy Mystagogue' (622) who returns in the guise of psychopomp just as he is about to apply the symbolic indigo turns out to be a very treacherous guide for Hurtle's projected journey 'to the Infernal River' (621). Moreover, his longings for transcendence or revelation are always momentary and the real world of people and things, of confusion, desire and change always asserts its own claims against the artist's half-hearted and unconvincing renunciations.

> If he could have chosen, if, rather, he had developed the habit of prayer, he would have prayed to shed his needled flesh, and for his psychopomp to guide him, across the river, into an endlessness of pure being from which memory couldn't look back.
>
> But how bloody dishonest! As if he could ever wish to renounce his memories of the flesh even when renounced by its pleasures: the human body, unbroken by its own will, leaping and bucking to unseat, but rapturously, the longed-for, the chosen, though finally abstract rider; yellow light licking as voluptuously as

tongues; green shade dribbled like saliva on nakedness; all the stickinesses: honey, sap, semen, sweat melting into sweat . . . (627)

As he approaches death Hurtle longs for release from the body and the intellect that are now failing him into a Platonic 'endlessness of pure being' beyond memory and desire which both torment and enrapture him (627). He cannot, however, abandon the body that has given him so much delight and the physical world which has given him the shapes, the colours and the energy of his art. Finally it is not only doubtful that Hurtle discovers the infinite, it is also largely irrelevant. God remains a problematic and confused projection of his divided response to the world: 'O God of mercy and straitjackets' (588).[59]

In Hurtle's conflict between desire and renunciation, we find continuing evidence of White's concern to explore the contradictions in a man's response to the world. In *The Vivisector* the physical world most clearly and cogently asserts its claims against those of the spirit.

> '. . . it was going to be a long trudge to the Elysian Fields'. (629)

At the same time the world of Australia – inescapable, changing, vulgar and beautiful – asserts its claim on the artist against his romantic postures and transcendental impulses.

*   *   *

The question of the place of religious ideas in White's fictions cannot be separated from his complex and ambivalent response to Australia. Australia, for White, is never merely the country in which he chose reluctantly to settle. It is both the most Edenic of all possible worlds, being associated with childhood vision, and the most fallen, being associated with the terrible disenchantment of adult vision. The continent is thus, for White, not a world, but *the* world; it focuses his ambivalent reponses towards modernity and towards material reality itself. In its Edenic condition it encourages a religious celebration of the immanence of deity within the world; in its fallen condition it encourages the religious idea of transcendence, the urge to abandon the actual, fecund, changeable world in favour of a world of permanent forms. Between these two impulses White's fiction vacillates and we miss the dynamic that arises from that vacillation if we insist on associating the author's viewpoint too dogmatically with either pole of the opposition.

We must acknowledge that, for all the signs of White's cantankerous presence in his novels, he remains detached (though not, like Stephen Dedalus's artist-God, indifferently paring his fingernails). Neither the religious nor the sceptical school of interpretation is satisfactory because each understates the degree of authorial ambivalence that surrounds the various metaphysical structures to be found in the novels. What we need is a way of allowing both for the religious seriousness in White's work and for the irony that surrounds *all* fragile human structures, including human constructions of the Deity and of the Deity's relation to the world.

4

Mirrors and Interiors

From his return to Australia in 1947 until the end of the 1960s White was chiefly preoccupied as a novelist with the problems of adapting an international modernist style and outlook to the material of a country which seemed to him provincial and inimical to art and to the spirit. All his novels, from *The Aunt's Story* to *The Vivisector*, explore and dramatise the problems of the artist and of artistic representation and reflect his feelings of alienation as an artist from the society in which he found himself. Nevertheless, during that same period we discover an increasing acceptance of the artist's place within that society, of the artist's dependence on the forms and practices of society for the production of novels, paintings and so forth. *The Vivisector* is both a romantic celebration of artistic vision in the face of philistinism and a subversion of the romantic stereotypes that allow the artist to assert his separateness and superiority.

In the seventies White's concerns with the artist and with nationality are less prominent. It would seem that after addressing the problem so directly in *The Vivisector*, he feels that he can at last relax about the whole business. The themes of the fifties and sixties do not, of course, disappear from his later work. *The Eye of the Storm* explores the egotism of yet another artist, this time an actor. *A Fringe of Leaves*, like *Voss*, dramatises Australian history. But the old preoccupations are less overweeningly present. The romantic gestures of the prose are more restrained. The novels of this period are less tortuous than those of the fifties and sixties; the central characters are not so extreme or intense. The epic sweep of *The Tree of Man* and *Voss* has gone, but a quality of leisurely expansiveness appears. After the self-appointed effort of 'reinventing' the Australian novel according to his own anti-naturalistic preferences, White apparently can at last take the matter of Australia for granted.

This new mood reflects a shift in White's sense of his own relation to the several traditions that had shaped his writing. In the late 1930s White had set about becoming a novelist by adapting the high modernist style to characteristically thirties concerns. In the post-war period he had drawn on both the tradition of nineteenth-century epic realism and on modernism to remake himself as an 'Australian' novelist, and in the process to establish an oppositional style to that which he saw as ruling contemporary Australian writing. (In fact, there was a strong element of self-mythologising in White's stance towards Australian writing, which has never been as straightforwardly 'factual' as he has claimed; from Joseph Furphy to Peter Carey, there has been an honourable tradition of 'lying' in the Australian novel.) [1] In the novels of the seventies he adopts a new stance towards the traditions on which he draws: he takes up various traditional forms and uses them as frames on which he imposes the impasto of his own by now richly various style.

The Eye of the Storm is modelled loosely on the novel of sensibility, *A Fringe of Leaves* is a version of the historical novel. What is significant is the stance adopted towards those forms. Where *Voss* offered a strained rewriting of the historical epic, a violent reconfiguration of the form, *A Fringe of Leaves* refers to the historical novel, the diary, the novel of sensibility in an easy and familiar tone. *The Eye of the Storm* is playfully subversive of the religious themes and stylistic concerns that have figured in White's previous fiction.

The whole business of adapting English literary styles and international forms to Australian conditions, which had been so central a part of his writing in the 1950s, is evidently boring to White by the seventies; hence he sends it up in *The Eye of the Storm.* Dorothy de Lascabanes finds herself at a dinner party beside an Australian writer who affects a 'Dickens hairdo'.[2] Unimpressed by Stendhal, he is busy 'adapting the Gothic novel to local conditions' (292).

White's relation to tradition is crucial to his practice as a writer and to our understanding of his work. His traditionalism up to the sixties is fundamentally modernist: it involves a sense that the modern world with its broken forms and mass tastes represents a tragic decline from previous periods in which religion and high culture were integrated within the social order. In *The Vivisector* the attitude of disdain for modern urban life remains largely intact, but a new sense of the artist's *creative* need of the forms of that life is also noticeable. The anxieties about the lack of depth in modern life, the degradation of language by mass media and popular culture, that were so insistent in *The Living and the Dead,* have given way to an equivocal acceptance. By the seventies the concern with simplicity and directness that was so strong in 'The Prodigal Son' and *The Tree of Man* has given way to a pleasure in fabrication, an acknowledgement that artifice is inseparable from art. This acknowledgement will be expressed most exuberantly in *The Twyborn Affair,* but it is discernible in *The Eye of the Storm.*

In this sense White's conservative modernism is moderated over the post-war period. We still find passages in *The Eye of the Storm* in which modern urban life is depicted as ugly, banal and meaningless, as when Basil Hunter walking on a Sydney beach sees 'an aimless bobbing of corks which have served their purpose, and scum, and condoms, and rotting fruit, and rusted tins, and excrement' (352). This passage could have been lifted straight from *Riders in the Chariot,* but in that novel it would have expressed the disgust of Himmelfarb, a sympathetic Whitean outsider. In *The Eye of the Storm* the passage expresses the spiritual emptiness of Basil Hunter, a hollow man with little authorial sympathy.

White is also traditional in the sense that he writes at times in the manner of a previous generation. The debts of his fiction to the nineteenth-century novel are obvious and pervasive. The novels of the fifties owe much to Tolstoy and George Eliot. His comic sense, particularly his love of caricature and exaggeration, owes much to Dickens. His psychological studies in extremity owe much to Dostoevsky. White's narrative method, even in the later work, has strong links to the nineteenth-century novel. The author does not hesitate to enter the fictional worlds he has created, speaking to us apparently directly in his own voice, commenting on the characters. All those authorial intrusions signal lack of sympathy with the postmodern notion of the death of the author. Moreover, White's sense of the novel form is centred on an essentially realistic understanding of character: 'my novels usually begin with characters . . . I always think of my novels as being the lives of the characters'.[3]

This sense of traditionalism in White's work also undergoes a change in the post-war period. The author's voice, while not absent from the work, becomes more and more elusive. The characters become more caught up in artifice and disguise. The honesty of Stan Parker moves towards the relentless self-fabrication of

Eddie Twyborn in *The Twyborn Affair*. Language, which in *The Tree of Man* aspired to a condition of simplicity, becomes a 'jungle' from which the characters cannot escape. In his post-war fiction White progressively parodies the assumptions, myths and 'master narratives' that had underlain the realist novel. The persistence of family, the stability of character, the meaningfulness of history, the continuity of the individual – all the traditional humanist systems of meaning and value are broken down. The religious focus that appears in his post-war work reinforces this subversive tendency. The spiritual realities intuited by his major characters do not shore up the old orders of meaning and authority, they are a means of recording their loss. They themselves remain mythic possibilities rather than achieved facts.

At the same time White has included traditional elements and tendencies in his work without committing his writing to them. They serve as stylistic manners to which he turns in the way a painter may adopt various styles to solve particular formal problems. At the centre of his concern as a novelist is what Frank Kermode calls 'research into form'.[4] This means that White has consistently adopted an exploratory and inclusive stance towards the various possibilities taken by the novel as a form since the eighteenth century. Connections between his writing and that of novelists as diverse as Jane Austen, Graham Greene and Wilson Harris can fruitfully be made, depending on which aspect of his astonishingly eclectic writing one seeks to highlight. He is one of those authors of whom it is useful to discuss influences precisely because he transcends all his influences and works them into a narrative manner which is recalcitrantly his own. But that narrative manner or voice is White's not by excluding other voices. It is a kind of 'conversation' that includes many different, sometimes conflicting, voices, manners, styles, tendencies within itself.[5]

Categories such as modernism, realism and postmodernism can only be usefully applied to his work so long as we acknowledge that none of these tendencies has been allowed to dominate the others. The mixture of conflicting styles in his mature fiction and the variety of stances adopted by the authorial voice are White's means of expressing and including the diversity of voices in his own experience as a social being who felt himself always to be at odds with the allegiances of class and nation, in his own profoundly contradictory make-up as an individual, and in the heterogeneous country in which he chose to live and write.

The Eye of the Storm

In *The Eye of the Storm* through the mind of a dying old woman – sensual, proud, vain, selfish – White explores the dichotomies of immanence and transcendence, sensuality and sensibility. Elizabeth Hunter is a wealthy former beauty and socialite, now blind and apparently senile. Although she is eighty-six and has recently suffered a stroke, vestiges of her former beauty remain to captivate those around her. Moreover, her mind remains formidable enough to terrorise her attendants so that they are torn between affectionate admiration for their generous and helpless charge and contempt for a vain, self-indulgent, cruel old woman. Elizabeth herself is aware of her effects on others, but feels that her victims resent her because she tells them the truth about themselves and that she sees things more clearly than they.

Elizabeth Hunter has the ability to make others accept her conceptions of them. She turns the surrounding world into a kind of stage for self-projection and casts those in it as aspects of her own self. Her two nurses represent the opposing poles she recognises in her own personality, roles they accept with varying degrees of good grace. Mary de Santis is quite willing to see herself as 'Saint Mary', psychopomp to the old woman's aspiring soul. She takes on night care because she sees Elizabeth, in spite of her worldliness and selfishness, as 'also a soul about to leave the body it had worn, and already able to emancipate itself so completely from human emotions, it became at times as redemptive as water, as clear as morning light' (12).

Mary's version of Elizabeth Hunter reflects her desperate 'need to worship' (167). At the same time, having led a sheltered life, Mary hopes to live vicariously through her worldly charge: 'She wanted a belief, which perhaps this ageing, though still beautiful woman could give her: secondhand experience must be more enlightening than that which may never come your way' (160).

In spite of her eagerness to assist in Elizabeth Hunter's spiritual liberation, Mary de Santis remains subject to very human desires. On the one hand, like Laura Trevelyan in *Voss*, she sees love as self-abnegation: 'love is a kind of supernatural state to which I must give myself entirely, and be used up, particularly my imperfections – till I am nothing' (162). On the other hand, she must acknowledge that she herself is still 'weak, sensual enough, to crave intermittently for the luxury and refreshment of physical beauty'

(166). Her attraction to Basil, Elizabeth's actor son, which she sees as prompted by pity, grows, in fact, on 'decomposed lust' (351).

Mary's mystical aspirations are threatened by the complexities she discovers in others and suspects in herself. She is forced to admit that she cannot resolve the duality between human nature and aspiration. Her priestly office is a vulnerable self-deception, threatened by her 'thumping bust' as well as by her repressed sexuality (14).

Flora Manhood, the day nurse, is the 'animal presence' Elizabeth Hunter continues to crave, in spite of her spiritual preoccupations (85). Flora enters the novel apparently determined to live up to the expectations occasioned by her name and by the old woman's condescending, if affectionate, view of her: 'legs apart, thighs radiating light and strength below the dazzle of minimal skirt' (80). Here Flora is presented to the reader through the snobbish, disapproving gaze of Dorothy de Lascabanes, but Flora herself does not contradict the role Elizabeth Hunter has assigned her: 'What she herself liked she sometimes wondered: rich, yummy food; sleep; cosmetics; making love; not making love' (84). With her golden skin, perspex ear-rings and violently coloured dress, she looks the mindless sensualist constructed by the old woman and her envious, frustrated daughter.

Flora, like the saxophonist Wally Collins in *The Living and the Dead*, is one of those Whitean characters who reflect the ways in which popular culture shapes individuals, especially those without the will to separate themselves from the conformist and materialist urgings of society. Her personality has been constructed out of paperbacks and records. Classical music bores her: '"All I can do is think of other things at music"' (114). Yet, Flora is allowed a self behind the inauthentic gestures of personality. She is not merely hollow, as is Wally.

Flora, moreover, is another of those Whitean victims of the projections of dominating egotists and, like Hurtle Duffield's Nance Lightfoot, she reveals an inner life that calls into question the terms in which she has been considered. Flora is more complex than Elizabeth Hunter's view of her as a 'breeder' allows (445). She is an ordinary, modern, pretty girl threatened by sexually voracious men, the impending drudgery of marriage and, above all, by the arrogance of those who reduce her to a stereotype. She is pathetically conscious of the emptiness of her own life which is caused largely by the refusal of others to see her as a person in her own right. Her awareness of her entrapment is no less acutely felt for her inability to express it except in clichés: 'What am I living for?' (86). Like Hurtle's Nance, she sees herself as a victim of her sexuality and resents being used by men, although she is powerless to resist. Like Nance also, she sees the penis as a weapon, bludgeoning her into 'childbirth and endless domestic slavery' (86).

Flora has her own hidden aspirations which Elizabeth Hunter, obsessed by her own supposed spiritual superiority, cannot discern, in spite of her claims to a special insight into human beings. At times the old lady herself becomes a symbol of the richer life to which the girl vaguely aspires: 'Momentarily at least this fright of an idol became the goddess hidden inside: of life, which you longed for, but hadn't yet dared embrace; of beauty such as you imagined, but had so far failed to grasp . . . and finally, of death, which hadn't concerned you, except as something to be tidied away, till now you were faced with the vision of it' (121). Moreover, Flora has been troubled by '[i]nklings' of that state of transcendence Elizabeth Hunter and Mary de Santis consider their elect preserve (442).

At one point satiric inspiration and resentment lead Flora to strike a blow against her main persecutor. Elizabeth Hunter, to assist herself towards the illusion of physical beauty her vanity still desires, has made Flora, 'guardian of the wigs' (120), an ironic counterpoint to Mary de Santis, the psychopomp. In heretical mood Flora presents a savage, parodic version of the 'sacred image' entrusted to her (539). Elizabeth Hunter, who desires to be trans-formed cosmetically into the goddess of life, is transformed instead into a grotesque 'idol' (539). The victim of Elizabeth Hunter's truth-telling thus presents another version of the true Elizabeth Hunter: 'Nobody could accuse you of malice when you had only emphasised the truth' (541).

Flora is threatened on all sides by people with simplistic and self-serving views of her: Col, her lover, sees her as a whore; Elizabeth sees her as a 'breeder'; Dorothy sees her as a slut; Basil sees her as Flora Primavera, potential nurse and wife. In desperation she turns to Snow Tunks, her lesbian cousin and her only link to a more innocent past. But Snow, like all the rest, wants to force her onto a narrow bed.

Flora decides to have a child to offset her feelings of inadequacy. The mythical child she hopes to conceive with Basil Hunter's help will be 'the embodiment of unselfish love' (315). 'Unselfish love', however, cannot issue from Basil's bankrupt sensuality or her own emptiness. She greets her period with relief, and Basil's non-baby confirms that: 'Nothing will come of nothing'. Just after the 'trickling [of the] . . . blessed BLOOD' signals that she is not pregnant, Flora is reminded by Elizabeth's little bell of the communion bell that is rung to signify what she cannot believe, that 'nothing can become something' (548–9).

A knotty web of religious and literary references is to be found here. 'Nothing will come of nothing' is, of course, Lear's line, hence appropriate where a Shakespearian actor, Basil, is so intimately involved in the action. The allusion to the communion service and the doctine of transubstantiation, 'nothing can become something', reflects Flora's dilemma with a neat irony. The language and imagery of Flora's catholic childhood, which persist after belief has fled, invest her present seedy situation with unexpected resonances. Flora is a 'modern' girl without recourse to religious faith, yet she is not a mere hedonist and experiences her own spiritual emptiness as a nagging lack. She would like to fill that emptiness ('nothing') with spiritual meaning ('something') if she could. But how? Without the apocalyptic experience that transforms Elizabeth Hunter from sensualist to secret visionary, Flora's religious sense can only have a parodic function in the novel. She serves as a priestess in the cult of Elizabeth Hunter, goddess or idol, depending on the viewpoint.

If Mary de Santis's religious role is to guide Elizabeth Hunter's soul through the stages of dying towards spiritual life, Flora's is to minister to the body which still craves the sensual life it is abandoning. She also serves in the cult of Elizabeth Hunter, preparing the old woman for worship. Elizabeth Hunter dies on her commode, fully made up and wigged by Flora, a grotesque idol. Thus a bizarre juxtaposition is affected: the exiting soul journeys towards spiritual being; the deserted body in savage parody of religious worship looks back towards earthly life.

Such parodies of religious significances are pervasive and disturbing in the novel. The Christian associations of transubstantiation are subverted when they are used as a metaphor for the flow of blood that signals Flora is not pregnant. On Warming's Island Elizabeth Hunter tastes a chip from a cut tree and finds a 'transmuted wafer' (418). By 'reverently' fitting Elizabeth Hunter in her lilac wig, Flora assists in a 'resurrection' (120). Seated on her commode, dreaming back over her life and sensing that the 'flimsy soul' is about to be ejected from the body, Elizabeth herself discovers that 'souls have an anus they are never allowed to forget it' (194). Spiritual aspiration and gross carnality, mysticism and heresy, the desire for transcendence and unbearably nostalgic memories of physical love – all these opposites continually entwine. At night, after Basil leaves the Hunter house, Sister de Santis finds that '[p]aradox and heresy mingled with the night scents' (155).

It is difficult to avoid the thought that White here is deliberately playing with the expectation of his religiously-minded readers that his work embodies a particular religious viewpoint. Considerable scorn is directed at a variety of religions: Roman Catholicism through Dorothy, Protestantism through Sister Badgery. Christian Science is mocked because of its denial of the reality of suffering. More important than these attacks on specific kinds of Christianity are parodic versions of Elizabeth Hunter's mystical aspirations. The pervasive imagery of cultic worship shifts the perspective disconcertingly from the religious understandings represented by Elizabeth Hunter, which confirm traditional understandings of mystical experience, to grotesque forms of mockery and subversion. A continual ironic parallel is drawn in the novel between the spiritual aspirations of the dying woman and imagery of perverted or revalued religious significances.

The effect is not unlike that in *Paradise Lost* where the Hellish world made by the fallen angels inverts and parodies the Heavenly world from which they have been expelled. This ought to point the reader away from diabolical mockeries of Truth towards the divine reality itself. In fact, as the Romantics pointed out, it is difficult for modern readers not to side with Milton's Devil, who has all the best lines, against his God. Milton, of course, did not intend or approve such a reading, but he made it possible by the dramatic force with which he evoked Hell. Similarly, White makes it possible for his readers to interpret on the side of the angels (Mary de Santis) or the attractive devils (Flora), and provides cults that serve both viewpoints.

Flora, of course, is unaware of the complex inversions of religious meaning that surround her. Yet, although her concerns are primarily immediate and mundane, she is not wholly worldly. Hence the poignancy of her sense of personal worthlessness. Unable to produce anything pure out of herself, Flora accepts Elizabeth Hunter's harsh and limited view of her: 'She understood me better than anybody ever. I only always didn't like what she dug up out of me'

(573). Laying out the corpse of the old woman who has tormented her, she waits pathetically for the 'illumination' she knows she will never be granted.

> . . . it did not prevent her touching the body several times when she had laid it on the bed, not expecting evidence of life (she was too experienced for that) but illumination? that her emptiness, she ventured to hope, might be filled with understanding. (552)

Elizabeth Hunter is torn between her sensuality and sensibility, between her longing to liberate herself entirely from her memories of physical desire and ultimately from her own body and the continuing force of her own sensual, self-indulgent past: 'The past has been burnt into me . . . ' (32). Like Hurtle Duffield she finds the task of transcending her human 'self', its desire and imperfections, no easy matter. Like Hurtle also, she 'creates' her lovers, family and friends according to the dictates of her own imagination. Thus she invents 'Flora Pudenda' and 'St Mary de Kleenex' (196), to both represent and minister to the opposing poles of her being.

Elizabeth Hunter even 'invents' her children as she herself comes to admit: 'But I made them into mine. That is what the children resent' (529). Dorothy and Basil resent more than this. Unconsciously they are both aware that their mother saw them as 'barbs he [her husband] had planted in her womb' (35). Much later she guiltily recalls her lack of milk and imagines Basil sucking 'the pus from everything begrudged' at her breast (423). Moreover she encouraged her children to compete for her love, thus setting them one against the other. She dreams that they were twins 'fighting each other to be first out of the womb' (431), and 'blaming [her] because [she] prevented them loving each other' (528). Accordingly, in collaborating to 'murder' the mother who divided them in the beginning, Dorothy and Basil establish a temporary truce in which they almost come to terms with themselves and their failures as spouses, lovers, parents.

In the 'circle of love and trust' at Kudgeri, their childhood holiday home, Dorothy finds the acceptance which she has so far been denied (511). Basil, also, rediscovers his youth and glimpses that 'sanity' that was his at the beginning when he 'saw clearly, right down to the root of the matter' (273). In this atmosphere they are drawn closer together, waiting for the telephone call that will announce the death of their mother. Simultaneously they discover a childhood they never had: 'So the Hunter children held hands for the return' (518). This closeness culminates in an act of incest performed on the very night on which their mother dies in the bed in which they were probably conceived. They fail, however, to achieve the nostalgic renewal they seek as Arthur and Waldo Brown failed in similar circumstances. They are too accustomed to sterility to fulfil themselves through an identification with the landscape of their childhood, with an illusory view of the past, or simply through their belated attempt at love: 'They lay huddled together, and he tried to conjure their former illusion of warmth, under a reality of wretched blankets' (527).

The mother who divided and dominated them as children, defeats them as adults desperately seeking a link to the past. By dying, Elizabeth Hunter provides them with the money they sought by 'murdering' her, and simultaneously breaks the tenuous link that binds them. Without their mother to remind them of their spiritual bankruptcy and their common interests, the Hunter children return to their former illusions of worldly success, Basil less eagerly than Dorothy who 'lock[s] a door' on their one pathetic act of mutual recognition (558). Returning to France, Dorothy is lulled by her new protection against disorder and desire, though she is momentarily racked by doubt and fear, no doubt an augury of things to come (587–9). Basil finds himself standing 'on the brink of something; or was it nothing?' (585).

Elizabeth Hunter has a talent for justifying to herself all her shortcomings. She does not want merely to transcend her human imperfections, she wants to excuse them to herself by seeing them in a new, redemptive light. In senescence her mind returns to the dolls she tortured as a child and the people she tortured as an adult. But she will not accept the charge of cruelty that is levelled at her by others, Dorothy in particular. She sees herself as a truth-teller and visionary, who hurts people by acquainting them with the truth about themselves which they will not acknowledge. She uses the symbol of the 'skiapod' to further justify herself: 'You couldn't say the expression looked deceitful, or if it was, you had to forgive, because it was in search of something it would probably never find' (404). Above all, she excuses her failure to love her family by claiming to pursue a purer, spiritual love: 'There is this other love, I know. Haven't I been shown?' (162).

Elizabeth Hunter will not direct at herself the ability to perceive the truth beneath appearances which she directs so mercilessly at others. Dorothy, her daughter, clings to her conviction of a nobler self than that rejected by the world, 'her actual self, as opposed to the one which others saw' (410). But that 'actual self' is an illusion fostered by resentment. She resents her mother for possessing 'the physical attributes which belong to your [Dorothy's] true, invisible, hence unappreciated self' (399). Elizabeth clearly perceives the tormented, dishonest little girl beneath the horsefaced princess, and counters Dorothy's accusation of cruelty with her own unflattering version of 'truth'. she refuses, however, to recognise similar contradictions in herself. She claims to have discovered and submitted to a superior, apparently divine, will during her experience in 'the eye of the storm'. But her own will remains uncompromising in the face of people or fate. She repeatedly proclaims that she will not die until she is ready to do so (63, 414). All her life she has refused to recognise her own lust that exists 'alongside those unrealizable aspirations' as an inescapable and 'true' part of herself (96). Elizabeth Hunter, rather like Voss, has split herself into a 'true' spiritual self that seeks release from the world, and a 'false', sensual, cruel, vain, human part.

Elizabeth sees only what she wants to see in herself. By refusing to see her opposing 'selves' as potentially complementary parts of a complex whole she constructs a self image as limiting as those she foists on her nurses. Similarly, the old woman Dorothy meets at the Cheesman's party, Lady Atkinson, sees her beloved grandchildren as perfect beings, while Cherry Cheesman sees them as '"Nasty little bastards"' who torture live chickens (297). Both look at the world through spectacles tinted to suit their own prejudices. Elizabeth Hunter wishes at the end of her life to be taken over by a superior Will, but continues to pursue salvation by pure will. She attempts to bully God into providing what she seeks: 'Now surely, at the end of your life, you can expect to be shown the inconceivable something you have always, it seems, been looking for' – as though salvation were a sweet to be wheedled out of a capricious father (544). But God turns out to be an efficient and ironical bully in his own right, with more power at His disposal than Elizabeth Hunter ever possessed. Flora Manhood's God, when she believes in Him, is very like Elizabeth Hunter in this respect: 'they had given her [Elizabeth] the power which can't help trampling. Doesn't God? On whole nations, as well as decent inoffensive individuals' (300).

Elizabeth Hunter's death appears to provide the release into a

Platonic 'endlessness' of pure being she has sought: 'myself is this endlessness' (551). Here at last she seems about to realize that intuition she has already had that 'the splinters of a mind make a whole piece' and that the human individual is 'a detail of the greater splintering' (93). In other words, rather like Himmelfarb in *Riders* (although Himmelfarb is no Platonist), she sees the human soul as a segment of a unified spiritual reality from which we come at birth and to which we proceed at death. If we accept this Platonic position, the function of the storm in the novel is to render down the inessential, 'human' components of Elizabeth's self so as to prepare the essential, 'spiritual' part for its journey beyond life. Like Voss's desert or Stan Parker's fire, the storm strips away the socially constructed garb of self.

However, forceful ironies surround this mystical level of meaning in the novel. Elizabeth Hunter dies grotesquely painted and wigged as an idol of gaudy life seated on her commode. We are reminded of the death of her husband, Alfred. Elizabeth had nursed him through the last stages of cancer to atone for her long neglect. She had hoped to assist at his 'miraculous transformation' (204), but Alfred himself dies outside her 'boxes'. His last word is simply: '"*Whyyy?*"', a question that mocks the various theodicies concocted by the more hopeful among White's characters (204). Human suffering in White's novels is inescapable and inexplicable; no efforts to justify it in terms of some divine plan can make it acceptable.

In the dichotomy of flesh and spirit, sensuality and sensibility, that runs through the novel, the former is never denigrated. The landscape around Kudgeri which Basil and Dorothy rediscover is celebrated in language as richly lyrical as any in White's writing. Sexual pleasure is also celebrated. Elizabeth's adulteries are not impediments to or lapses from her spiritual journey but affirmative moments in their own right. At the end she can no more deny the world of flux and flesh than Hurtle Duffield could at the close of *The Vivisector.*

Moreover, in a novel preoccupied with role-playing and disguise of the self no single, secure core of subjectivity is discovered, even by Elizabeth. She remains detached from and indifferent to the judgmental versions of her constructed by others, but her own inner self remains changing and myriad rather than fixed and unified. Given the multiplicity and instability of the self, then, what part of our human egos might survive death?

The Eye of the Storm is a novel of sensibility in that it explores

the rich inner life of a consciousness possessed of great subtlety
and expansiveness. White opens up a subjective world to us fully
and convincingly. But the sensibility he explores is surrounded by
ironies. Elizabeth Hunter aspires to the Truth, but is herself a mar-
vellous fabrication of wigs and make-up and socially determined
roles – wife, lover, mother and so on. She seeks the clarity and
stillness of spiritual being, but must continue 'struggling through
the wicked jungle of language' (72). She wishes to transcend the
world and the self, but cannot resist looking back longingly to
the many guises she has adopted as a woman and to the sensual
experiences she has enjoyed. Like the speaker of Yeats's 'Sailing to
Byzantium', his mind's eye fixed on eternity but unable to stop the
flow of images of fecund life, Elizabeth Hunter remains '[c]aught
in that sensual music'.[6]

A Fringe of Leaves

When W. B. Yeats wrote 'Labour is blossoming or dancing
where/The body is not bruised to pleasure soul' he envisaged
a harmony between mind and body, wisdom and sensuality, that
is generally absent from White's work.[7] Nevertheless, the violent
dualities that characterise White's novels of the fifties and sixties
are modified over the following decades. *Voss* is structured around
an absolute antagonism between matter and spirit. *A Fringe of Leaves*
returns to the world of *Voss* – the Australian wilderness as a setting
for love, torment and discovery – but in a new spirit, closer to Yeats's
reconciliation than to Voss's violent prising apart of the two halves
of human experience. In a sense, *A Fringe of Leaves* rewrites *Voss*,
but with a woman as the protagonist and without the extreme
metaphysics of the earlier novel. The old dualities are present,
but they are not manifest so violently nor so irreconcilably in the
novel.

In both novels human aspiration is set against human nature.
In both, individuals of strong will and imagination who desire
'something deeper'[8] from their lives than material success, hap-
piness or even love are placed in an extreme situation where their
egotism and presumption are exposed by their sufferings. Both
novels explore the ambiguous and inconclusive evidence of a divine
plan operating in human lives or in the material world. Both are
concerned with self alienation and the opposing demands of love.

Above all, both novels powerfully describe the desert landscape of Australia that is both terrifying and beautiful, and both ironically explore its effects on 'civilised' Europeans.

Voss sets out determined to subjugate the country of Australia to 'the country of the mind', to impose his vision on the landscape and on his followers by force of will alone. Ellen Roxburgh, on the other hand, is led by circumstances over which she has no control to reshape her limited view of the world and herself according to the demands of the strange landscape in which she finds herself and of its inhabitants. The Aborigines who kidnap her respond to the world in a way that she finds both attractive and disgusting. Their way of life is so opposed to the conventions of class and religion which the Roxburghs had taught her that she rediscovers her own primitive childhood self long repressed by her marriage above her class. Similarly, Jack Chance, the convict who rescues her, reacquaints her with the compassion and sensuality she has suppressed in herself. Ellen Roxburgh only finds self knowledge and an unexpected form of love among 'savages' to whom the rituals and conventions of Christianity are meaningless, in a landscape inimical to 'civilised' men and women.

From the start Ellen Roxburgh lacks Voss's surpassing arrogance. In place of the uncompromising 'vision' which he held up against the world, she has only self doubts and an openness to experience and to self modification. Moreover, the 'moral strength' for which she prays continually eludes her (33). While Voss had set out to redeem himself from his humanity by self-deification, Ellen hopes more mundanely to 'redeem [herself] through [her] husband' (137). Nevertheless, like Voss, she is drawn closer to the unfamiliar country in which she finds herself 'than to any human being' (104), although at this stage she has largely experienced the landscape from a carriage window. In a less presumptuous fashion than Voss, she too aspires to some undefined, presumably spiritual understanding, but has little hope of achieving her aspiration 'this side of death' (104).

Born into a humble, rural, Cornish family, Ellen Gluyas is early troubled by a 'presentiment of an evil' (110). From the start she believes 'more intently in the Devil than in the Deity' (123). This morbid fear of a vague threat appears to have a partly sexual cause. As a young girl she manages to exorcize it for the time being by immersing herself naked in a pool associated with some 'darker myths of place' (111). Years later with Jack Chance she discovers the continuing power of this sexual energy that neither the rituals of her Cornish girlhood nor those of her Christian adulthood could permanently suppress.

Her elevation to the leisured, cultured classes by marriage to Austin Roxburgh acquaints her with a conventional moral and intellectual world view that sits uneasily on the primitive myths and energies of her origins. The Roxburgh's abstract and comforting 'Divine Being' (123) does not eradicate her former demonism, however tractable she is to instruction. Her childhood desire to see Tintagel, a village not far from her own birthplace, is not obviated by her marriage, although she is able to travel far beyond that Cornish village. Her continuing dissatisfaction shows her aspiration to have been more than geographical. In Australia she discovers a force of sexual passion that shocks her, long conditioned as she is to her role as faithful wife in a dutiful but asexual marriage. Her adultery with her brother-in-law, Garnet, opens her eyes unwillingly to possibilities in herself for which she had not allowed. Her husband's behaviour during the shipwreck accelerates this process of self-discovery. Faced by the prospect of immediate death, Austin Roxburgh is primarily concerned to rescue his volume of Virgil. His obtuseness undermines her faith in 'the many-faceted role she had been playing' (175). The roles imposed on her by the Roxburghs – wife, nurse, 'courageous woman', 'expectant mother', and 'compliant adulteress' – all now seem equally unconvincing (175).

In the course of the shipwreck and the subsequent journey in small boats, the Roxburgh veneer of rationality, duty and convention is stripped from Ellen and her original, more primitive self emerges. A squall they encounter seems to her to be driven less by capriciousness than by 'an almost personal rage or malice', and Ellen dares to wonder if God is not punishing them for 'their human shortcomings' (224). But Ellen Roxburgh has only just begun to experience the intractability of those aspects of herself – sexuality and superstition in particular – which she had learnt to dismiss as 'human shortcomings'. By breaking her marriage vows she discovers love; by abandoning the God of the imperial class she discovers the inscrutability of the divine presence. With the murder of her husband (who dies bravely according to the conventions of his class and sex), Ellen's faith in Christianity collapses, and with it the conventional ritual that has protected her against her childhood 'presentiment of an evil' (110).

She could not, would never pray again. 'Oh, no, Lord! Why are
we born, then?'. (240)

So she is forced painfully to begin again the business of being
educated in an unfamiliar set of social conventions. The Aborigines
present her with a way of life as alien to her now as 'the drawing-
rooms of Cheltenham' were to her as a young bride (243). They
do not, however, offer her any system of belief that might satisfy
her doubts. She searches for, but is unable to discern, 'evidence of
a spiritual design' in the bizarre behaviour of these 'savages' who
are manifestly human (247). She is completely exposed to her own
doubts and weaknesses without the protection of the roles assigned
her by the Roxburghs or their now implausible system of belief. She
is no longer able to believe in 'a merciful power shaping her own
destiny' (247).

Ellen is curiously drawn to the Aborigines who torment her,
and whose behaviour disgusts her as a formerly civilised, leisured
woman. She discovers that behind the conventions erected by a culture and the platitudes of organized religion, 'truth' is obscure, and
good and evil depend on one's point of view. After participating in
a cannibalistic ritual she discovers not so much 'an abomination
of human nature' as a sense of having partaken in a 'sacrament'
(272). The lesson she had only partly assimilated as a girl is finally
driven home: 'there are conventions in truth as in anything else'
(74). After gnawing on the human bone she experiences some of
the disgust demanded by 'the light of Christian morality', but she
is impressed above all by the strangeness of the impulse in herself
that 'moved [her] to do it' (272). The energies of her primitive,
repressed self remain as mysterious as they are undeniably forceful.
She discovers that nothing human is alien to her.

With Jack Chance, the convict who rescues her, Ellen at last
reaches self knowledge, but not through duty, religion or intellectual learning. By submitting to her passionate, 'sensual' self, Ellen
discovers a compassionate, 'selfless' self. More importantly, she
cannot clearly distinguish between the two types, or interpretations
of love (316). Disgust gives way to tenderness as material privation
gives way to spiritual plentitude. The instinctual Ellen Gluyas at
last puts aside the unconvincing, rational Ellen Roxburgh and is
rewarded with a direct experience of 'love' that subsumes old
Mrs Roxburgh's categories ('sensual' and 'selfless'), that restores
her youthful skin, her singed hair, her beauty. When her life is

turned upside down, when all the civilising props and comforts
are removed, Ellen discovers a passionate love for a human being
although he is a murderer, and for the country in which she finds
herself although it is barren and inhospitable: 'As she covered him
with her breasts and thighs, lapping him a passion discovered only
in a country of thorns, whips, murderers, thieves, shipwreck, and
adulteresses' (311–12).

Nevertheless, she chooses to return to civilisation where her new
self-knowledge is a source of 'embarrassment, even danger' (341).
She is unable to adjust to the cruelties and dishonesties of 'civilised'
society after having seen such richness in the lives of 'savages' and
'criminals'. Like Theodora Goodman, Ellen retreats into what the
world sees as madness because of her acute sensitivity to the pain,
cruelty and stupidity that characterise normal society. The 'liberal'
commandant of the penal settlement, Captain Lovell, who takes her
in as one of his own class, exercises his authority over his family as
well as the convicts with a mixture of humane platitude and violent
punishment. The chaplain, Mr Cottle, eager to strengthen Ellen's
faith in the benevolence of God, condones the cruel punishment
dealt to the convicts (387).

Ellen understands the sufferings of the convicts because she has
suffered herself, and because she has encountered the humanity of
the convict, Jack Chance. The measure of her self-knowledge is her
new ability to enter into the sufferings of others. She is not granted
any mystical insight, but she comes to see the world as a place of
both suffering and great beauty, life as both a precious gift and
a hateful curse. She cannot explain these contradictions in the
light of a benevolent divine plan: 'Over all, the sun, which she no
longer knew whether she should love as the source of life, or hate
as the cause and witness of so much suffering and ugliness' (348).
In the little chapel built by Pilcher, the mate, she finds a moment of
peace and understanding similar to Stan Parker's 'vision' towards
the end of *The Tree of Man*. This is not achieved through prayer
or reason and she does not attempt to 'interpret' this sudden
peace of mind she experiences (391). Certainly, her insight owes
nothing to the rituals or beliefs of conventional Christianity. The
Roxburghs' 'LORD GOD OF HOSTS . . . charging in apparent
triumph' is merely a noisy and unconvincing impediment to her
contemplative state of mind' (390). For a moment Ellen is at
one with a world whose contradictions she cannot explain. Like
Theodora Goodman, she must 'accept'.[9]

Austin Roxburgh is reminiscent of Waldo Brown. Like Waldo he is a writer manqué. Like Waldo he attempts to transform those around him into aesthetically pleasing works of art shaped by his own stale, literary imagination (61). Like Waldo he is always undertaking, but never completing, great projects: 'the resolution to follow an ascetic rule, to love all humankind, to give thanks to the supreme Being, to round out his miserable fragment of a memoir, to undertake Sanskrit, Arabic, Hebrew, Russian, while there was yet time' (199). Above all, like Waldo, he lives according to literary stereotypes and conventions. However, while Waldo lived out his staid life in suburbia, Mr Roxburgh is precipitated into a situation where his literary prescriptions for behaviour are grotesquely and tragically inappropriate. On the small island on which the survivors pause to repair their boat, Austin Roxburgh is stripped of 'the trappings of wealth and station, the pride in ethical and intellectual aspirations' (208) that have protected him from his own insignificance and inadequacy. He discovers too late that 'his experience of life, like his attitude to death, [has] been of a predominately literary nature' (209). He discovers actual death not the 'literary conceit' he has expected. He approaches his death in the unlikely role of a man of action, but dies as a puzzled, grotesque man overwhelmed by a reality he has avoided.

> Austin Roxburgh was keeling over. On reaching the sand his body would have re-asserted itself, but the attempt petered out in the parody of a landed shrimp. (240)

The similarities between *Voss* and *A Fringe of Leaves* are marked, but a change of emphasis has occurred. Voss's singular arrogance was both horrifying and perversely admirable. Voss aspired to transcend his humanity and failed. Ellen Roxburgh neither aspires so high, nor falls so low. Accordingly, she is both more sympathetic and less fascinating than Voss. Through their common failure, both Voss and Ellen Roxburgh achieve a greater humanity, a recognition of their weaknesses and doubts, and above all their need for love.

The 'truth' about material events or metaphysical problems, remains as elusive as ever. Captain Lovell believes that 'by hearing different versions of the same incident . . . we arrive at the truth' (362). Ellen knows that 'the truth is often many-sided, and difficult to see from every angle' (378). She herself suspects, correctly, that she projects 'emanations' from her own troubled mind onto her surroundings (381), so that, finally, she has no way of knowing whether she sees the truth of things or not.

The 'fringe of leaves' of the novel's title is, of course, the veils civilisation imposes on our primal nature. The attraction of tearing away the veils springs only partly from the recognition that civilisation represses our sexual, moral and religious instincts. More fundamentally still, civilisation obscures the true complexity, obliquity and multiplicity of the self. Ellen's journey towards self-knowledge repeats Voss's into the burning centre of Australia. For Ellen, however, it is not so much the landscape as the discovery of love across the gulf of class and dialect which demolishes the whole structure of meanings and confidences that constitute 'civilisation'.

The process of burning away the veils of civilisation ought to expose what lies beneath: innocence or depravity, innate knowledge or mere blankness. What is discovered, finally, is not any graspable presence, good or bad, but an enigmatic silence that lies behind all our socially constructed fronts. Whatever reality lies at the heart of human beings cannot be named or known, yet it is not a wholly tragic discovery for Ellen. In the end she finds a more encompassing version of the love she has been seeking through various disguises than she had ever suspected. This love, however, is not a presence or a fixity that might be identified with any human individual. It is a mysterious presence that White's characters intuit but which they cannot grasp or define.

*   *   *

In both *The Eye of the Storm* and *A Fringe of Leaves* White's point of view remains as obscure as ever. White directs irony at his characters, both the more and the less sympathetic, from a variety of apparently contradictory standpoints. Dorothy de Lascabanes is rejected by her aristocratic French family as a colonial, but herself despises Norwegians, Dutchmen and Australians by identifying with her French oppressors. Her Catholic contempt for the Protestant Dutchman who experienced the eye of the storm is mocked because she uses her piety to excuse her viciousness and to repress the sexual impulses that disgust her. Sister Badgery and Lal Wyburd are mocked for their squeamish, anti-Catholicism (43, 536). Mary de Santis, who pursues salvation by rejecting her physical self and her desires, is shown to limit her response to the world as much as Flora Manhood who comes to accept Elizabeth Hunter's view of her as a purely physical being.

The characters in both novels in varying degrees respond to the world in a limited fashion. Understanding is not achieved by cutting off the 'sensual' self to please the 'spiritual' self. Nor is 'truth' perceived by those whose eyes are 'too deeply concentrated on an inner self' no-one else is ever privileged to meet.[10] Elizabeth Hunter discovers a moment of peace in the eye of the storm, but returns to the confused, violent, ordinary world because of the impaled sea-bird, an image of unexplainable suffering. After her moment of peace in the little chapel, Ellen Roxburgh returns 'to the settlement in which it seemed at times she might remain permanently imprisoned' (391).

Although the novels seem to move in such different directions, the one towards death and mysticism, the other towards life and passion, and although they express common doubts and ambiguities rather than a common message, they are fundamentally complementary. Both explore the mysteriousness of being, human and divine, always supposing the latter exists. If Heaven does indeed love us, it loves in a most 'perverse' fashion, as the second epigraph to *The Eye of the Storm* suggests: 'He felt what could have been a tremor of heaven's own perverse love'. On the other hand, as the final epigraph to the later novel asserts: 'Love is your last chance. There is really nothing else on earth to keep you there'. Those who pursue knowledge of Absolute truths, like Elizabeth Hunter, are doomed to failure. Those who seek to love, like Ellen Roxburgh, may discover a measure of understanding, but no certainties:

for however much crypto-eagles aspire to soar, and do in fact, through thoughtscape and dream, their human nature cannot but grasp at any circumstantial straw which may indicate an ordered universe. (405)

5

Flaws in the Word

> everywhere
> Echo or mirror seeking of itself,
> And makes a toy of thought.
>
> Samuel Taylor Coleridge, 'Frost at Midnight'

The Twyborn Affair is White's last great novel. He was to produce one more novel, *Memoirs of Many in One*, before his death. The latter is a slight work by comparison with any of his previously published novels, even *Happy Valley*. Thematically, however, the two late novels are connected. More importantly, they show a late flowering of a tendency that has always been present in his work but which has not previously been so dominant, nor so inventively worked into the texture and structure of the writing: White's late fictions are intensely self-consciously preoccupied with the relations between art and the world.

This metafictional tendency does not indicate that White has adopted postmodernism in any doctrinaire sense. Game-playing, fabulation, the love of puns and double meanings, the recognition that the worlds invented by novelists are never the 'real' world – all these are particularly associated with the novels of John Barth, Donald Barthelme and Thomas Pynchon, but they are also found at the inception of the novel and are as fundamental to the novel as a form as is mimetic realism. Major novelists have always recognised that if the novel is a mirror moving along a highway, the distortions in what it shows can be as interesting as the life-like reflections. Even Jane Austen is capable of adopting in *Northanger Abbey* the fabular techniques of the gothic novelists, albeit for parodic purposes. From *Don Quixote* (1605) to Graham Greene's *Monsieur Quixote* (1982) by way of Sterne, Joyce and Nabokov the sense of the hyper-realist possibilities of the novel has always been part of the genre.

140

For White, as for his great precursors in this tradition, the anti-
(or hyper-) realist possibilities of the novel are not a function of
its unbridgeable distance from life. They do not exclude the moral
and mimetic aspects of the genre. They are a manifestation of the
endless possibilities for play, for invention and for disguise that are
inseparable from life itself. White richly draws on his own existing
body of fiction, on the ancient possibilities of the novel as a form,
and on his sense of the strangeness and wonder of reality to explore
'lying' as a fundamental human activity, of which art is merely one
manifestation.

It is true that linguistic self-consciousness was present even in
White's early novels, but a significant change has occurred in the
way it figures between *The Living and the Dead* and *The Twyborn
Affair*. In the earlier novel White was unable to discover any substance in the world; the novel can only offer the gestures and
symbols it condemns. Hence, the self-enclosedness of *The Living
and the Dead*, the sense that the novelist has found himself trapped
within a circle of what he most wishes to transcend: words. This
sense of entrapment is everywhere present in spite of White's
evident and fashionably thirties desire to condemn solipsism in
favour of 'the actual plane'. The novel offers us symbols about
symbolism such as the Bristol box. The characters – particularly
Catherine and Eden Standish – are uncomfortably conscious of
their lives as 'narrative' or 'symbol' or 'hieroglyph'. Their lives
are composed of gestures void of meaning. Their words have no
connection to things. Unable to find a way out of the impasse it
describes, the novel is forced into an extreme self-consciousness.
The Living and the Dead becomes unavoidably what its author most
deplores: an enclosed world of self-reflexive words.

In *The Twyborn Affair* White no longer sees language and life as
separate orders. The novel teems with rich, sensual and varied
forms of life – a London brothel, an Australian sheep station, an
air raid in the Second World War. But all this is focused through
a character who, unlike Elyot Standish, knows that we touch the
'real' not by commitment to a cause or a class but by way of
the imagination, by invention. Elyot Standish retreats from life
into a cerebral literariness and in the process impoverishes both
his experience of others and his writing. Eddie Twyborn in his
incarnations as Eudoxia Vatatzes and Eadith Trist discovers the
endless possibilities for transforming the self that are part of lived
reality and in so doing becomes perhaps White's most compelling

and convincing artist figure. The bizarre deceptions he practises as a man and as a woman are his art form *and* his life. There is no longer any difference.

The Twyborn Affair

For a writer who has been said to endorse 'orthodox Christian mysticism' Patrick White is embarrassingly interested in heresies, in non- and anti-Christian religions and sects, and in an extraordinary range of sexual practices, chiefly unorthodox. In his last two novels the old themes of God, visionary experience and the religious nature of the self reappear, but in a more playful, even self-mocking sense than before. This is not to say that White at the end dismisses the religious impulse or retreats into a tragic scepticism. The old preoccupations are, however, reconfigured in the light of a new mood of playfully ironic acceptance. The protracted searches of White's protagonists for vision or God or transformative self-knowledge give way to a more relaxed, humorous rather than bleakly sardonic, sense of the inevitability of failure in all such undertakings. The failings of the characters are neither so protracted nor so painful.

The Twyborn Affair is about sexual ambivalence. The central character, Eddie Twyborn, raised a man, masquerades as Eudoxia Vatatzes and is reborn as a woman, Eadith Trist. White thus moves into the centre of the novel's interest a theme that has long been important in his work. What is significant here is that the sexual theme does not replace the longstanding concerns with religious and existential meaning, it is shown as intrinsically part of those concerns. Sexual ambivalence is celebrated as a condition that is quintessentially human and at the same time religiously significant. Even its attendant 'vices', especially transvestitism, are seen as states and acts that have a metaphorical relation to the deep problems of meaning and design with which White has consistently been preoccupied. Sexuality is also closely associated with art, as an essentially *imaginative* activity.

Transvestitism in *The Twyborn Affair* is representative of the inescapable inauthenticity of human beings, our need to dress up our personalities and the lack of any essence behind the disguises we adopt. Clothes are intimately related to sexual identity. By altering our dress we alter the signals we give to others about our sexuality.

Those who cross-dress assert that we are not born simply male or female; we have the capacity to make – or invent – our own gender. More importantly, the transvestite cannot escape the knowledge that implicates us all: that the reality of selfhood behind the fictive masks we adopt is always shifting and elusive. This same knowledge links the transvestite to the artist.

Clothes are consistently associated in *The Twyborn Affair* with deception and disguise. Behind these disguises lies enigma or absence. 'Nothing is mine,' says Eudoxia, 'except for the coaxing I've put into it. For that matter, nothing of me is mine, not even the body I was given to inhabit, nor the disguises chosen for it.... The real E. has not yet been discovered, and perhaps never will be'.[1] Yet the sense that human personality rests on no essence of self, no permanent core, is not the occasion of despair in the novel. The use of makeup and cross-dressing are seen as 'poetic' activities, opposed to the prosy naturalism of those who see the self as predictable and stable (310) There are, of course, limits to how far we can take our fantasies. Eadith cannot have sex with Gravenor without confronting him with a reality other than that which she has studiously cultivated. The elegant fiction she has achieved as a woman would be subverted by a violet jaw with stubble (404).

The 'self', then, that intractable egotism which has been an article of faith for romantically conceived artist figures like Hurtle Duffield, is revealed as ultimately illusory. The artist, like the trans-vestite, 'dresses up' reality in order to present others with versions of the self, of the world and of Truth. As much as any conjuror (from the Syrian peddler in *The Aunt's Story* to Angelos Vatatzes in *The Twyborn Affair*) artists are committed to appearances, however fervently they may believe that their work touches the axis of reality. By this identification of artist, conjuror and transvestite, White parodies and subverts the romantic self-conceptions of his artist figures and the Platonising tendencies of his religiously oriented critics.

Eddie finds he is unable to escape from role-playing and thereby from fostering illusions in others. Even as a jackeroo, enacting the thirties belief that working people are closer to the real, Eddie cannot believe in his rough (and in the terms of Aus-tralian naturalism, 'realistic') garb: 'Would he ever succeed in making credible to others the new moleskins and elastic sides? At least people were more ready to accept material facade than glimpses of spiritual nakedness, cover this up with whatever you will, pomegranate shawl and spangled fan, or moleskins and elastic sides' (183).

This sense that we can never quite grasp the reality that lies behind what we see applies to more than the disguises adopted by sexually ambivalent individuals. The land itself, which Eddie comes to believe holds some spiritual meaning, is grasped only incompletely. The written word also fails to illuminate: 'he sat looking at the word which promises so much, yet never illuminates to the extent that one hopes it will' (242). Similarly love which is 'the core of reality itself', that force which hopefully lies beneath all the disguises of personality, always eludes the seeker (336).

The problem here is whether humans possess an essence, some inviolable core of self, or whether they are no more than gestures, mannerisms and imitations. Do we have depth, as the romantics and modernists affirmed, or are we merely shifting surfaces, as the postmodernists maintain? White's fictions find a position somewhere between these two apparently irreconcilable views. Again and again his novels invoke the concepts of essence, presence, depth, the author, God and meaning. But precisely at the point where we seem about to touch the realities behind those concepts, where his visionary characters come closest to achieving vision, a shift of perspective occurs, so that the presence we are ushered towards becomes elusive or disappears. We are brought continually to the house wherein the mystery is supposedly contained, but when the door is at last opened we find that nothing is there. We cannot be sure whether the god was never there or whether he (or she) is merely hiding.

This does not mean that White is a non-believer any more than he is a mystic. As always, he explores specific structures of meanings, metaphysical and existential, in terms of the ironies in the lives of those who hold them. As always, White is interested as a novelist in 'myth', in the positive sense of the word, rather than in the revelation of Truth. As always, whatever ultimate reality there is to confront lies outside the categories of human thought and language.

White, then, is a mystical sceptic, as he is a modernist romantic. Both terms of each opposition apply to his late work, but only provisionally. Neither cancels the other out. In *The Twyborn Affair* the sense that meaning is discoverable in nature or in the self appears as in White's earlier novels, but the irony that now surrounds it has deepened and strengthened. The gap between aspiration and fulfilment has lengthened. At the same time a shift has occurred in favour of the sexual and religious heresies which have long figured in White's fiction. Sexual and doctrinal heresies are not merely ironic and subversive counterpoints to various orthodoxies as they are in *Voss* and *A Fringe of Leaves*; they have supplanted them. Even sodomy is invested, not wholly ironically, with metaphysical significance in the novel.

The linked themes of sodomy and religious quest are introduced through Angelos Vatatzes, Greek lover of Eddie Twyborn (called Eudoxia by Angelos), who is an expert on Byzantium, on Greek orthodoxy, on heresies, and on buggery. Among the heresies he studies is Bogomilism. The Bogomils were a sect of Christian Gnostics who, according to the Church Fathers who recorded their heretical doctrines, believed that matter was evil but that whatever the body did was unimportant because the soul was separate. Hence they found themselves in the position that they were sexual libertarians but believed that procreation was evil. Their solution to this dilemma, according the Fathers, was to practise sodomy. Hence, one possible derivation of the word 'bugger' is from a French corruption of the words Bulgar or Bogomil.

A. P. Riemer, in a fascinating article on the place of Bogomilism in *The Twyborn Affair*, argues that the Fathers misrepresented the Bogomils who were essentially an ascetic sect, although they degenerated and eventually adopted 'certain notorious practices'.[2] Riemer notes that the Bogomils were dualists, holding that the created world was utterly separate from God, that matter was evil, that Christ was not material and that 'the soul may be liberated through mortification of the body'. The Bogomils, then, strove to achieve an extremely ascetic way of life. At the same time, they exhibited an ambivalence characteristic of dualistic religious sects: their doctrines justified both abnegation of the flesh and extreme libertinism, and it would seem that at various times adherents of the sect tended towards both extremes.[3]

Riemer contends that Bogomilism has an important structural function in the novel. Superficially, the allusions to the heresy involve a gross joke: that Angelos, as a sodomite, 'for all his heretic-hunting, is himself guilty of "Bogomilism"'. However, Riemer detects a serious aspect to this joke. The jesting and irreverence that surround the French section of the novel where Eddie plays the role of Angelos's catamite, reveals, according to Riemer, 'a purpose, an intellectual coherence, centred on these fleeting references to the Bogomil heresy'.[4] In part this is achieved by the contrast White establishes between Sydney life and the ancient Byzantine world. As in *Voss* (or Evelyn Waugh's *A Handful of Dust*), a parallel is drawn between life in the interior, a savage or exotic place, and life in the normal world. Our sense of the proper relations between normality and abnormality are undermined by the continual sudden transitions between one world and the other. These cross-references form 'bewildering mirror-images, reflections of the human condition, wherein nothing is but what is not'.[5] Appearance and reality are thus blurred. All this, according to Riemer, establishes the novel's central theme of radical dualism and prepares us for further sudden shifts of perception and underminings of orthodoxies.

Riemer sees this opening section with its air of strangeness and ambivalence, its 'shifting perspectives and deceptive shadows' as 'highlighting the absurdity of humankind and of its endeavours'. This is true, and Riemer is also right when he asserts that the novel 'challeng[es] . . . received notions about Patrick White's art', but Riemer pushes his reading to a dubious conclusion.[6] Riemer sees dualism as fundamental to the novel's vision, worked into its structure. He argues that *The Twyborn Affair* is charged with a Manichaean disgust towards physical existence. He sees the novel as exploring and dramatising the dualistic position that there is an 'absolute gulf between the soul and created matter'.[7] In spite of the constantly shifting surfaces in *The Twyborn Affair*, in spite of Eddie's lack of coherent character traits and the inconclusiveness of his quest, Riemer maintains that 'there are constant intimations that Eddie's sensibility, spirit, or perhaps soul, is unified, integral and whole'. In other words, Eddie's experience conforms to the Manichaean dualism in terms of which the Bogomils experienced the world. The world is evil and confusing, the soul canot reach fulfilment by way of flesh. The body is a prison. Thus the initial jest about Bogomils and buggers discloses a philosophical/existential significance.[8] The novel is structured according to the Bogomil idea of the initiate's struggle with flesh – with Eddie as an unlikely heretic/initiate.

There are certainly grounds for Riemer's reading. The novel is rich in allusions to dualism, and specifically to the Bogomils. These allusions have an important role in the novel's meaning and structure. *The Twyborn Affair* is not, however, a wilfully obscure exercise in dualistic theology, embodying an heretical metaphysics.

Above all, the novel's meaning is not to be identified with the Manichaean/Bogomil aversion to the flesh. White is not treating his readers to an enormously complicated and sly disclosure of his personal dislike of the world. If there is a Manichaean tendency in White's fiction it is manifest in the persistent ambivalence displayed towards physical love from *The Living and Dead* to *The Twyborn Affair*. But sexuality is scarcely depicted with unmixed repugnance, and the urge to transcend the flesh felt by so many of White's major characters is balanced by the urge towards physical life, towards flux and towards pleasure. That genuine ambivalence about sexuality – the attraction *and* the repulsion – is prior to the religious themes that derive from the will towards transcendence of so many of White's characters.

We need always to allow for the deflating humour which White directs at his characters' otherworldy aspirations. When Eddie is raped by Don Prowse and then becomes the active partner in their fierce couplings, Riemer sees a sign of Eddie's Bogomilism: 'the heretic must, in order to shed the trammels of orthodoxy, liberate himself to its degradations'.[9] Yet the unequal measures of acceptance and disgust in these joinings may more readily be seen to reflect the usual positions of love – dominant/passive; penetrator/penetrated; masculine/feminine (even if the latter terms are used here parodically) – than to dramatise obscure Gnostic doctrine. The philosophical and esoteric levels of implication are undoubtedly present, but they play around the psychosexual dimensions of human love, particularly of homosexual love. All White's novels, including *The Twyborn Affair*, explore the responsiveness to matter and to physical love of familiar Whitean characters. Eddie is merely one in a line of these characters: Stan Parker, Mordecai Himmelfarb, Hurtle Duffield, Elizabeth Hunter, Ellen Roxburgh. Bogomilism in *The Twyborn Affair*, like cabbalism in *Riders in the Chariot* or Jungianism in *The Solid Mandala*, is not unequivocally endorsed by the author. It has the status of myth.

Riemer underestimates the humour in *The Twyborn Affair*, although he notes the levity and irreverence of the novel, which distinguish it from the portentousness of White's previous novels. In fact, *The Twyborn Affair* merely extends the ironic and playful tone – the deflation of the portentous strain in White's writing, the subversion of familiar religious themes – that has been marked in White's fiction since *The Vivisector*, at least. Riemer notes that Eadith Trist's brothel is presented 'in terms of a convent or house of retreat' as evidence of the novel's subversions of religion, but this is scarcely more mocking than the numerous anti-religious allusions in *A Fringe of Leaves* or *The Eye of the Storm.*[10] Eddie may see himself here as 'inwardly preparing for purification', but the novel is not controlled by his perceptions.[11]

If we allow for a Manichaean tendency in White's fiction, we must also acknowledge that the stance towards the body shifts between *The Living and the Dead* and *The Twyborn Affair.* In the earlier novel there was a palpable sense of disgust associated with the body. In *Voss* that disgust is dramatised in the person of the protagonist. In *A Fringe of Leaves* the body is a source of religious knowledge. In *The Twyborn Affair* the heretical material is made structural, not in the sense that novel is, in Riemer's words, an extended 'Manichean conceit' concluded by the image of Eddie's father as the Pantocrator, 'aloof from evil world of matter [having] become reconciled with the no-longer-captive soul' of his son.[12] Nor is the novel 'dedicated to the notion that the body, the flesh and the senses are utterly worthless'.[13] The dualism which informs Eddie's experience and which shapes his thought is another mythic system which White explores, and with which he entertains, teases and finally disconcerts his readers, still seeking the novelist's 'vision', the novel's essential meaning.

The source of all the Bogomil allusions in the novel is the unreliable and self-deceiving Angelos, who loves orthodoxy and abhors heresy. Angelos instructs Eudoxia (and us) in Bogomil doctrines. But he is unable to bring her to see what he considers to be the true meaning of the heresy. He speculates: 'Perhaps it's that way with any heresy, more than most others those of sexuality' (77). Himself a sodomite, he is infected by the heresies he studies once he grants the link between sexuality and religion. Both religion and sexuality have conveniently been categorised by the Fathers into orthodox and heretical, sound and unsound, divinely ordained and against nature. Angelos accepts the religious prejudices of the Fathers in theological but not in sexual terms. Yet the distinction he makes between sexual and religious heresies is unsustainable. The 'reality' that supposedly lies behind the orthodox concept of God is neither more nor less 'fictional' than the idea that innate sexual characteristics are the immutable determinants of gender. Like the Holy Ghost in orthodox theology the idea that gender roles are fixed or approved by nature serves to hold together a 'disintegrating structure' (78).

The 'structure' that is disintegrating, or has disintegrated, is orthodoxy. For Angelos, orthodoxy in religion is a necessary fiction. It is not 'true' in the sense that its claims can be affirmed or disproved on rational grounds. But it makes life coherent; it imposes order. The Byzantine world of his family in which orthodoxy held sway was more satisfying and meaningful than the post-sacramental world Angelos inhabits. Himmelfarb on his Jacaranda tree/cross discovered the limits of the religious construct in terms of which he had come to interpret his experience. Angelos lives outside any such system or construct, but he wishes the world were still interpretable inside a complete system of meaning, as it was once for his family.

For Eudoxia, Angelos is a magician. He conjures richness out of their sexuality. Yet 'she' is instinctively on the side of the heretics, by virtue of nationality as much as sexuality. Australians stand towards Europe as the Bogomils stood towards Orthodoxy: they are inescapably the barbarians. Such dualities, however, are subject to ironic reversal in this novel. Byzantium seems to stand for deception, complexity and art, Australia for simplicity and honesty. Yet it is Eddie/Eudoxia/Eadith, the sexually ambivalent self-disguiser and Australian, who is most closely identified with art in the novel because the artist is by nature on the side of the heretics against the 'Fathers'. It isn't simply that the artist is once again the outsider – that romantic stereotype White himself has frequently, albeit ironically, invoked. The old theme of exile and alienation has none of the romantic freight of suffering and earnestness which it bears in the figures of Frank Le Mesurier in *Voss* or Alf Dubbo in *Riders in the Chariot*. Eddie's exile from various orthodoxies – sexual, suburban, religious – is marked by self-delighting subversion and playful ironies.

Through her relationship with Angelos, Eudoxia comes to understand the religious nature of sexuality. Sexuality is seen as partaking of the fundamentally religious nature of all experience. Eudoxia learns about the enigma of the world by way of sexuality and sexual ambivalence. Transvestitism itself has an existential, even a metaphysical, dimension for her. The act of disguising the self by dress has the same relation to human subjecthood that religious systems have towards God. Religions, creeds, orthodoxies are merely unconvincing disguises humans choose to wear. In seeking God or Truth or the Reality behind appearances, they subject themselves to the same fruitless task as those readers of White's novels who seek the author's 'vision', as some fixed essence which determines meaning everywhere.

The novel is also about the ways in which language constructs our selves and the effects of swapping language, even if it is only different class registers of English. The Golsons, wealthy Australians touring Europe before the First World War, find the English aristocracy formidable because their 'casually incorrect version of the English language' shows an ease, a sense of belonging, which they lack. When Lady Tewkes exudes, '"the Hôtel Splendide is an 'otel, dear gel, I can recommend with confidence"', Joanie Golson of Golson's Emporium, Sydney, feels intimidated (12). Language and class are the great dividers, as in *The Living and the Dead*, but now there is no need for painful reconstructions of the self as the earnest hero sets out in search of the reality to which only poor and working people supposedly have access. One simply changes clothes, or adopts a new way of speaking. The novelist exults in his character's and his own capacity for evasion and disguise. Writing itself is seen in the novel as a baroque facade built on colonial wattle and daub (355).

As the various versions of the name Edward which appear in the novel hint, one of its themes is the long lapse of modern culture away from the Edwardian world of graziers with vast incomes travelling through Europe from their Hunter Valley seats, the world into which White was born and to which he has returned again and again in his fiction.

At the opening of the novel the Edwardian world is already under threat. E. Boyd Golson, the Australian gentleman, represents Edwardian solidity. He loves objects that remind him of his prosperity, but he is threatened by forces over which he has no control and which he does not understand (90). Looking from the window of the hotel he sees the formal bourgeois world menaced by some unseen threat. He puts it down to the war, which he might otherwise avoid by not understanding the French papers (91). What threatens him personally is not the violences war will unleash. He will be exempt from terror, but he cannot escape the effects of the war on the world order he represents: the high bourgeois world inherited from the Victorians, plush, self-confident, reasonable. The war will end that world and usher in the fierce ideologies, relentless violences and displacements of peoples and ideas of the twentieth century. All the confidence in human reason founded on the Enlightenment, the faith in material progress and the general

betterment of human beings, will collapse under the pressure of the
irrational forces released by the destruction. After the war reason
will become a frail raft 'threatened with extinction by the seas of
black unreason on which it floated, sluiced and slewing' (71).

At close of the novel another World War looms amid equal
unreality (375). In their 'protected room' the English upper classes
ignore the violences that will consume them (377). The Australian
rich still tour Europe cringing over their lack of 'culture-tradition'
– already redundant, or at least nostalgic, terms (385). In the
final pages the east is blazing as civilisation crumbles once again.
History becomes unavoidable for individuals, however protected
by wealth. At the same time 'history' as continuity and meaningful chronology, a term with the transcendent force that God
or Truth once possessed, is itself collapsing. In the face of this
general collapse the individual can find value and meaning only
in those moments of perception or memory when the particulars
of experience come into sharp focus. Walking through the air raid
towards his own death (recalling Elyot Standish's walk home from
seeing his sister off to an earlier war in *The Living and the Dead*)
Eddie finds that only the memory of his Australian childhood is
real (431). The snatches of childhood detail he recalls are 'the
minutiae to which Eudoxia Vatatzes had clung as insurance against
the domes of Byzantine deception' (175). Whatever reality such
moments possess has little do with their concrete materiality. They
are moments of perception, occasioned by something as mundane
as combing the fleas from a dog's genitals, that resist the hazy
abstractions of the intellect.

There is no escape from unreality, within the self, in the forms of
nature, or by appeal to history. Disguise, role-playing, imitation are
the inescapable conditions of modernity, indeed of being human.
The citizens of suburbia, as much as the artist or the homosexual,
are faced with 'an impersonation of reality' (172). The return of
the alienated hero to the land is unsettling rather than spiritually
nourishing because it fails to provide access to the permanent forms
sought. Eddie sets out expecting that the landscape will respond to
his need for a reciprocal relation with nature. He sees 'the brown,
scurfy ridges, fat valleys opening out of them to disclose a green
upholstery, the ascetic forms of dead trees, messages decipherable
at last on living trunks' (161). He seeks 'the reality of permanence'
(179), the Platonic forms behind the outward appearances. He is
granted partial access: 'the scene's subtler depths were reserved for

the outcast-initiate' (194). But this is long way from the discovery of the permanent forms of reality. All that Eddie discovers finally are mirrorings of his own mind. The landscape becomes sexual: 'they were driving down the moonlit clefts, between the stereoscopic buttocks of hills' (268).

Finally, the novel celebrates the endless permutations of human love. Even an act of masturbation becomes an expression not only of the malaise of the individuals involved (the swimmer and the voyeur) and of the world sliding into another war but also somehow of a triumphant leap into light and colour (76). The affirmation offered is, characteristically, a frail and equivocal one. Love is not celebrated as a Platonic ideal, however many of White's visionary characters have sought that ideal. Nor is it an absolute that, by transcending the failures and limitations of the individual humans who seek it, offers a means of holding the fragile human personality together. Love, like human subjectivity, is shifting, multiple, limitlessly open to possibility. It is subversive of all those structures of meaning that aim to fix and define the self. It does not rescue or redeem us, but by allowing us to see our humanity in unfamiliar, often heretical, ways, it affirms a central value in White's novels.

William Walsh sees *The Twyborn Affair* as embodying a tragic vision, but the novel is finally comic. It celebrates the artist's powers of invention and the author's powers of escape. In the last line of the novel a bird raises its little jester's cap and White cocks another snook at his too-earnest readers.

Memoirs of Many in One

Memoirs of Many in One, like *The Twyborn Affair*, is full of echoes of White's previous novels. This self-reflexiveness is not a new development in White's work, it may be found in *The Vivisector* where the narrative of *Voss* appears in diminished and parodic form in the ill-fated journey of Hurtle's grandfather. In that novel it was as though White were deliberately deflating the epic and grandiose features of his earlier fiction. In *The Twyborn Affair* we find a pleasurable ranging across the established scenes and stylistic manners of the White oeuvre. Eddie's return to the land is enacted, after so many previous treatments of the theme, as a literary topos. The scenes in the Grand Hôtel Splendide des Ligures recall the middle section of *The Aunt's Story* where European hotel life is evoked with expressionistic exaggeration. In *The Twyborn Affair* the ladies eating become parrots and macaws with ferocious mouths and upholstered claws (84–5). In the latter novel Eddie's moment of epiphany while 'stranded in [the] landscape' at Fossickers Flat watching a little hen wren recalls a famous moment on a Greek hillside in *The Vivisector* (174). Again White draws us away from abstraction towards the 'everyday embroidery of life' (175). Even the description of a masturbating kiosk proprieter watching Eddie Twyborn swimming recalls the scene in which Voss watched the sun rise (72).

In *Memoirs* such repetitions are even more pervasive. Alex Gray's memory and experience are littered with events and characters which have featured in White's previous novels. When she recalls killing a beloved dog we are reminded of Voss. Escaping from her daughter, she journeys around the wealthy seaside suburbs familiar from White's Australian fiction and comes upon an elderly couple on a bench outside their weatherboard house. They might be Stan and Amy Parker preserved through forty years and subjected to a visit from their own author. They are 'seated on a homemade wooden bench, surrounded by a forest of gaint dahlias'.[14] The prose, apparently in nostalgic homage, becomes suddenly charged with the epithets of goodness, simplicity and humility that figured so prominently in both *The Tree of Man* and 'The Prodigal Son': 'there was such inherent goodness in these old people, they could only welcome me as parents welcome a long lost child' (40).

The tone of these repetitions or returns is not so much nostalgic, however, as deflating, even parodic. The old couple exist in a mock suburban idyll in which only the '"[t]ermarters are holy"' (48). The novel returns to Stan's garden epiphany, but in the light of a new shaping perspective, which is neither wholly parodic nor nostalgic but which sees the protracted struggle of White's characters to wrest significance from life as somehow both comic *and* tragic, doomed and capable of achievement, ironic and valuable. Alex says: '"What they don't understand is that joy and suffering are interchangeable"' (86). Joy and suffering, meaning and non-meaning, plenitude and emptiness – the oppositions that have driven and tormented White's seekers are now not so much healed or resolved as turned into mirror images of one another. Stan Parker found ultimate significance in a gob of spittle. Alex, suffering from phlegm, remembers the French mystic who demonstrates her piety by swallowing a gobbet of beggar's spittle (94).

In the earlier novel the ordinary became extraordinary. Now, in an extension of that counter-movement Riemer observes in *The Twyborn Affair*, the extraordinary continually becomes ordinary.[15] Stan's gob of spittle was God grasped in a moment of blinding illumination; Alex's gob of spittle is God and nothing, depending on how the observer looks at it. Joy and suffering, insight and blindness, ecstasy and blankness – are all now interchangeable terms. The same facts cause tragic irony or comic acceptance. Alex sets out 'to rise above ordinariness' but finally confronts the truth that her journey for meaning or purpose is prompted by life's banality, its awfulness (104). The mystic derelict from whom she had expected guidance must be led back to the Park 'where [he] belong[s], along with the garbage, the plastic, and the flashers' (113)

In *Memoirs* White not only recalls his previous novels, he also situates himself within the novel, again with a mixture of nostalgia and self-mocking deflation. The 'Patrick' we meet in the novel is not another version of the romantic artist/writer/visionary egotistically placing himself at the centre of the novel's action. The author, as well as presenting himself as merely the editor of another's memoirs, appears in the novel as a character, not a major one, living on the edge of the park and at the edge of the narrative.

Such entries of the author into the narrative are not new in White's fiction. In *The Aunt's Story* we find, among the exotic names that bestow an uneasy grace upon the squatters' homesteads, three stolid English ones, and among these is one of the author's own Christian names: Patrick Victor Martindale White. White thus acknowledges his own ambivalent placing in the Australia he describes. There is a coy self-consciousness in this sly entry of the author into his earlier novel. It suggests White's unease in the post-war period with his Australianness. It also draws attention to a persistent habit of White's of using names drawn from fairy tales or literature or names that overtly signal the characters' traits to disturb the realistic surface of his novels. In *The Living and the Dead* we find a too-good character named Harry Allgood. In *The Tree of Man* a passing digger relates to Amy Parker a small narrative that has no relation to the larger narrative which deals with Jack Horner who 'sits around and spits'.[16] In *Voss*, we find a harlequin figure composed of shadows and patches of light named Jack Slipper.

This predeliction for breaking the narrative illusion by way of the characters' names reflects White's increasingly cavalier stance towards realism in his post-war fiction. In *Happy Valley* the narrator's intrusions had the effect of interrupting the illusion of reality established by the narrative, but this was the result less of authorial design than of narrative uncertainty. In the later fiction anti-illusionistic strategies are employed for more calculated effects in terms of the overall economy of the novels. In *Voss* the variety of styles in which the landscape is conveyed, realistic and non-realistic, reflect the violent antagonism of the country to *all* the categorising systems which the European characters impose on it. In *The Vivisector* the painter's progressive move towards abstraction indicates White's impatience with mimetic kinds of art. In *The Twyborn Affair*, however, White returns to a form of radical mimesis. Eddie's disguising and distorting of reality suggests that there is no source of 'Truth' behind appearances. Yet in a world where imitation is so pervasive, given the absence of originals, this compulsive invention of possible selves reflects the only available reality. By dressing up appearances Eddie performs an act of self-invention that is characteristic both of artists and of human beings generally. He is merely more flagrant than the rest of us.

'"Names'", Alex Xenophon Demirjian Gray observes, 'give a clue to character'" (100). In *Memoirs* the names of places give a clue to the character of the novel itself by their blatancy, their flagrant self-consciousness. Touring through the outback with a theatrical troupe ('our journey into the wastes of Philistia' [125]) Alex passes through Peewee Plains, Lone Coolabah, Ochtermochty, Kanga Kanga, Toogood, Baggary Baggary, [and] Aberpissup' (127). There is an inspired mixture here of Australian twee, Aussie outback iconography, obscenity (the play on buggery) and punning satire of favourite outback activities ('ave a pissup). We recall the sardonic joke at the expense of the Australian social scene in *Riders in the Chariot* where the name of the suburb, Barranugli, conceals the words barren and ugly. Now the longstanding theme in White's work of the relation of the romantic artist to Australian philistinism is being sent up through the aural puns in the names of the outback towns. At the same time the pretensions of 'the Artist' are being deflated. Alex Gray is a Whitean romantic elitist in flamboyant drag bringing culture to the desert of Australian philistinism. Alex herself acquires names 'as other women encrust themselves with jewels' (9).

In *The Vivisector* a passing reference was made at a party to an unpleasant person named Patrick. In *Memoirs* the joke is extended as the public perception of Patrick White, encouraged in the fiction, of a fussy, bitchy, pompous egotist is exposed to scathing satire. The whole history of White's treatment of the interconnected themes of illusion, self and the author is recapitulated as the author places himself in his own text. The novel is attributed on the cover and title page to 'Alex Xenophon Demirijian Gray' and Patrick White is merely mentioned as the editor. Thus we are made to feel that we are finally encountering the elusive author who has appeared under so many disguises, while at the same time we are further distanced from the author as a person behind the novel. The structure of *Memoirs* both invites identification with the author and frustratingly removes the author once again.

In White's last novel, the author, whose fiction has included more and more of the author's biographical and subjective experience, teasingly presenting the self to the reader and snatching it away at the same moment, at last offers himself as a character, seemingly undisguised, in his fiction. Moreover, 'Patrick' is exposed to continual mockery in novel in his role as author/mystic/romantic. Patrick is seen by Alex as 'the ersatz Reverend Mother . . . in search of the unanswerable, the unattainable' (88). It is, however, not Patrick, the novelist, but Alex, the mother-figure dreaming maliciously in her bed like Elizabeth Hunter, who encompasses the fullest range of human possibilities in the novel. In a sense she even encompasses Patrick White, the famous Sydney novelist in the popular conception. It is she who sees herself in danger of 'becoming Centennial Park's Very Own Saint' (107).

Alex herself is like Elizabeth Hunter, a rich Whitean feminine sensibility, a tyrannical mother, vain, selfish, egotistical, yet with conviction of inner spiritual election: 'She knows me, not the essential part, but she knows – the worst' (24). She knows that the illusion of art is 'far more real than what is known as life' (120). She is another version of the self-deified Creator (166). Above all, she is the Whitean mother wholly triumphant, leaving behind her memories to be worked up by Patrick, the pompous, plodding novelist and vehicle of her own greater spiritual power: 'Patrick will be the spirit guide at the great seance' (164).

Patrick himself is the gray figure in the book. '"He's sick of writers . . . He's sick of himself. Literature, as they call it, is a millstone round his neck"' (177). He ends up a captive of Hilda, Alex's daughter, her possession, cosseted and protected. As 'I – the great creative ego' he had been given the task of seizing Alex Gray's life and transforming it into art (192). But he ends as victim of her posthumous power.

White presents himself to us in *Memoirs* modestly as the editor of a pile of notes left by Alex Gray, a disordered narrative in which he himself figures. Thus the author disguises himself as the editor of a work in which he presents a satirical view, not so much of the true, the essential Patrick White, as of the various versions of himself that have been constructed from his own writing by his earnest readers and exegetes. As White, the 'editor' remarks dryly at outset: 'some of the dramatis personae of this Levantine script could be the offspring of my own psyche' (16).

Memoirs is rich in complex narrative play involving the categorical distinctions between memoirs, autobiography and fiction. According to Alex, memoirs are archives with a 'soul' (21). They also have shape, of course. The disposition of significant events is determined by an authorial will, but that will is always opaque to the reader, however assiduously he or she seeks out the underlying 'vision' which supposedly signifies the essence of authorial self. The problem in this novel which presents itself as memoirs edited by the author's hand, is that the relations between author, subject and reader have been wilfully and perversely subverted. We are invited to chase the author, who seemingly offers himself to us. But the author is revealed as no more than yet another fiction.

Writing in *Memoirs* is a means not only of concealing the self but also of controlling the infinite possibilities of subjectivity. Alex confesses that she writes 'To confirm that I am I' (89). '[T]hat most important pronoun' is the organising centre of a deliberately disorganised book which is finally neither a memoir, an autobiography nor a novel, but a meta-form combining elements of all these genres while showing their specific limitations (89). White dramatises the self by dissolving the self; the subject of the novel is finally subjectivity itself – the elusiveness of that experience designated unsatisfactorily by the pronoun 'I'. '"[C]an I believe that I AM I?"', writes Alex in her memoirs, both begging the question and recalling the question Frank Le Mesurier heard Voss intoning in the earlier novel (96). Voss attempted to make the self secure by self-deification. In White's last novel the links between the human and the divine have been severely strained. As the sense of the transcendent becomes more unstable, so the whole structure of meanings – including language and the self – in terms of which White's visionary characters have sought ultimate realities progressively collapses.

Patrick appears in *Memoirs* not in the guise of visionary artist, anguished truth-seeker, tragic cynic or bedazzled mystic, but as one who cultivates disguises of the self by dramatising its various possibilities. He is a somewhat pompous figure, condescended to by luminary Alex. She dismisses him as 'too piss-elegant by half' (124). Alex, the first-person narrator, reflecting on her life as an actress, notes that Patrick also 'is a performer' (25). He is, however, a far less extravagant and entertaining performer than she. Alex herself is more adept not only at self dramatisation but also at self-concealment: '"I am protecting myself by cultivating this jungle of words. None of the Boobies will investigate me if I plait the branches densely enough"' (51). Yet in the end, it is Patrick White – the author as distinct from the fictional editor of Alex Gray's memoirs – who by placing 'himself' in his own text, by seemingly dissolving the distance between author and character, entraps his readers ('the Boobies') most cunningly in the jungle of language.

In *Memoirs* it is not only the police and Alex's bossy daughter, Hilda, who are the 'Boobies' chasing the cunning escape artist, Alex. Alex, by virtue of her powers of invention and disguise is the novel's true artist figure. She has 'invented' her own son, Hal (53). When Hal appears, or is conjured up, she considers biting off his delicate nose and 'return[ing] it to the womb of [her] imagination' (55). Alex is the author eluding the vulgar readers, especially critics, and especially those from the University of Sydney. We, the readers and determined pursuers of the author, are the 'Boobies', and once again the author, like Alex, escapes and mocks our efforts. White even takes a swipe at his most ferocious exegete of the Jungian persuasion, David Tacey, along with all his religio-mystical critics when Alex remarks: 'I have studied practically nothing beyond my own intuition – oh, and by fits and starts, the Bible, the Talmud, the Jewish mystics, the Bhagavad Gita, various Zen masters, and dear old Father Jung who, I am told, I misinterpret' (54).

In White's last novel the gnomic pasages of the familiar Whitean narrator are curiously absent. In part this is a function of the distancing perspective White's narrative method in the novel achieves. The Whitean narrator himself is a minor character within the novel rather than a God-like overseer of the narrative and the characters. Hence his role as unfolder of the mysteries has been radically diminished. There are, however, some revisitings in the novel of Whitean portentousness. After a familiar passage of Swiftian loathing at the disgusting aspects of modern life – grease, alcohol, semen, wine underfoot – Alex is granted an angelic vision:

> Then I look up and he is kneeling opposite in exactly the same position. We are a few yards apart. I cannot see his face, because it is gilded by the sun's glare, but sense that it is smiling, and know that it must be as dark as the smooth dark kneeling thighs. I can feel the stream of understanding which flows from this miraculous Being, bathing my shattered body, revitalising my devastated mind. (138–9)

Such moments, however, are surrounded not only by the usual Whitean irony, the faintly raised eyebrow at the too-earnest reader's expense, but also by a *structural* irony. The author cannot be associated with such statements because he has placed himself, or the versions of him accumulated over years by his readers, within the novel and exposed those versions of 'Patrick White' to comprehensive irony. Not only the other characters but also the narrative organisation of the novel itself are charged with irony at the expense of those familiar constructions of the author. By placing 'himself' within the novel, then, White both offers himself and denies that we can ever, as readers, know the author. If the author is like God, he is so in the sense that once again he escapes the seeker who asks in a letter: '"I will believe you love me if you reveal yourself. But you never do. Surely you can give me a clue, at some humble, earthly level?" (84).

In *Memoirs* White even mocks the mystical outcasts who have figured so prominently in his fiction when he introduces the narrative of the tramp taken in from the park by Alex. 'There is an old man with matted hair and a hand down his back, scratching. Probably a mystic' (85).

In this novel only one human artifact is granted reality: excrement. The self is a construct, sets of clothes worn to hide nothingness, art is a system of disguise and evasion. Only shit is 'real' (21). White's novels have copiously referred to farts, excretia, bodily fluids. Genitals and buttocks, often grossly exaggerated, have been obsessively dwelt on. In *Voss* and *The Solid Mandala* characters have shown their humility and faithfulness by cleaning up human shit. Hurtle Duffield ends his life painting with his own excretia.

Perhaps all this confirms that homosexual subtext that has always been present in the novels. But in making the subtext explicit as he does in *The Twyborn Affair* White does not embrace the homosexual cause or produce a 'gay' novel. The results of having done so at any point in his fiction would probably have been no more successful than was E. M. Forster's *Maurice* (1971). Indirections, in these matters, are often more productive of narrative power than explicitness, especially where a 'cause' as contentious as homosexuality is concerned. White is not interested in confessing his sexual preferences to his readers or preaching at them about the sufferings of homosexuals. Nor is his obsession with bodily wastes a sign of a Manichaean sensibility or an anal fixation. He is engaged in his old practice of fooling the boobies. He is satirising human pretensions, rubbing our readerly noses in the unpleasant realities beneath our noble self-conceptions. Shit is a human not a homosexual product, and it is human vanity that White once again condemns – including the reader's.

*   *   *

White's last two novels are his most European. That is not to say that they are 'English' as was *The Living and the Dead*. Rather, they exhibit a cosmopolitan sense of the world and an international sense of possibilities of the novel as a form. A useful comparison may be made to Vladimir Nabokov, a writer who would probably have detested White had he been aware of him and classed him as an antipodean Dostoevsky. Yet both White and Nabokov achieve that sense of the novel as supremely civilised medium – playful and detached. Both regard 'design' in fictional terms as a problem involving all human fabrications and one related to the possibility of a divine design behind the apparent randomness of the world.

There are, however, important differences between White and Nabokov. Nabokov's understanding of human beings and of the world is ultimately optimistic. For all the sufferings he saw, there is little place for evil in his conception of the world. For Nabokov, if we look into the heart of humanity we find an imaginative richness, and this outweighs even the nihilism implied by the concentration camps. He suspects that a benevolent purpose might exist beyond the evidence of human suffering.

For White, the argument from design is a treacherous one. He continually affirmed his own religious faith and his major novels are informed by this faith. But the nature of the deity demonstrated by the hints of design we discover in the world is profoundly ambiguous for White, who sees not only the darkness and terrible egotism worked into human nature, but also the capacity for mischief in whatever purpose shaped the world. The world itself, for all its beauty, is full of suffering that denies our dreams of perfect transcendent orders. That is why the games he plays with design in his fictions are not resolved as neatly as Nabokov's are. Nabokov leads us through mazes until we glimpse the artificer and behind him the shadow of another artificer. White plays more troubling games with his reader. He traps us, plays with us, and leads us not to resolution but to enigma. It may be that some 'purpose' lies behind the world. If so, its nature is unknowable, as is that of the author who seems to be so palpably present to us within the novels of 'Patrick White'. All that we can know about those purposes (authorial or divine), we learn by way of the deceptions they practise on us as readers of the worlds they prolifically invent.

Yet for all this pessimism, White's last novels reveal a deep sense of acceptance and even celebration – of life, of sexuality, even of Australia. Ever since *The Tree of Man* White's dissatisfactions with Australia as it is have been marked. He treats 'ordinary' life but invests it with an imaginative richness that makes it bearable to his fastidious sensibility. He discovers in the quotidian what he calls in 'The Prodigal Son' 'the extraordinary' in order to make bearable a social world he finds inimical. In other words, he invents, and in invention lies his consolation. But only in the late fiction do we find the poetic play which is, as Schiller pointed out, the sign of aesthetic freedom.[17] It is not that White simply snips the string that holds the world of art to the actual world and watches it vanish into pure aesthetic space. He has always been aware of the distances between words and things, between the world in the mirror and the highway along which the mirror moves. He finds in these distances not a source of anxiety as in the early novels but the enabling condition of play, of imaginative invention.

In his last work White has rearranged his fictional landscape so that the familiar features are present, but are viewed from new and disorienting perspectives. The notions that God can only be interpreted in terms of necessarily limiting systems, private or conventional, or that sexuality is a construct rather than a biologically determined function of fate have long figured in White's fiction, but in *The Twyborn Affair* playful, even celebrative ironies surround them. A comic and affirmative stance is adopted towards problems that have previously been invested with great angst. Failure is seen not only as inescapable but also as a potentially *positive* result of all human efforts at self transcendence. The elusiveness of truth, the instability of the self, the fundamental inauthenticity of human gestures towards self-disclosure – all these are now celebrated as both ineluctably human and as the fundamental conditions of art.

Conclusion: Patrick White and the Modern Novel

In the early 1960s Patrick White came across the work of Janet Frame. With characteristic generosity he wrote to his New York publisher, Ben Huebsch, drawing his attention to her strange genius. He also wrote to Frame herself, and did not receive a reply to his letter for 22 years.[1] It is not surprising that White should have admired Frame's work. They have in common a love of outsiders, of those wounded by 'normal' society. Both people their novels with alienated figures whose brand of separateness is that they 'construe as miracle the hieroglyphic commonplace'.[2]

Both opposed with their idiosyncratic and difficult styles the 'dreary, dun-coloured' realism that dominated fiction in their respective countries in the 1950s.[3] Above all, both chose to remain in societies for which they evidently felt little sympathy. Both combined in their writing a modernism that was steeped in the great tradition of European literature and a nationalism which aimed to make a distinctively new kind of writing out of the new worlds in which they found themselves.

In the third volume of her autobiography, *The Envoy from Mirror City*, Frame recalls her decision to return from London to New Zealand in 1963:

My reason for returning was literary. Europe was so much on the map of the imagination (which is a limitless map, indeed) with room for anyone who cares to find a place there, while the layers of the long dead and the recently dead are a fertile growing place for new shoots and buds, yet the prospect of exploring a new country with not so many layers of mapmakers , particularly the country where one first saw daylight and the sun and the dark, was too tantalising to resist. Also, the first layer of imagination mapped by the early inhabitants leaves those who follow an access or passageway to the bone. Living in New Zealand would be for me, like living in an age of mythmakers; with a freedom of imagination among all the artists because it is possible to begin at the beginning and to know the unformed places and to help form them, to be a mapmaker for those who will follow nourished by this generation's layers of the dead.[4]

The language in which Frame expresses this decision is very similar to that used by White in his 1957 essay, 'The Prodigal Son', in which he explains his own decision to return to his native land from the Europe in which he felt culturally much more at home. For both, Europe is dense with tradition and culture, receptive to the imagination and to the artist. Yet for both, the attraction of the new countries is irresistible. There lies the possibility of fresh beginnings, of the discovery of the extraordinary and the poetic within the commonplace and the banal. There lies the possibility of new forms of language, new ways of seeing. And there lies the opportunity to take part in the epic task of making a new literature.

What is significant in both White's and Frame's attitudes to the countries they chose to live and write in is the mixture of affirmation and repugnance. Both have been reluctant nationalists, choosing to remain in their respective countries but consistently condemning the materialism and puritanism of those societies and calling for a respect for spiritual values. What drew them back was partly the force of a remembered landscape, partly the (self-mythologising) belief that by doing so they were participating in the making of a new literature, and partly the sense that in the new worlds lay realities that were 'local and special'.[5] Not to return involved the risk of becoming a beach-comber or travel writer – rootless, drifting, removed from any familiar reality. As Frame expressed the problem in Whitean prose:

The writer . . . may find herself spending a lifetime looking into the mists of a distant childhood, or becoming a travel writer who describes the scene, then leaves it, pocketing the uprooted vegetation, erasing the sea and the sky without hearing the cries of a world that has been torn from itself into the fictional world, from people whose very skin is left hanging in the centuries-old trees; the unmistakable cry of a homeland truthfully described and transformed.[6]

Seeing themselves as removed from the social scenes of their respective countries, both White and Frame tended to interpret adverse criticism of their work as resistance to their speaking the 'truth' about those cultures. The dingoes howl and the reviewers cry 'insane' because the works too trenchantly oppose the myths in which the society habitually clothes itself.

Yet neither Frame nor White set out to offer a truthful picture of the life of the place, if 'truthful' we mean accurate in naturalistic terms. White determined as early as the mid-1940s that he would show the worlds that lie within the ordinary in high romantic colours; Frame was determined to 'transform' the world she fictionalised so as to arrive at a higher kind of truth, not truth *to* appearances but the truth *behind* appearances.

It is by comparison to writers like Frame and Lowry that we grasp White's place in modern literature. Each chose to live and write away from the centres of London or New York that were available to them. Yet none embraced the rhetorics of nationalism or post-colonialism that have become fashionable in the former colonies. Each directed a satiric eye at the country he or she chose to remain in and condemned the various shortcomings of social life there. Eluding all the competing categories that have been imposed on them – nationalist, internationalist, modernist, postmodernist, and so on – White, Frame and Lowry have emerged in the last twenty years as crucial, perhaps *the* crucial, post-war novelists. All address in their fiction – by their attention to form, style and narrative stance, not simply at the level of theme – the collapse of traditional centres and authorities that terms like postmodernism and post-colonialism attempt to account for.

Yet while we should avoid the reductive criticism that seeks to explain all the complexities and ambivalences in a writer's work by consigning him or her to some fashionable category such as post-colonialism or postmodernism, it is important to recognise that White's fiction *is* susceptible to such readings. White is not an aesthete, as was Vladimir Nabokov . His writing is too grounded in contemporary history, too directly involved with issues of nationality, gender, power, colonisation and postmodern culture.

Towards the end of his massive biography of Nabokov Brian Boyd seeks to account for the decline in Nabokov's prestige in the 1960s and 70s. Although Nabokov was still hailed as probably the greatest living novelist, he had already reached the curious position of being 'at once admired and forgotten'.[7] Boyd notes the rise of feminism and the change in intellectual fashion that meant that Doris Lessing and Margaret Atwood were arousing 'excited attention' while the author of *Lolita* was vaguely under suspicion. He also notes another profoundly important shift in taste prompted by the emerging issues of post-colonialism and postmodernism.

> In the 1960s and 1970s, as the world tried to shake off the legacy of colonialism and to recognise the limitations of a Eurocentric view of history, readers turned to Latin American, Caribbean, and African novelists as different as García Márquez, Naipaul, and Achebe. Nabokov, on the other hand, was more decidedly European in emphasis than any other writer of his time, less sympathetic to 'boring ethnopsychics' or to any kind of folk or primitive art. On the other hand he also dismissed much of the Western heritage, from mediaeval Christianity to modern Marxism, from Greek drama to French neo-classicism; he had no illusions about the savagery of colonization; he strongly opposed racism of all kinds. But by the 1970s that seemed not enough to balance his unswerving allegiance to the best of Western culture, the best of Western freedoms.[8]

Boyd here usefully sketches an historical shift that is profoundly important to White's position in twentieth-century writing. White is not a magic realist. Nor is he in any limiting sense a post-colonial writer. In many respects he is closer to Nabokov than to writers like Achebe. He works out of and continues the general European high cultural tradition. An element of aestheticism runs through his work. He shares some of Nabokov's metaphysical preoccupations, especially the sense that there is a more than metaphorical link between creativity and creation.

Nevertheless, that shift in taste to which Boyd refers involves White as it does not involve Nabokov. White belongs with writers like Janet Frame, Wole Soyinka and Wilson Harris who manage to reflect the full complexity of the post-colonial situation without adopting either the Eurocentrism of Naipaul or the ethnic nationalism of Ngugi Wa Thiongo. At the core of White's concern as a writer is the complexity of cultural inheritance in colonised countries like Australia. For White, as for Harris and Soyinka, countries born out of the colonial process contain layers of cultural traditions – imported and indigenous, colonial and settler – and the trick of writing novels in such places is to include the variety of kinds of knowledge and cultural experience they contain. In White's fiction this is achieved above all by the inclusiveness and elusiveness of the narrative voice.

The voice we hear in the narrative asides and comments throughout White's novels seems to us very much the author's – the cantankerous, querulous, bullying voice that we recognise in the autobiography. In this sense White is a very *present* author who has not unseated the writer's ego. Yet the point of view of the narrative in any White novel changes continually, rapidly and disconcertingly. The narrative voice in White's novels, individually and collectively, is not a unified and consistent one behind which we may detect the lineaments of a given personality or authorial vision. It is voice composed of many voices, a slippery, complex, fluent medium.[9] The elusiveness of voice in White's fiction, the variety of registers and styles he employs, are strategies that reflect the complexity of his sense of subjecthood, nationality and belonging.

In this respect White can most fruitfully be compared to Lowry and Frame. The knotty complexity of voice in their works reflects not only the modernist sense of the self as multiple and changing (a reflecting glass cut on several planes, in one of White's favourite metaphors) but also their acute sense of displacement everywhere. The question is, what kinds of communities or nations provide the range of linguistic, cultural and social resources on which these writers draw and how is each particular writer placed in respect of that community? In their works they represent communities composed of a wide range of dialects, idiolects and styles. Their works, in fact, *are* the communities or nations they never managed wholeheartedly to belong to as individuals.

Lowry once observed in a letter to Gerald Noxon '[t]here are queer and unique difficulties that ever beset the transplanted'.[10] This truism ignores the immensely positive effects that transplantion or exile have had on most of the major writers in English of this century who have not been English. Indeed, there seems to be a productive link between 'the sense of discomposure *anywhere*' Katherine Mansfield felt so acutely and modernism itself.[11] This has been noted of high modernists like Lawrence and Pound, both of whom chose self exile from the

London of the 1920s. But the traffic away from the 'centre' did not stop with them. A similar exasperation with the provincialism of English literary culture in the late thirties through the early fifties led writers like White and Lowry to abandon London for various kinds of exile (Lawrence Durrell is another example). The effect of transplantation on these writers was to liberate them from the remarkable homogeneity of voice – a curious kind of decorum – that characterised the post-war English novel, even when practised by the angriest of the 'Angry Young Men'.

The nature of this liberation is indicated by the use of 'traditional' material from English literature in White's novels. In the opening sections of *Voss* we find pastiches of the nineteenth-century novel that serve to draw attention to the radical otherness of the environments in which they have been placed. Nowhere in roughly contemporary the fiction of Amis, Cooper, Snow or Wain do we find anything similar.

Throughout the period from the mid thirties to the late fifties, while mainstream English fiction was retreating into a more and more confined linguistic space, White and Lowry were diligently struggling to incorporate into their fiction a range of neglected dialects. In Ezra Pound's terms they were not simply writing in dialect, a necessarily limiting procedure, but were making use of dialect 'to keep their diction in the living language' and thus they were 'extending the language to make it cover wider ground than before'. They incorporated various aspects of dialect 'into the very essence of their work so that sometimes these elements are completely absorbed or invisible'.[12] They did not merely substitute working-class speech for educated English or the speech of middle-class English people for the mandarin dialect of the upper classes. They set about drawing on a range of dialects, often parodically including the dialects of the classes from which they themselves had come and which they were determined to escape.

Linguistic pluralism, then, is a response to the variety of styles and traditions which impose themselves upon the works of these writers. It is also part of their effort to extend the range of linguistic elements which have been represented in fiction. Here we find most forcefully the extent of White's achievement as a twentieth-century novelist.

In the end terms like modernism, postmodernism, realism and so forth are inadequate to a writer on White's scale. They account for impulses within his writing but never for the whole thing. He escapes the categories. John Berger's words, speaking of the sculptor, Ernst Neizvestny, are relevant: 'His profoundest works defy explanation by resort to any established concept. They remain – like the experiences they express – mysterious'.[13]

Notes

Introduction: Places, Tribes, Dialects

1. Dylan Thomas, 'A Visit to America', *Dylan Thomas Reading*, Vol. 4, Caedmon, TC 1061, n.d.
2. Patrick White, 'The Prodigal Son', in *Patrick White Speaks* (Sydney: Primavera Press, 1989), p. 13.
3. As David Marr shows, White failed to acknowledge his mother's assiduous promotion of his writing, particularly his juvenile poetry. Marr, *Patrick White: A Life* (Sydney: Random House, 1991), pp. 89–90.
4. Colin McInnes *et al.*, *Australia and New Zealand* (New York: Time, 1964), p. 140.
5. McInnes, pp. 52–5.
6. Patrick White, *Flaws in the Glass* (New York: Viking, 1981), facing p. 55.
7. Osbert Sitwell, Introd., *Escape with Me* (London: Macmillan, 1940), p. 20.
8. Virginia Woolf, *The Years* (London: Hogarth Press, 1965), p. 241.
9. White, *Flaws*, pp. 52–8.
10. See photograph in White, *Flaws*, facing p. 150.
11. Ezra Pound, Letter to James Joyce, [between 6 and 12] September 1915, in Forrest Read, ed., *Pound/Joyce* (New York: New Directions, 1967), p. 45.
12. White, *Flaws*, p. 123.
13. Sitwell, *Escape with Me*, pp. 3–4.
14. The term 'poofteroos', Australian slang for homosexuals, occurs in White's *The Solid Mandala* (Harmondsworth: Penguin, 1969), p. 9.
15. T. S. Eliot, '*Ulysses*, Order and Myth', *The Dial*, 75 (July/Dec. 1923), p. 483.
16. White, 'The Prodigal Son, p. 15.
17. Patrick White, *The Ploughman and Other Poems*, illus. by L. Roy Davies (Sydney: Beacon Press, 1935), n. pag.
18. Raymond Williams, *Culture and Society* (New York: Columbia University Press, 1960), p. 207.
19. F. R. Leavis and Denys Thompson, *Culture and Environment* (London: Chatto & Windus, 1933), p. 87.

20. Leavis, *Culture and Environment*, p. 85.
21. Patrick White quoted on the dustjacket of Maurice Shadbolt, *A Touch of Clay* (London: Hodder and Stoughton, 1974).

Chapter 1: 'The English' Patrick White

1. See Carolyn Bliss, *Patrick White's Fiction: The Paradox of Fortunate Failure* (London: Macmillan, 1986), p. 15.
2. Marr, *Patrick White*, p. 162.
3. William Empson, 'Proletarian Literature' in *Some Versions of Pastoral* (Harmondsworth: Penguin, 1966), pp. 11–25.
4. Marr, *Patrick White*, between pp 216–17.
5. T. E. B. Howarth notes that J. M. Reeves 'solemnly pronounced the final epitaph of Georgian poetry in *Granta* as follows: "I suppose the last word on Georgian poetry has been said a great many times"'. See Howarth, *Cambridge Between Two Wars* (London: Collins, 1978), p. 69.
6. John Davenport *et al.*, Editorial, *Arena*, 2 (Autumn 1949), p. 3.
7. Cecil Day Lewis, 'Letter to a Young Revolutionary', *New Country*, ed., Michael Roberts (London: Hogarth Press, 1933), p. 40.
8. F. R. Leavis, 'Mass Civilization and Minority Culture', *For Continuity* (London: The Minority Press, 1933), pp. 13–46.
9. Spender wrote an equivocal apologia, *Forward from Liberalism* (London: Gollancz, 1937). He notes there that 'the liberal individualist who turns towards communism is in a peculiar, isolated position', p. 175.
10. Aldous Huxley, *Ends and Means* (London: Chatto & Windus, 1937), p. 274.
11. Graham Greene, Introd., *Journey Without Maps*, 2nd edn. (1936; rpt. London: Heinemann, 1978), p. ix.
12. Christopher Isherwood, *Lions and Shadows* (London: Hogarth Press, 1938), pp. 75–6, 207. George Orwell shared this feeling. See Richard Rees, *George Orwell: Fugitive from the Camp of Victory* (Carbondale: Southern Illinois Press, 1967) pp. 145–6.
13. Virginia Woolf, *A Letter to a Young Poet* (London: Hogarth Press, 1932), p. 26.
14. W. H. Auden and Cecil Day Lewis, Preface to *Oxford Poetry 1927* (Oxford: Basil Blackwell, 1927, p. v; rpt., Samuel Hynes, *The Auden Generation: Literature and Politics in England in the 1930s* (London: Bodley Head, 1976) Appendix A, pp. 397–8.
15. David Lodge, 'Modernism, Antimodernism, and Postmodernism', *The New Review*, 4, No. 38 (May, 1977), p. 41.
16. This phrase is scattered through *Selected Letters of Malcolm Lowry*, ed., Harvey Breit and Margerie Bonner Lowry (New York: Capricorn, 1969), pp. 28, 42, 115, 143.
17. Michael Roberts notes that the figure of 'the returning hero' found in the poetry of Rex Warner, Auden, and Charles Madge 'is the

antithesis of Eliot's Prufrock', 'The Return of the Hero', *London Mercury*, 31, No. 181 (1934), p. 72.

18. White, *Flaws*, pp. 123–4.
19. Barry Argyle, *Patrick White* (New York: Barnes and Noble, 1967), p. 15.
20. Bliss, *Patrick White's Fiction*, p. 23.
21. Peter Wolfe, *Laden Choirs: The Fiction of Patrick White* (Lexington: University of Kentucky, 1983), p. 34.
22. White, 'The Prodigal Son', p. 16.
23. Patrick White, *Happy Valley* (London: Harrap, 1939), p. 115. All further references in the text.
24. White, *Flaws*, pp. 58–9.
25. White, *Flaws*, pp. 52, 63.
26. Patrick White, 'The House Behind the Barricades', *New Verse*, No.30 (Summer 1938), p. 9.
27. Geoffrey Grigson, 'Ucello on the Heath' and 'Mediterranean', *New Verse*, No. 30 (Summer 1938), p. 8.
28. Thelma Herring describes Elyot as 'a younger Prufrock' in 'Odyssey of a Spinster', in *Ten Essays on Patrick White: Selected from 'Southerly' (1964–67)*, ed. G. A. Wilkes (Sydney: Angus and Robertson, 1973), p. 6.
29. 'I have never liked *The Living and the Dead*', White, *Flaws*, p. 77.
30. W.H. Auden, 'September 1, 1939', *W.H. Auden: Selected Poems*, ed., Edward Mendelson (New York: Vintage, 1979), p. 86.
31. T. S. Eliot, 'Gerontion', *Selected Poems* (London: Chatto & Windus, 1937), p. 273.
32. Cyril Connolly, *Enemies of Promise* (1938; rev. edn. 1948; reissued London: Andre Deutsch, 1973), pp. 70–1.
33. Patrick White, *The Living and the Dead* (New York: Viking, 1941), p.108. All further references in the text.
34. Malcolm Lowry, Letter to Albert Erskine, June 5, 1951, *Selected Letters of Malcolm Lowry*, p. 242.
35. James Joyce, *Ulysses* (New York: Random House, 1934), pp. 45–7.
36. See F. R. Leavis, 'Introductory: Life *IS* a Necessary Word', *Nor Shall My Sword* (London: Chatto & Windus, 1972), pp. 11–37.
37. W. H. Auden, *Spain* in *Selected Poems*, p. 54.
38. William Walsh, *Patrick White's Fiction* (London: George Allen & Unwin, 1977), p. 7.

Chapter 2: Pastoral and Apocalypse

1. Greene, *Stamboul Train* (London: Heinemann, 1932), pp. 79–80.
2. John Wain, *Hurry on Down* (London: Secker and Warburg, 1955), p. 60.
3. See for instance: James Gindin, *Postwar British Fiction* (Berkeley: University of California Press, 1962), p. 11; Frederick R. Karl, *The Contemporary English Novel* (New York: Noonday Press, 1962), ch. 1; Rubin Rabonivitz, *The Reaction Against Experiment in the English Novel, 1950–1960* (New York: Columbia University Press, 1967).

Leslie Fiedler's 1968 comment that '[t]here is no scene in the arts in England' reflects a widespread American dismissal of the arts in England after the war. Fiedler's comment is found in 'The Invisible Country', *New Statesman*, 14 June 1968, p. 810.

4. See for instance Bernard Bergonzi, *The Situation of the Novel* (London: Macmillan, 1970), pp. 57–8; William Cooper, 'Reflections on Some Aspects of the Experimental Novel', *International Literary Annual*, No. 2, ed., John Wain (London: John Calder, 1959), pp. 29–36.

5. Malcolm Bradbury, *Possibilities* (London: Oxford University Press, 1973), p. 174.

6. See Bergonzi, *Situation of the Novel*, pp. 61–2.

7. Bergonzi, *Situation of the Novel*, pp. 81–103, particularly pp. 92–3.

8. Margaret Drabble, BBC Radio Interview 1967, quoted in Bergonzi, *Situation of the Novel*, p. 65; White 'The Prodigal Son', p. 16.

9. Malcolm Lowry, 'Through the Panama', in *Hear Us O Lord From Heaven Thy Dwelling Place* (New York: Lippincott, 1961), p. 85.

10. C. P. Snow, *The Conscience of the Rich* (London: Macmillan, 1958), p. 49.

11. Hermann Hesse, *Demian*, quoted in Malcolm Lowry, *October Ferry to Gabriola* (New York: World Publishing, 1970) p. 268.

12. Bradbury, *Possibilities*, p. 193.

13. Bradbury, *Possibilities*, p. 193.

14. Bradbury, *Possibilities*, p. 181.

15. Patrick White, *The Aunt's Story* (New York: Viking, 1948), p. 12. All further references in the text.

16. George Lukács, *The Theory of the Novel*, trans., Anna Bostock (Cambridge: Mass.: MIT, 1977), p. 30.

17. Walter H. Sokel, *The Writer in Extremis: Expressionism in Twentieth-Century German Literature* (New York: McGraw-Hill, 1959), p. 17.

18. Paul Klee, quoted in Herbert Read, *A Concise History of Modern Painting* (New York: Praeger, 1959), p. 180.

19. White, 'Prodigal Son', p. 16.

20. In *Flaws in the Glass* White confesses that he considered giving up writing altogether during the period in which he lived more or less isolated at Castle Hill, dejected by the indifference of Australian readers to *The Aunt's Story*. See Flaws, pp. 143–4.

21. Patrick White, *The Tree of Man* (New York: Viking, 1955), p. 416. All further references in the text.

22. A. D. Hope, 'The Bunyip Stages a Comeback', *Sydney Morning Herald*, 16 June 1956, p. 15.

23. White, 'The Prodigal Son', p. 15.

24. White, 'The Prodigal Son', p. 15.

25. White, 'The Prodigal Son', p. 16.

26. White, 'The Prodigal Son', p. 15.

27. Harry Levin, *James Joyce* (New York: New Directions, 1960), p. 4.

28. C. G. Jung, *Psychology and Alchemy*, trans., R. F. C., Hull, 2nd. edn. (London: Routledge and Kegan Paul, 1968), p. 54, passim. White mentions the influence of *Psychology and Alchemy* on *The Solid Mandala* in *Flaws*, p. 146. For a Jungian reading of White's work as a whole see

David J. Tacey, *Patrick White: Fiction and the Unconscious* (Melbourne: Oxford University Press, 1988).

29. Iris Murdoch, *Under the Net* (London: Chatto & Windus, 1956), p. 21.
30. Patrick White, *Voss* (New York: Viking, 1957), pp 151–2. All further references in the text.
31. *Flaws*, pp. 185, 227–33.
32. 'When New Zealand is more artificial, she will give birth to an artist who can treat her natural beauties adequately. This sounds paradoxical, but it is true', Katherine Mansfield, *The Letters and Journals of Katherine Mansfield: A Selection*, ed., C. K. Stead (London: Allen Lane, 1977), p. 26.
33. Plato, *Timaeus*, 48e. trans. and ed., John Warrington (London: Everyman, 1965), p. 53.
34. See Colin Roderick, '*Riders in the Chariot*: An Exposition', *Southerly*, 22 (1962), pp. 62–77. A useful discussion of the Gnostic sects in the Christian context is Hans Jonas's *The Gnostic Religion* (Boston: Beacon Press, 1963).
35. David Marr confirmed this in conversation.
36. Richard Poirier, *A World Elsewhere* (New York: Oxford University Press, 1966), p. 51.
37. See my '"Design of Darkness": The Religious and Political Heresies of Captain Ahab and Johann Voss', *Australasian Journal of American Studies*, Vol. 5 No. 1 (July 1986), pp. 26–40.

Chapter 3: The Artist and Suburbia

1. *Flaws in the Glass*, p. 49.
2. See, for example, 'The Prodigal Son' and 'In the Making', both collected in *Patrick White Speaks*.
3. Patrick White, *Riders in the Chariot* (London: Eyre & Spottiswoode, 1961), p. 488. All further references in the text.
4. The biblical parallels in the novel are treated most exhaustively by J. F. Burrows; 'Archetypes and Stereotypes: *Riders in the Chariot*', *Southerly*, 25 (1965), pp. 46–68.
5. R. F. Brissenden, *Patrick White* (London: Longmans, Green, 1969), p. 34.
6. Roderick, p. 73.
7. Roderick, p. 76.
8. Leonie Kramer, 'Patrick White's Götterdämmerung', *Quadrant*, Vol. 17 No. 3 (May/June, 1973), p. 9.
9. Kramer, p. 11.
10. Kramer, p. 10.
11. Alan Lawson, 'White for White's Sake: Studies of Patrick White's Novels', *Meanjin*, 32 (1973), p. 347.
12. Kramer, p. 17.
13. G. A. Wilkes, 'A Reading of Patrick White's *Voss*', *Southerly*, 27 (1967), pp. 170–1.

14. Patricia A. Morley, *The Mystery of Unity: Theme and Technique in the Novels of Patrick White* (Montreal and London: McGill-Queen's University Press, 1972), p. 158.
15. J. F. Burrows states: 'Mrs Flack embodies all that is stereotyped about White's Sarsaparilla', 'Archetypes and Stereotypes', p. 63.
16. Burrows, p. 65.
17. 'Less grand and ambitious in its design, . . . [*The Solid Mandala*] is enriched by a deeper warmth of understanding, a broader humanity', Thelma Herring, 'Self and Shadow: The Quest for Totality in *The Solid Mandala*', *Southerly*, 26 (1966), p. 180. See also Brian Kiernan, *Images of Society and Nature: Seven Essays on Australian Novels*, (Melbourne: Oxford University Press, 1971), p. 127, and A. A. Phillips, '*The Solid Mandala*: Patrick White's New Novel', *Meanjin*, 25 (1966), p. 32.
18. With regard to the argument over the 'stature' of *The Solid Mandala*, Alan Lawson notes that the novel was received in the U.S. 'with some disappointment', English critics 'were more eager to praise the novel', Australian critics and reviewers, on the other hand, greeted the novel with 'uncritical acceptance and extravagant praise', 'Unmerciful Dingoes? The Critical Reception of Patrick White', *Meanjin*, 32 (1973), pp. 388–9.
19. Manfred Mackenzie claims that the novel 'examines very deep ambiguities in . . . sainthood', 'The Consciousness of "Twin Consciousness": Patrick White's The Solid Mandala', *Novel*, Vol. 2, (1968–9), p. 242; John B. Beston sees the novel as an 'ambivalent' exploration of White's notions of salvation and damnation, 'Unattractive Saints and a Poor Devil: Ambivalence in Patrick White's: *The Solid Mandala*', *Literary Half Yearly*, Vol. 14, No. 1 (1973), pp. 106–14.; Thelma Herring sees the novel as a religious allegory built on the 'perennial philosophy' of the Theosophists, Herring, 'Self and Shadow', p. 187.
20. Herring, 'Self and Shadow', p. 187.
21. A. P. Riemer, 'Visions of the Mandala in *The Tree of Man*', *Southerly*, 27 (1967), pp. 3–19.
22. See Tacey, pp. 121–48.
23. Morley, pp. 187–8.
24. Morley, p. 206.
25. Morley, p. 185.
26. Morley, p. 206.
27. Herring, 'Self and Shadow', pp. 187–8.
28. Kiernan, *Images of Society and Nature*, p. 133.
29. White, *The Solid Mandala*, p. 248. All further references in the text.
30. Morley, pp. 85–95.
31. Brissenden, *Patrick White* p. 38.
32. Kiernan, p. 132.
33. Morley, p. 207.
34. Morley, p. 206.
35. Patricia Morley suggests that Mrs Poulter abandons a heretical position, alien to White's vision ('Christ has been to her more divine than human') in favour of that affirmation that lies behind

all his novels of 'the goodness of matter, and the fusion of matter and spirit of nature and grace', *The Mystery of Unity*, p. 206.

36. Quoted from Patrick White, *White as Playwright*, by J. R. Dyce (St Lucia: University of Queensland Press, 1974), p. 138: White's description of *A Cheery Soul.*

37. Compare: 'The Mandala is a symbol of totality ... Its protective circle is a pattern of order super – imposed on – psychic – chaos', *The Solid Mandala*, p. 238; 'The archetype [of the mandala] ... represents a pattern of order which ... is superimposed on the psychic chaos ....', C. G. Jung, *Memories, Dreams, Reflections* (London: Collins and Routledge & Kegan Paul, 1963), p. 353.

38. Jung, *Psychology and Alchemy*, p. 256. The close references in White's novel to *Psychology and Alchemy* have been noted by Herring, 'Self and Shadow', p. 187.

39. 'As the shadow continually follows the body of one who walks in the sun, so our hermaphroditic Adam, though he appears in the form of a male, nevertheless always carries about with him Eve, or his wife, hidden in his body', *The Solid Mandala*, p.281; *Psychology and Alchemy*, p. 151.

40. *Patrick White Speaks*, p. 19.

41. Patrick White, *The Vivisector* (London: Jonathan Cape, 1970), p. 177. All further references in the text.

42. See Terry Smith, 'A Portrait of the Artist in Patrick White's *The Vivisector*', *Meanjin*, 31 (1972), p. 169.

43. R. N. Coe points out that *The Vivisector* re-echoes 'almost episode by episode the life of Romain Rolland's *Jean-Christophe*, written nearly sixty years earlier', 'The Artist and the Grocer: Patrick White's *The Vivisector*', *Meanjin*, 29 (1970), p. 527. Veronica Brady suggests that 'The title, *The Vivisector*, echoes what James Joyce has to say in *Stephen Hero* about "the modern spirit"', 'The Artist and the Savage God: Patrick White's *The Vivisector*', *Meanjin*, 33 (1974), p. 136.

44. Coe, p. 527.

45. Coe, p. 527.

46. Thelma Herring, 'Patrick White's *The Vivisector*', *Southerly*, 31 (1971), p. 11.

47. 'Vilis Vilissimus', in Jung's terms, *Psychology and Alchemy*, p. 430.

48. Robert Hughes, *The Art of Australia* (Harmondsworth: Penguin, 1966; rev. edn. 1970), p. 315.

49. 'The Shandeleer', review of *The Vivisector* in *The Listener* (BBC), 5th November, 1970, Vol. 84, p. 635.

50. White, 'The Prodigal Son', p. 15.

51. Mathew, 13: 46.

52. White, *Voss*, p. 446.

53. 'Cosmas' name puns upon cosmos. The black Vivisector God, as cruel and domineering as an oriental satrap, is also "the doomed god ... as tragic as the cats he has condemned"', Morley, *The Mystery of Unity*, p. 220.

54. Veronica Brady, 'The Artist and the Savage God: Patrick White's *The Vivisector*', *Meanjin*, 33 (1974), p. 144.

55. The puns in the novel are most extensively analysed by Patricia Morley in *The Mystery of Unity*, Chapter 11, from which I have borrowed.
56. Morley, p. 228.
57. Morley, p. 229.
58. Veronica Brady connects indigo with 'the colour of God in the alchemical spectrum', 'The Artist and the Savage God', p. 140. John Docker suggests that the painter himself has become 'indiggoddd . . . [when] the universe (or God) penetrates his female self', 'Patrick White and Romanticism: *The Vivisector*' *Meanjin*, 33 (1973), p. 60. Geoffrey Dutton uncovers INRI in 'indi – ggoddd', *Patrick White* (Melbourne: Oxford University Press, 1971), p. 43.
59. Hurtle's view of God as divine vivisector remains with him to the very end of his life. In his conversation with Cutbush on the park bench he defined the concept in these vague terms: '"Yes, I believe in Him [the divine vivisector] . . . Otherwise, how would men come by their cruelty – and their brilliance?"' (269). His description of Rhoda as 'a body only *malice* could have created' (639, my italics), shows that he still considers God to be both malevolent and benevolent.

Chapter 4: Mirrors and Interiors

1. See Helen Daniel, *Liars: Australian New Novelists* (Ringwood, Vic.: Penguin, 1990).
2. Patrick White, *The Eye of the Storm* (London: Jonathan Cape, 1973), p. 291. All further references in the text.
3. Patrick White, 'In the Making', in *Patrick White Speaks*, p. 21.
4. Frank Kermode, *Modern Essays* (London: Fontana, 1971), p. 60.
5. See Bill Manhire, 'Dirty Silence: Impure Sounds in New Zealand Poetry' in *Dirty Silence: Aspects of Language and Literature in New Zealand*, ed. Graham McGregor and Mark Williams (Auckland: Oxford University Press, 1991), pp. 143–57.
6. W. B. Yeats, *The Collected Poems of W. B. Yeats* (London: Macmillan, 1963), p. 217.
7. Yeats, 'Among School Children', *Collected Poems*, p. 244.
8. Patrick White, *A Fringe of Leaves* (London: Jonathan Cape, 1976), p. 104. All further references in the text.
9. White, *The Aunt's Story*, p. 272.
10. White, *A Fringe of Leaves*, p. 254.

Chapter 5: Flaws in the Word

1. Patrick White, *The Twyborn Affair* (New York: Viking, 1980), p. 79. All further references in the text.
2. A. P. Riemer, 'Eddie and the Bogomils: Some Observations on *The Twyborn Affair*', *Southerly*, 40 (1980), p. 14. On the Bogomils see

Dimitri Obolensky, *The Bogomils: A Study in Balkan Neo-Manichaeism* (Cambridge: Cambridge University Press, 1948).
3. Riemer, p. 14.
4. Riemer, p. 14.
5. Riemer, p. 15.
6. Riemer, p. 16.
7. Riemer, p. 19.
8. On the connections between ancient Gnosticism and twentieth-century Existentialism see Jonas, *The Gnostic Religion*, pp. 320–40.
9. Riemer, p. 21.
10. Riemer, pp. 22–3.
11. Riemer, pp. 23.
12. Riemer, p. 25.
13. Riemer, p. 26.
14. Patrick White ('editor'), *Memoirs of Many in One, by Alex Xenophon Demirjian Gray* (London: Jonathan Cape, 1986), p. 40. All further references in the text.
15. Riemer, p. 27.
16. White, *The Tree of Man*, p. 209.
17. Friedrich Schiller, 'Aesthetical Letter, 27', in *Essays Aesthetical and Philosophical* by Friedrich Schiller (London: George Bell, 1916), p. 113.

Conclusion: Patrick White and the Modern Novel

1. David Marr drew my attention to this in conversation.
2. Janet Frame, *Faces in the Water* (London: the Women's Press, 1980), p. 251.
3. White, 'The Prodigal Son', p. 16.
4. Janet Frame, *The Envoy from Mirror City, An Autobiography: Volume Three* (Auckland: Century Hutchinson, 1986), pp. 151–2.
5. Allen Curnow, Introduction to *The Penguin Book of New Zealand Verse*, in Allen Curnow, *Look Back Harder: Critical Writings, 1935–1984*, ed., Peter Simpson (Auckland: Auckland University Press, 1987), p. 133.
6. Frame, *Envoy from Mirror City*, p. 153.
7. Brian Boyd, *Vladimir Nabokov: The American Years* (London: Chatto & Windus, 1992), p. 654.
8. Boyd, *The American Years*, p. 655.
9. See Manhire, *Dirty Silence*, pp. 143–57.
10. Malcolm Lowry, Letter to Gerald Noxon, 28 September 1943, held in Humanities Research Centre, University of Texas at Austin.
11. Vincent O'Sullivan, *Finding the Pattern, Solving the Problem: Katherine Mansfield the New Zealand European* (Wellington: Victoria University Press, 1989), p. 5.
12. Quoted in Noel Stock, *Poet in Exile* (Manchester: Manchester University Press, 1964), p. 5.
13. John Berger, *Art and Revolution: Ernst Neizvestny and the Role of the Artist in the U.S.S.R* (London: Weidenfield and Nicolson, 1969), p. 125.

Select Bibliography

Argyle, Barry. *Patrick White* (Edinburgh: Oliver and Boyd, 1967).

Beatson, Peter. *The Eye in the Mandala. Patrick White: A Vision of Man and God* (London: Paul Elek, 1976; Sydney: Reed, 1977).

Beston, John B. 'Alienation and Humanization, Damnation and Salvation in *Voss, Meanjin*, 30 (1971) 208–16.

——. 'Unattractive Saints and a Poor Devil: Ambivalence in Patrick White's *The Solid Mandala*', *Literary Half Yearly*, 14 (1973) 106–14.

Björksten, I. *Patrick White: A General Introduction*, trans., S. Gerson (St Lucia: University of Queensland Press, 1976).

Bliss, Carolyn. *Patrick White's Fiction: The Paradox of the Fortunate Failure* (London: Macmillan, 1986).

Brady, Veronica. 'The Artist and the Savage God: Patrick White's *The Vivisector, Meanjin*, 33 (1974) 136–45.

Brissenden, R. F. *Patrick White* (London: Longmans Green, 1966).

Burrows, J. F. 'Archetypes and Stereotypes: *Riders in the Chariot*', *Southerly*, 25 (1965) 46–68.

Coe, Richard N. 'The Artist and the Grocer: Patrick White's *The Vivisector, Meanjin*, 29 (1970) 526–9.

Colmer, John. *Patrick White* (London: Methuen, 1984).

——. '*Riders in the Chariot*', *Patrick White* (Melbourne: Edward Arnold, 1978).

Docker, John. 'Patrick White and Romanticism: *The Vivisector*', *Southerly*, 33 (1973) 44–61.

Dutton, G. *Patrick White* (Melbourne: Oxford University Press, 1971).

Gray, Martin (ed.). *Patrick White: Life and Writings: Five Essays* (Centre of Commonwealth Studies, University of Stirling, 1991).

Green, Dorothy. 'The Edge of Error', *Quadrant*, 17 (1973) 36–47.

——. '*Voss*: Stubborn Music'. In *The Australian Experience*, ed. W. S. Ramson (Canberra: Australian National University Press, 1974) 284–310.

Heltay, Hilary. 'The Novels of Patrick White', *Southerly*, 33 (1973) 92–104.

Herring, Thelma. 'Self and Shadow: The Quest for Totality in *The Solid Mandala, Southerly*, 26 (1966) 180–9.

——. 'Patrick White's *The Vivisector*', *Southerly*, 31 (1971) 3–16.

Kiernan, Brian. *Images of Society and Nature: Seven Essays on Australian Novels* (Melbourne: Oxford University Press, 1971).

——. *Patrick White* (London: Macmillan, 1980).

Kramer, Leonie. 'Patrick White's *Götterdämmerung'*, *Quadrant*, 17 (1973) 8–19.

Laidlaw, R. P. 'The Complexity of *Voss*', *Southern Review*, 4 (1970) 3–14.

Lawson, Alan. 'Unmerciful Dingoes? The Critical Reception of Patrick White', *Meanjin*, 32 (1973) 379–91.

——. 'White for White's Sake: Studies of Patrick White's Novels', *Meanjin*, 32 (1973) 343–9.

——. *Patrick White* (Melbourne: Oxford University Press, 1974).

Mackenzie, Manfred. 'The Consciousness of "Twin Consciousness": Patrick White's *The Solid Mandala'*, *Novel*, II (1968–69) 240–54.

McAuley, J. 'The Gothic Splendours: Patrick White's *Voss'*, *Southerly*, 25 (1965) 34–44.

McCulloch, A. M. *A Tragic Vision: The Novels of Patrick White* (St Lucia: University of Queensland Press, 1983).

——. 'Patrick White: *Riders in the Chariot'*, *Quadrant*, 6 (1962) 79–81.

Marr, David. *Patrick White: A Life* (Australia: Randon House, 1991).

Morley, Patricia A. *The Mystery of Unity: Theme and Technique in the Novels of Patrick White* (Montreal and London: McGill-Queen's University Press, 1972).

Phillips, A. A. 'Patrick White and the Algebraic Symbol', *Meanjin*, 24 (1965) 455–61.

Ramson, W. S. (ed.). *The Australian Experience: Critical Essays on Australian Novels* (Canberra: Australian National University Press, 1974).

Riemer, A. P. 'Visions of the Mandala in *The Tree of Man'*, *Southerly*, 27 (1967) 3–19.

——. 'The Eye of the Needle: Patrick White's Recent Novels', *Southerly*, 34 (1974) 248–66.

Roderick, Colin. '*Riders in the Chariot*: An Exposition', *Southerly*, 22 (1962) 62–77.

Shepherd, R. and Singh, K. (eds). *Patrick White: A Critical Symposium* (Adelaide: Centre for Research in the New Literatures in English, 1978).

Shrubb, P. 'Patrick White: Chaos Accepted', *Quadrant*, 12 (1968) 7–19.

Smith, Terry. 'A Portrait of the Artist in Patrick White's *The Vivisector'*, *Meanjin*, 31 (1972) 167–77.

Stern, J. 'Patrick White: The Country of the Mind', *London Magazine*, 5 (1958) 49–56.

Steven, Laurence. *Dissociation and Wholeness in Patrick White's Fiction* (Waterloo, Ont.: Wilfrid Laurier University Press, 1989).

Tacey, David J. *Patrick White: Fiction and the Unconscious* (Melbourne: Oxford University Press, 1988).

Tanner, Tony. '*The Solid Mandala'*, *London Magazine*, 6 (1966) 11–7.

Walsh, William. *Patrick White's Fiction* (London: George Allen & Unwin, 1977).

Walters, Margaret, 'Patrick White', *New Left Review*, No. 18, (1963) 39–50.

Watson, Betty L. 'Patrick White, Some Lines of Development: *The Living and the Dead* to *The Solid Mandala'*, *Australian Literary Studies*, 5 (1971–2) 158–67.

Weigel, John A. *Patrick White* (Boston: Twayne, 1983).

White, Patrick. *The Aunt's Story* (New York: Viking, 1948).

———. *The Eye of the Storm* (London: Jonathan Cape, 1973).

———. *Flaws in the Glass* (New York: Viking, 1981).

———. *A Fringe of Leaves* (London: Jonathan Cape, 1976).

———. *Happy Valley* (London: Harrap, 1939).

———. *The Living and the Dead* (New York: Viking, 1941).

———. *Memoirs of Many in One* (London: Jonathan Cape, 1986).

———. *Patrick White Speaks* (Sydney: Primavera, 1989).

———. *The Ploughman and Other Poems* (Sydney: Beacon Press, 1935).

———. *Riders in the Chariot* (London: Eyre & Spottiswoode, 1961).

———. *The Solid Mandala* (Harmondsworth: Penguin, 1969).

———. *The Tree of Man* (New York: Viking, 1955).

———. *The Twyborn Affair* (New York: Viking, 1980).

———. *The Vivisector* (London: Jonathan Cape, 1970).

———. *Voss* (New York: Viking, 1957).

Wilkes, G. A. 'A Reading of Patrick White's *Voss*', *Southerly*, 27 (1967) 159–73.

——— (ed.) *Ten Essays on Patrick White Selected from 'Southerly' (1964–67)* (Sydney: Angus and Robertson, 1973).

'An Approach to Patrick White's *The Solid Mandala*', *Southerly*, 29 (1969) 97–110.

Wood, Peter. 'Moral Complexity in Patrick White's Novels', *Meanjin*, 21 (1962) 21–8.

Wolfe, Peter. *Laden Choirs: The Fiction of Patrick White* (Lexington: University of Kentucky, 1983).

———. (ed.). *Critical Essays on Patrick White* (Boston: G.K. Hall, 1990).

Index